Camping in the 90s
Tips, Techniques & Secrets

Camping in the 90s
Tips, Techniques & Secrets

Victoria Logue

Illustrations by Leigh Ellis

MENASHA RIDGE PRESS
BIRMINGHAM, ALABAMA

Library of Congress Cataloging-in-Publication Data
Logue, Victoria, 1961-
    Camping in the '90s / by Victoria Logue;
        p. cm.
    Includes bibliographical references and index.
    ISBN 0-89732-181-2
    1. Camping—United States—Handbooks, manuals, etc.
    2. Camping—Equipment and supplies—Handbooks, manuals, etc.
    3. Wilderness Survival—United States—Handbooks, manuals, etc.
    4. Recreational vehicle living—United States—Handbooks, manuals,
    etc. I. Title.
    GV191.4.L64 1995
    796.54'0973—dc20   95-35481
                                                            CIP

Text and cover design by
Carolina Graphics Group

Cover illustration by Victoria and Frank Logue

Menasha Ridge Press
3169 Cahaba Heights Road
Birmingham, Alabama 35243

This book is for Frank, without whose help
I would never have seen it through.

And also for my father,
who introduced me to camping

· Contents ·

Introduction

Remember thy creator in the days of thy youth. Rise free from care before the dawn, and seek adventures. Let the noon find thee by other lakes, and the night overtake thee everywhere at home. There are no larger fields than these, no worthier games than may here be played.

—Henry David Thoreau
Walden

Some of my fondest memories of camping have occurred during the day's golden hours—dawn and dusk. From quiet and solitary moments spent watching the sun peek over the horizon to the times spent with friends and family as brilliant sunsets faded into blue-dark—days spent outdoors have provided me with many exquisite memories.

But even the coldest, rainiest and hottest of camping trips have left a lasting impression of something special shared with nature—a mug of hot chocolate thawing cold fingers, the music of rain pattering against a tent, frigid spring water

flowing through parched lips, the ghostly apparitions of trees in the fog, brilliant red salamanders on rain-soaked rocks, the fairy-tale vistas of snow-covered forests . . .The list goes on and on. The secret is finding the ability to appreciate the small things, particularly when the environment seems overwhelmingly brutal.

I have written this book to introduce you to the potential pleasures inherent in camping. It will provide you with the background knowledge necessary in order to enjoy the outdoors. Because food and water (beverages) are always our main concern, I begin in Chapter 1 with an overview of the types of food you will need for camping, including recipes and ideas for menus. Water, though readily available at most camping areas, is also discussed in detail for those who enjoy backcountry camping. Stoves and other gear needed to prepare your meals are discussed in Chapter 2.

Toiletries, first aid kits, day packs and fanny packs are among the items discussed in Chapter 3. These are the miscellaneous items you will need to make your trip the most comfortable. The type of clothes and footwear you bring on a camping trip are also important and may vary according to the trip you have planned. Chapters 4 and 5 will present the various kinds of clothing and shoes and what is appropriate for the climate, terrain or season.

Sleeping gear, primarily sleeping bags and tents, is discussed in detail in Chapters 6 and 7. Because a third of your day will be spent in your bag and in your tent (or under the stars or in your RV), you will want to purchase the gear that is most appropriate for you and your type of camping.

Recreational vehicles have become increasingly popular and Chapter 8 is included to provide you with the knowledge necessary for choosing the RV that will best suit your needs. Packing tips and driving tips are included as well.

Once you have assembled your gear and chosen your method of transportation, you might have trouble choosing where to go. Chapter 9 offers some suggestions on places to camp throughout the United States (the appendix offers information on Canada).

In Chapter 10, you will learn a few tips on packing your gear for the trip to camp as well as how to select and set up your camp. There are also a number of suggested activities with which to occupy yourself once camp is set up in this chapter.

In these days of minimum impact, or Leave No Trace, camping, it is important to learn how to reduce your affect on the environment. Chapter 11 provides a number of suggestions on how to do just that. This new ethic must become a way of life if we are to leave the pleasures of camping and the outdoors to our children and our children's children or, as the famous quote says,"unto the seventh generation."

Problems arise even in paradise. Chapters 12 and 13 cover what to do should a problem arise. Nearly anything (from a bruise to hantavirus) that can happen in the outdoors is discussed, although only training can really provide you with a knowledge of what to do in any emergency situation.

The final two chapters provide you with a general background on special types of camping trips. Backpacking, canoeing, cycling, winter and desert trips as well as camping with children are among the trips covered at the end of this book.

Once you have acquired the basic gear and the necessary skills, camping is simple. The only impediments are time and rare severe weather (tornados, hurricanes, blizzards and floods). The slight chance of a rain shower or partly cloudy skies shouldn't deter you from an overnighter any time of year. Remember, joy can be found in the swirl of fog that embraces your tent or the rime ice that glitters in the trees. There is no need to confine your camping memories to those "perfect" days of azure skies and spring-like temperatures.

You road I enter upon and look around, I believe that you are not all that is here. I believe that much unseen is also here.
—Walt Whitman

· 1 ·
Food and Water

Dreamily, deliriously, I waded into the waist-deep water and fell on my face. . . . I had no fear of drowning in the water—I intended to drink it all.

—Edward Abbey
Desert Solitaire

Camp cookery can be as simple as hydrating a freeze-dried meal or as involved as preparing a lavish gourmet dinner. As at home, it all depends on what you want (and what the cook wants to prepare). Honestly, most people go camping for rest and relaxation, to take a break, to take it easy. This means that lots of chopping and dicing won't seem very enticing come meal time.

Fortunately, there are thousands of options when it comes to camp foods, and most of them are easy. Fresh foods will keep well in a cooler on short trips and can be bought at a trading post, camp store or a supermarket near the campground on longer trips. Nothing beats a grilled steak for supper or a fresh omelet at breakfast. You are only limited by your cooler size and the amount of time you want to spend cooking.

Dehydrated and freeze-dried foods are the most popular when it comes to bicycle camping, backpacking and canoe camping. These compact, lightweight foods are also good for walk-in campsites offered in some state and national parks. At these sites your equipment is hauled only a hundred yards or so and resorting to backpacking gear isn't necessary, but you will appreciate lightweight food just the same. For the most part, these types of meals (if you purchase the backpacker brands) are expensive and less than filling. Taste has greatly improved over the years, but thanks, no doubt, to the ever increasing number of women in the workforce, supermarkets are now filled with easy-to-fix, just-add-water style dinners.

From the universal children's favorite macaroni and cheese to pasta salads and the wide variety of sauces for pastas, there is much to choose from at your local grocery store. There are packaged rice, potato and noodle dishes, dehydrated soups that include more than the mundane vegetable soup offerings—lentils, curries, black beans, creoles and more—and even stuffing and less common (though increasingly popular) grains including couscous, bulgur wheat, quinoa, and TVP (textured vegetable protein). And most of these meals call for nothing more than boiling water.

Another option is to dehydrate your own food. Although it takes time and effort, dehydrating your own food can be an inexpensive alternative to store-bought meals. My mother swears by her dehydrated tuna, and Bill and Laurie Foot by their dried beef. Cindy Ross and Todd Gladfelter, who have spent more nights than they can count in a tent, dry most of the food they eat on their trips.

Dehydrators can be purchased through most outdoors stores and cost between $50 and $100. All manner of food can

be dehydrated—fruit, meats and vegetables. Use before you go camping since they run off electricity.

No matter what type of food you choose to bring, you will want to plan out your menus before you leave home. Here are some ides for meals and snacks along with a few favorite recipes.

Breakfasts
Breakfasts are easy to choose because there are so many breakfast products on the market. Most are vitamin-fortified, a gimmick to make parents feel that they are providing a healthy breakfast for their child even when the product is stuffed full of sugar. If you are active when camping—dayhiking, portaging or paddling a canoe, or involved in any athletic activity such as swimming—the extra carbohydrates are a boon.

❑ Suggested Breakfasts

Eggs (omelet, egg sandwich, fried or scrambled eggs)
Bacon
Fresh or instant hash browns
French toast
Stuffed pitas (fill with Spam and cheese then fry)
Bagels with cream cheese
Cold cereal with powdered, boxed or fresh milk
Oatmeal (instant or quick)
Toaster pastries
Bread with peanut butter
Granola bars
Gorp or Granola in milk
Instant or quick grits
Cream of Wheat
English muffins
Breakfast bars (such as Nutrigrain)
Raisin bread
Cinnamon rolls (camp-baked)

Pancakes
(makes about 10 thin or 6 traditional pancakes)

1 cup Bisquick
2/3 cup milk
1 egg (For a low-cholesterol version use two egg whites or 1/4 cup cholesterol-free egg product.)

Beat ingredients until well-blended. Pour by the 1/4-cupful onto hot frying pan (grease pan, if necessary). Cook until edges of pancakes are dry, flip and cook until golden.

To make your pancakes a little more interesting, try adding fresh berries (blueberries, strawberries or blackberries) or walnuts or even a dash of cinnamon.

Lunches

Lunches have always been a problem for me, both at home and in camp. Unless it is really cold, I never feel like fixing a hot lunch in camp, but there are also only so many things you can do to improvise a cold lunch. Do what suits you best. Some people like a big, hot meal in the middle of the day, some do best with a simple repast. The temperatures while camping may also determine your midday meal as will how you are set up and what you are doing.

On the following page is a list of suggestions, but the sky really is the limit.

Black Bean Salad with lime dressing
(serves two)

1 cup corn kernels (fresh, frozen or canned)
1 cup canned black beans
1 cup cubed tomato
1 diced green onion
1 teaspoon diced jalapeño

Dressing
1/2 teaspoon ground cumin
2 tablespoons lime juice
1 tablespoon vegetable oil
2 tablespoons cilantro
1/4 teaspoon salt

This recipe can be made ahead of time and stored in a cooler or can also easily be made in camp.

Thaw corn, if necessary, and rinse and drain black beans. Combine the corn, black beans, tomato, green onion and jalapeño. Blend separately, the cumin, lime juice, oil, cilantro and salt. Pour over bean mixture. Serve or chill.

❏ Suggested Lunches

Fried Chicken (prepared at home)
Pasta salads (prepared in camp or at home)
Hotdogs
Hamburgers
Sardines
Cheese
Nuts
Cookies
Crackers
Beef jerky
Peanut butter sandwiches
Dried soups
Candy bars
Graham or other crackers with peanut butter
Pepperoni or sausage (salami, summer, etc.)
Fresh or dried fruit
Gorp
Tuna
Spam or corned beef
Hard boiled eggs
Cheese sandwiches (stuff a pita)
Granola bars
Snack foods and cakes
Vienna sausage
Fruit cake
Crudites
Sunflower or other seeds

❦ Camping Secret ❦

Boiling eggs for five seconds will increase their pack life. Eggs will keep several weeks, even in the summer, if first treated in this manner. Another secret to increase the life of eggs is to coat them in petroleum jelly.

>> Camping Tip <<

If drinking instant coffee in camp, you save room, time and trouble by preparing a mix at home. If you use sugar and/or creamer in your coffee, add them (with the coffee) to a zipper-locked bag. In camp, just shake the bag to mix, and add the necessary amount to your mug before adding water.

Suppers

Supper is usually the most time-consuming meal of the day. It is time to relax, settle down for the night and enjoy the great outdoors. Camp is set. Dinner is your only concern. There are thousands of options. From grilled steaks, pit-baked potatoes and a freshly prepared salad to macaroni and cheese, you should be able to find something that suits your needs.

The following is a list of easy-to-prepare options, but don't be afraid to let your imagination run wild:

❑ **Suggested Suppers**
Steak
Hotdogs
Hamburgers
Chili or Stew
Quesadillas (add canned chicken to the cheese)
Pita pizzas
Lentils
Instant rice dishes (instant gravies or sauces can be added)
Macaroni and cheese (add dried soup or tuna)
Noodle dinners
Instant mashed potatoes
Instant stuffings
Canned or jarred sauce and pasta
Instant soup

Ramen soup
Pasta salads
Couscous
Pilafs
Instant potato dinners
Tuna and other canned meats
Pepperoni, dried beef and sausages
Sardines and fish steaks
Specialty dehydrated meals
TVP or tofu
Quinoa with black beans

Foil-Wrapped Meal
(serves one)

1 hamburger patty
1 diced medium potato
1 diced carrot
1/2 diced onion (optional)
seasonings—salt, pepper, oregano and/or other spices
    to taste
Aluminum foil

Multiply the ingredients according to the number of "meals" you wish to make.

Take a large piece of foil and place the hambuger patty in the center. Cover the patty with potato, carrot and onion and then season. Fold the foil over the ingredients securely so that no juice is lost as it cooks. Set foil packs in amongst the coals or on grill above coals and let cook half an hour to an hour depending on the heat of the coals. If set on a grill, it will take longer to cook. You may have to check your meal a couple of times before it is ready.

Desserts

Desserts are a nice way to finish your evening meal. They help fill that last empty spot in your belly and make the evening special, particularly if you do not usually eat dessert. Although pudding is a favorite, there are a number of other easy-to-make desserts on the market.

❑ **Suggested Desserts**

Instant puddings or cheesecakes
Cookies
Instant mousse
Jello or other flavored gelatins
Snack cakes
Easy-bake cakes
Specialty dehydrated desserts
S'mores (graham crackers sandwiching chocolate
    and baked marshmallow)
Baked apples (wrap in foil stuffed with chocolate chips, nuts, etc. and bake in the fire)

Banana Boat
(serves one)

1 banana
1/2 cup chocolate chips
1/2 cup marshmallows
aluminum foil

Multiply the ingredients by the number of people to be served.

Peel the banana and slice in half, lengthwise. Place in center of foil that has been cut large enough to enclose the banana. Stuff the center of banana with chocolate chips and marshmallows. Encase in foil and set in hot coals or on grill for 15 to 30 minutes depending on heat of coals. Unwrap and serve.

Snacks

I have never been a snacker, but I find in the outdoors, particularly when day hiking or swimming, that it is important to snack every now and then. Because you do not need to stuff yourself at meals—for comfort's sake as well as the fact that a too-full stomach can make you drowsy—it is a good idea to snack on high energy food, particularly after lunch and before supper.

❑ **Suggested Snacks**

Gorp
Hard candy
Skittles candy
Chocolate
Mixed nuts
Fruit bars and rolls
Snack bars

GORP recipe

One of the most popular camp snacks is Gorp, a mixture of nuts and other goodies. Mix and match your favorites:

Peanuts	Almonds
Pecans	Walnuts
Filberts	Cashews
Macadamia nuts	Reese's Pieces
Shredded coconut	Chopped dates
Raisins	Currants
Banana chips	Dried fruit
Figs	Prunes
Sunflower seeds	Cheerios
M&M's (plain, almond, peanut or peanut butter)	

Beverages

Drinking is a very important part of camping, particularly if you intend to be active. Becoming dehydrated will seriously impair your body's ability to perform normal functions. The best thing to do is drink water, but when the water tastes bad (as it can, even at established camp sites), you'll probably want to disguise its taste with a powdered drink mix such as Kool-Aid. Because I prefer the flavor, I have developed the practice of constantly carrying a full liter of flavored water for sipping on, and I keep a separate stash of water for cooking and washing. Even squeezing some fresh lemon in my water is preferable to the stale taste some water has.

The next best thing to water is an electrolyte solution such as Gatorade or Gookinaid ERG. These help replace the electrolytes, as well as the water, that you lose when you perspire, respire, etc. Some physiologists debate this claim and believe that electrolyte solutions do more harm than good.

There are few of us willing to give up our morning cup of coffee when we are camping. If you do drink coffee, cocoa or tea (unless decaffeinated), keep in mind that they are diuretics and you will need to drink more water to compensate if you will be expending more than the average amount of energy.

❏ **Suggested Beverages**
Water
Powdered fruit drinks
Powdered teas
Powdered fruit teas
Jello mix (a tasty hot drink particularly in hypothermic situations)
Instant coffee
Powdered spiced cider
Powdered egg nog
Gatorade (powdered)

>>Camping Tip<<

Keep hydrated even in cold weather. Believe it or not, dehydration impairs your body's ability to keep you warm, as does an empty stomach. Load up on carbohydrates before turning in at night.

Gookinaid E.R.G.
Hot tea (herbal or other)
Hot chocolate
Soft drinks (if you have a cooler)
Camp coffee (brewed on your camp stove or fire)

Spices and Condiments

Not everyone uses spices, and no one brings all those indicated below along on a camping trip; but those who bring spices tend to use a variety. Spices and condiments can add a lot to a meal.

It was once popular to carry spices in empty film canisters. Special caps were even manufactured to fit the canisters. But, Eastman-Kodak says that the chemicals from the film are dangerous and have been absorbed into the canister walls, making the canisters potentially harmful to use.

When carrying mayonnaise and other egg products, be sure that the cooler it is in stays cold throughout the trip, because they spoil quickly.

❑ **Suggested Spices and Condiments**
Garlic
Salt
Pepper
Italian Seasoning
Seasoned butter
Tabasco brand pepper sauce
Red pepper

Curry powder
Chili powder
Oregano
Cumin
Onion powder
Squeeze margarine
Ketchup
Mustard
Mayonnaise
Relish

Food For a Week or More

If you are camping for a week or more, will you be able to buy food where you are going? On short trips, I usually plan the meals ahead and carry the food with us. But, if I intend to be at a site for a week or more, I prefer to come up with a meal plan and purchase food at the nearest supermarket to the campground. This way I don't have to worry about transporting food that needs to be kept cold, saving on both weight and room.

This might mean, of course, that you have to either substitute if you can't purchase a hard-to-find item at an unfamiliar grocery store or that you bring hard-to-find items with you. Couscous, for example, is an ingredient I use a lot but only some grocery stores carry it. I usually bring it with me.

Packing Your Food

Car campers have seemingly endless room to pack gear and food. One of the big problems is not being able to find what you need. By creating a system used on trip after trip, you can avoid the annoying "where are those #@*! tongs" problem. One solution is to use color-coded milk crates (available in discount and office supply stores). Pack non-perishable food items in the same crate or crates each time, with cooking gear in yet another crate. This will make them easy to pack and simplify the task of finding hot dogs buns, for example, once you're in camp. Writing the contents on the outside of a paper bag is a no-cost solution to the problem, but the bags are more easily crunched by other gear in the trunk of your car.

Packaging is only a problem if you are unable to repackage the food yourself or if you have little storage space available to you. If you plan to buy food near the campsite, bring along plenty of zipper-lock bags (several sizes) if you are short on room. If you have an impenetrable screened dining fly or intend to keep the food in the car, space may not be a problem.

Proper packing is essential when room and weight are a problem, as it would be with a backpacking, cycling or canoeing trip and on some camping trips. In the interest of space, weight and waterproofing, you will want to repackage your food into plastic bags or some other waterproof container. Campers joke that the "yellow-and-blue-makes-green" Gladlock brand plastic bags are one of the great camping inventions of our time. This might be a little exaggerated, but not much. Other options include reusable, plastic squeezable food tubes. A clip at the bottom is used to squeeze the food upward toward the spout. I have seen these used only for peanut butter and jelly; but because peanut butter and jelly now come in plastic containers, it is just as easy to use them in their own containers. Also, it isn't a simple process to transfer these sticky foods from one container to another.

Rigid plastic egg cartons are available for less than $3 from most outdoors stores. They come in both the dozen and half-dozen size and are a wonderful way to carry eggs if you eat a lot of them while camping. However, these containers will hold small and medium size eggs only.

If space is a problem, sort your boxes and other packages

> ## >>Camping Tip<<
> If you do not like the taste of powdered milk, try adding a powdered non-dairy creamer—one tablespoon per cup of mixed milk.

into meals. Open the boxes and pour the contents into plastic bags of appropriate sizes. You do not need to do this to meals that come in foil or other waterproof pouches. On some trips, you may want to cut down on weight and space by adding the powdered milk, salt, pepper, etc. to a bag at home and leaving the condiments behind. If you need the directions, cut out the portion of the box the recipe is written on and put it in the bag with the meal.

Some food products do better in plastic bags with twist ties. If you are carrying powdered milk, for example, it is best to double bag it and shut it with a twist tie, because the grains of milk tend to get caught in the "zipper" and keep it from closing properly.

Once at the campground, everything that needs to be kept cold is stashed in the cooler and the rest is put out of reach of raccoons and other pests.

Coolers
The type of cooler and/or jug you need depends on the type of camping you plan to do. Backpackers, canoeists and hikers do not have room for this luxury, but car campers, even those camping on a small scale, will often want some type of cooler. Coleman, Igloo and Rubbermaid are some of the main manufacturers of coolers.

The variety of coolers available to the public is astounding. Everything from a lunchbox-sized cooler to coolers in excess of 100 quarts can be purchased for your camping trip. Most coolers are modified to make them useful for specific purposes. Some are built to hold 12 to 24 canned drinks; others will hold 1- and 2-liter bottles, and some have detachable lids that become serving trays.

Some coolers are constructed with drains so that as the ice melts, the water can be poured off. Food trays can be purchased with some cooler models and Coleman has recently introduced a cooler that lights up when you open it, just like a refrigerator. These coolers also feature a drain and storage tray and range from 48 to 68 quarts in size. Coleman's KwikServ cooler offers several options of access so that the entire lid does not have to be opened to pull out a drink or other item.

Another new Coleman product is the personal size thermoelectric cooler, which can be plugged into your vehicle's cigarette lighter to keep food either warm or cold. Igloo also makes a cooler that both cools and warms food.

Other types of coolers include those designed to hold both the fish you catch and the refreshments you'll need while fishing. Some even contain a bait well and tackle box to make them extra useful. Thermos-style jugs can be purchased to hold only liquids in sizes from 1 to 10 gallons.

Cleaning Up After Meals

Cleaning pots, dishes and utensils is an absolute necessity. Many campers have found out the hard way that giving cleaning the short shrift can result in severe gastrointestinal problems. Cleaning should be done away from the campsite, as well as 300 feet or more from any body of water.

There are several reasons to clean your pots and pans as soon as you finish eating, not the least among them being the growth of bacteria. Dirty pots also beg for the appearance of animals such as raccoons, skunks, mice and even bears.

First, any leftover food scraps go in the bag with the trash that you are packing out, unless your campground offers safe trash disposal. Dumping food near the campsite isn't just unsightly; even buried food scraps can attract raccoons and other animals. Once tempted, the scavengers will go through everything looking for more food.

Wash the dishes and utensils in warm water with biodegradable soap. Clean the pots, dishes and utensils with a scrubber. Many campers use steel wool, but I prefer a non-abrasive scrub pad. When finished, scatter the wash water over a wide area, well away from both the water source and the campsite. Rinse with water and scatter again.

If worried about giardia, boil some water for a final, purifying rinse. Or, if you have a filter, filter some water and rinse with that. Iodine water works well here, too, because in a rinse it leaves less trace of its taste.

Some camping areas offer a large sink near the bathhouse for washing dishes. However, don't use the bathhouse sinks themselves for this purpose. They are only for washing hands and faces and brushing teeth.

Scrubbing a dirty grill with steel wool will usually return its sheen after each use. If you want to save this dirty job for home, you can double bag the blackened grill in garbage bags and store it away to clean up later.

Water

Depending on where you camp, the quantity and quality of water will vary. How much water you will need, even how much you carry (backpacking, canoeing, etc.) is always a matter of personal preference.

Keep in mind that like the earth, the human body is seventy-five percent water. If you lose one-and-a-half liters of water (through respiration, perspiration, etc.), you lose twenty-five percent of your body's efficiency. And if you're expending any energy during a 100-degree, dry, desert day, you could easily double the amount of water lost and lose another twenty-five percent of your body's efficiency.

Fortunately, this is a worst-case scenario; death from

dehydration is rare. Still, it is always wise to be conservative when it comes to keeping yourself hydrated. Drinking at least four liters a day will replace the minimum you expend. Water is essential for life.

Remember that your body does not always warn you that it needs water. As a matter of fact, your body's thirst indicators are usually overridden when you start to dehydrate. Whether you feel like it or not, do not pass up an opportunity to drink water. The worst that can happen to you by drinking too much is that you'll have to head to the bathhouse or bushes a little more often.

One of the first warning signs of dehydration is the color of your urine. If it is dark gold in color, you're heading into trouble. Drink now, not later. Coffee, tea, soft drinks (unless they are caffeine-free) are a no-no because they are diuretics and will increase your fluid loss. Alcohol, too, is dehydrating. Obviously, if you have nothing else, you'll have to drink them; but the best way to avoid this situation is not to carry these drinks at all.

Most campgrounds offer water spigots at the site. It is only when backpacking, canoeing or cycling that you might have to search for water. Guidebooks often tell you where to find water, but don't count on them. Springs can run dry, for example, and are often intermittent.

Water sources in the wilderness vary from stagnant pools dribbling from their source to clear, ice-cold springs gushing

---

>>Camping Tip<<

There is a widespread myth that water tumbling clear and cold over sun-washed rocks is naturally purified. Don't fall for this notion. Actually, moving water is more likely to be contaminated because the motion stirs up bacteria and disease-causing protozoa. If you must take your water from a stream without disinfecting or filtering it, take it from a still spot.

forth from rocks, the earth and even trees. Although there are exceptions, the higher you are, the harder it will be to find water. Conversely, the lower you are, the more water there is, and the more likely it is that you'll have to treat it.

Water Containers
There are a number of options when it comes to holding water for camp or personal use. Large thermos-style containers (mentioned under coolers), water bags and dromedary bags all hold large amounts of water. Milk jugs can be rinsed out, filled with tap water from home, and refilled in camp. Bottled water can also be bought, though, because of the cost, this is an option we have only used when traveling in Third World countries.

Canteens are another option, particularly for carrying enough water for a day hike or trip to the beach. Nalgene bottles are the most popular and even come with holsters so you don't have to hold onto the bottle. The squeeze-style bottles made popular by athletes are another option.

If you are on a trip where you might have to filter your water, MSR offers containers that can be fitted with their filter to treat your water. An adaptor for the filter must be purchased through the manufacturer. The MSR Deluxe Dromedary bags range in size from 2 to 10 liters and work with their Waterworks Filtration System.

Another option is a collapsible water bag. They're wonderful at camp because they hold more than enough water for dinner, cleanup, and sometimes even a sponge bath (if camping primitively). Water bags, however, are unwieldy to carry, tend to stay damp, and leak a bit. Another alternative to the water bag is to recycle the bladder found in the five-liter "boxes" of wine. They're strong, lightweight, and fold up easily when empty. They are susceptible to punctures, though, so use them with care.

Treating Water

If you get your water from a questionable source, don't succumb to the urge to drink it before you've purified it. If you are careful, your chances of contracting Giardia are few. But Giardia cases are increasing at an alarming rate—an estimated figure (because so many cases go unreported and/or misdiagnosed) is more than 120,000 cases per year nationwide.

Giardia is a parasite normally found in the feces of mammals. When mammals defecate in or near a water source, Giardia can leech into the water. This is, for example, why beaver ponds are a notoriously bad source of water. Unless killed or filtered from the water before drinking, the parasite will cause intestinal cramping, bad gas and diarrhea. Symptoms usually appear well after the outdoor enthusiast is home, making Giardia sometimes difficult to diagnose. Giardia will not go away on its own, but it is easily treated by a physician.

Suspect water should always be treated, and portable devices with microstrainer filters are the only way to filter out Giardia. A pore size of one micron or less will filter out Giardia as well as bacterial and viral organisms.

There are many water filters on the market. General Ecology offers several, including the First Need Deluxe, which has an accessory that can connect it to a Nalgene bottle. Other filters are the Katadyn's Water Purifier and Minifilter, Timberline's Filter, Sweetwater's Guardian micro-filtration system, Pur's Explorer, Hiker and Scout

---

>>Camping Tip<<

Remove large particles from debris-filled water by filtering it through a bandana first. This will save wear and tear on an expensive replacement filter.

> ## >>Camping Tip<<
> Add an iodine tablet to a liter of water, and, once it is dissolved, heat that water to boiling. Then, divide it into two or three containers and top those containers off with unpurified water. The heated iodine water kills contaminants more effectively and doesn't taste as bad once it is diluted.

filters and Microlite's waterfilter. Many of these filters now come with adapters to fit Nalgene and other bottles.

Another way to treat your water is by boiling it. Giardia is killed at a lower temperature than boiling point, but by boiling your water for a minute or more, you will also kill viruses, other parasites and bacteria. The drawbacks to heating water is the time it takes, both to heat it and wait for it to cool down sufficiently to drink. If it is cold out, this is less a problem.

Iodine and Halazone also kill Giardia. One tablet in one liter of relatively clear, not too cold water for half an hour will effectively kill Giardia. Unfortunately, iodine leaves an unpleasant taste in the water, and once again, you have to play the waiting game. If you leave your water uncovered for a while, the iodine taste will dissipate somewhat. The Potable Aqua system with P.A. Plus by Wisconsin Pharmacal comes with tablets that neutralize the taste of iodine, but the tablets can be used only after the water has been treated.

Never use chlorine (as in the form of bleach) to treat your water as there are too many variables that affect just how well the chlorine will work, including water pH, water temperature, organic content of the water, chlorine contact time, and the concentration of chlorine.

When camping in the snow or on cold days . . .
• Never drink icy water in the winter or even on cool days. The cold water can cause your body temperature to drop.

To avoid this, warm snow or water in your mouth before swallowing.

- Protect your water when temperatures drop below freezing by stashing it in your tent or at the end of your sleeping bag. You can also turn water bottles upside down so that the ice won't block the spout.
- Keep your bottles full of water by topping off with snow after each drink.
- Use water to melt snow. An inch of water in your cook pot will melt snow more quickly. Add the crustiest, iciest or wettest snow to your pot—it will produce more water.
- It probably goes without saying to avoid yellow snow, but also steer clear of pink or "watermelon" snow. This snow gets its name from its color, taste and scent produced by microorganisms that can cause diarrhea.
- Burying your water in the snow will help insulate it. A lidded pot buried a foot or so under snow will not freeze. Remember to mark the spot carefully.
- Keep in mind that melting snow will take more fuel and more time. With a cold wind blowing, it can take an hour and a stove full of fuel to melt and boil a quart of water.

· 2 ·
Stoves and Cooking

. . .as the days went slowly by we came to live for the moment, taking limitless pleasure in the small adventures that came our way.

—*G.B. Schaller*

"**I**'ve just put some brownies on to bake. They'll be done and we'll have a taste test about the time the talk is over."

With those two sentences, the audience's attention was fixed on the Outback Oven perched on top of a small Coleman backpacking stove. No matter how interested they were in the forty-five-minute seminar on cooking for campers and backpackers, their eyes would occasionally wander over to the stove, no doubt drawn in part by the smell of brownies baking.

Frank and I were demonstrating cooking techniques at an Outdoor Expo that drew 30,000 attendees during the weekend. As the talk and then question and answer session drew to a close, the fudge brownies could be smelled through-

---

>>Camping Tip<<

For starting camp stoves in the cold, carry along fire paste. If the stove refuses to start, let it cool completely before each re-lighting. Vaporized gas is highly volatile.

---

out the lecture area on the floor of the convention center. Everyone eagerly lined up to taste the fresh-baked treat. There were a number of oohs and aahs during the tasting. It's not that the brownies were unbeatable. They were tasty, but wouldn't have drawn so much praise if they had been pulled out of an oven at home. Everyone seemed entranced by the idea of baking brownies on a backpacking stove.

If you have done much camping, you have probably lowered your expectations a bit about what you can cook on your camping trips. With the right equipment and a little imagination, however, you can pull off some memorable meals from a camp stove.

Camp Stoves

The king of the two-burner camp stoves is Coleman, which makes a variety of two- and even three-burner stoves to choose from. Primus also makes a well-built line of camp stoves, but they are not as easily found as the dominant Coleman brand stoves. These well-built stoves offer adjust-able temperatures like any home range. The primary differ-ences among Coleman's full line of stoves are the fuels they use and the size of the stove.

The fuel options for Coleman stoves include dual-fuel stoves (which burn either unleaded auto gas or white gas), white gas stoves and propane stoves. The dual-fuel stoves are the cheapest to operate, as auto gas is cheaper than white gas and propane. However, auto gas is more volatile than white gas and doesn't burn as cleanly. Propane stoves are easy to use and have the advantage of no fuel spills. Coleman offers

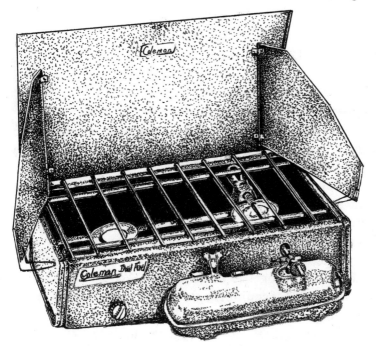

nine models of propane two- or three-burner stoves. Each works with the company's 16.4-ounce propane fuel bottles. Many of their stoves (of all fuel types) are available with matchless electronic ignition, which is reliable down to 32 degrees Fahrenheit. Below that point, you must use a match.

A second difference among the stoves is the overall stove size. For example, you can buy a two-burner, duel-fuel stove in the standard size (22" x 13.75" x 6.25") or in a compact model (18" x 11.5" x 4.8"). The standard size stove has a 3.5 pint fuel capacity, with 2.5 pints capacity in the compact model. Coleman also offers ultralight versions of their stoves that are thinner and lighter. The right stove for you depends on how much space you have to carry your gear and how big a pot you need to cook with after you set up.

Coleman's camp stoves cost about $30 to $75, and most weigh 7 to 15 pounds.

>>Camping Tip<<

A closed-cell foam pad (perhaps the one you use as a seat!) should be placed under your stove when the ground is cold to act as an insulator and to increase your stove's productivity. Another foam pad can be used as a windbreak. Fasten it with a clothes pin. If a pad isn't handy, create a wind break with water bottles, food sacks, rocks or whatever is handy.

Coleman sells a number of accessories to augment its line of camp stoves, including a stand to raise the stoves up to a good cooking height, an oven, a griddle sized for their stoves and even a Coleman Kitchen. The kitchen weighs 35 pounds, folds up like a suitcase to fit in your car trunk and carries everything including the kitchen sink. When unfolded, it gives 72.75" x 20" of counterspace and a removable ABS sink with drain plug and hose. Though a bit much for many camping trips, it might be worth a second look for hunting camps and use by serious tailgaters.

Grills

Many parks and campgrounds have grills in place. With a bag of charcoal, lighter fluid if your charcoal requires it, and matches, you're ready to cook. The hefty steel grates on institutional grills often make it difficult to keep hamburgers from dropping between the cracks. To grill smaller items (vegetables for example), cover the thick grate with a double layer of aluminum foil. It will distribute the heat more evenly and keep you from sacrificing food to the fire. Carrying your own grill, such as a small hibachi, will not only ensure that your site has a grill, but the smaller grates on store-bought grills are easier to cook on.

If it is pouring down rain, your cook-out on the grill will be cancelled. Bringing a back-up meal, bailing out to a restaurant for the night or going home will be the only options for food. Watch your TV weather in advance and have a backup plan.

Pyromid Cooking Systems

Pyromid, Inc., makes stoves/grills in several sizes, starting with the 40-ounce Pack-Lite Plus which packs down to 6" x 6" x 1.25" for portability. The stainless steel Pack-Lite folds out to form a grill that, like all of Pyromid's stoves, can cook with Sterno, Butane, wood or charcoal briquets. The stove folds down into the mess kit (included with the stove) when not in use. The Pack-Lite is intended for backpackers, cyclists and canoeists. It is a little small for most other campers' needs and costs about $80.

Pyromid also sells Eagle Grills in sizes from 8 to 18 inches square. When setting up an Eagle grill, it is easy to see where Pyromid gets its name. A support collar that looks like a pyramid with the top third cut off supports a cone, which is an inverted pyramid, making an X-shaped silhouette when the two pieces are fitted together. The cone effectively spreads the heat from a small area to evenly heat the grill that sets into the top of the cone. Our 12" Pyromid has proven to be an easy-to-pack, efficient-burning grill for camping trips. Our preferred fuel is charcoal briquets. Only ten briquets are needed to effectively heat the 12" grill. We use the accessory hood to hold in heat while cooking. Like the Pack-Lite, Eagle grills fold down flat to fit in a stuff sack just larger than the grill.

>>Camping Tip<<

To save time and frustration later, fill your fuel bottle or stove after each meal. Because fuel expands, never completely fill the bottle—three-quarters is enough.

The Eagle Grills range in price from $40 for the 8" to $200 for the 18" grill. A variety of accessories, including smoker ovens, roasters and a sportsman's kitchen, are sold to go with Pyromid stoves.

Z.Z. Corp. Sequoia and Sierra

The Sequoia is a portable fire pit that burns wood or charcoal equally well. Temperature is controlled by adjusting the damper at the bottom of the stove. As the fire gets going, air is pulled through the damper into a chamber in the burner bowl that surrounds the fire. The air is preheated in this chamber before being pulled in the burner bowl to feed the fire with oxygen. The pre-heated air being pulled over the fire creates a much hotter blaze than possible in a wood or charcoal fire alone. The Sequoia and its smaller brother, the Sierra, are both approved by the Forest Service for use in areas where only stoves are permitted. The Sequoia is 12" tall and 12" in diameter with a 9" x 5.5" fire area. It weighs 8 pounds and costs about $45.

Z.Z. Corp. also makes the smaller Sierra Stove. The 15-ounce stove is made with backpackers and cyclists in mind, but it is not so small as to be overlooked by car campers. The Sierra uses a battery-powered fan to force air into the stove. Once a fire is lit, a pint of water will boil in just over four minutes on the Sierra. We have successfully started fires using a fire starter and all wet wood with the Sierra. A friend of ours hiked more than 1,000 miles on the Appalachian Trail using a Sierra Stove and experienced no problems. The AA battery that powers the fan lasts about six hours.

The Sierra Stove costs about $40. For an additional $15, you can get a 1-quart pot and pan/lid sized so that the Sierra nests inside of it. Though small, the pot and pan are well made.

Propane Cookers

Large gas cookers fueled with a bulk tank of propane can be used to feed a large crew easily. Propane cookers can be used to deep fat fry food for a group of hungry campers. They are also used with a large (12 or more quarts) pot to boil crab or lobster, corn on the cob and more.

These are particularly popular in coastal areas. One of the best camp meals we know of is a "low country boil" where shrimp, short chunks of corn on the cob, potatoes, sausage and seasonings are boiled together (the shrimp is added right before serving). This is one of those regional specialties that everyone seems to have their own recipe for, so ingredients may vary.

These cookers are a specialty item and they are not suitable for cooking everything. The fuel and stove are bulky, but the results can be worth the extra effort of getting them to camp, particularly if a large crowd is involved or a special feast is being prepared.

Backpacking Stoves

Many campers prefer to use the smaller, backpacking stoves. These types of stoves are particularly useful if you do a lot of small-scale tent camping or canoe camping. Easy to carry, set up and use, backpacking stoves are definitely worth considering when purchasing a camping stove.

White Gas/Kerosene Stoves

Stoves that use white gas are the preferred backpacking stoves because they are the most versatile. They are more likely to reach a boil in cold weather, and their fuel is more widely available.

All fuels have their advantages and disadvantages. White gas evaporates quickly, has a high heat output, and is widely available in the United States. However, priming is occasionally required, the spilled fuel is very flammable, and self-pressurized stoves using white gas must be insulated from snow or cold. On the other hand, kerosene stoves can sit directly on the snow, have a high heat output and fuel is available world-wide. Although kerosene will not ignite readily, it also does not evaporate quickly. All kerosene stoves require priming.

No matter what the stove type, a 16- to 22-ounce container of Coleman or MSR fuel generally lasts seven to twelve days. In the winter, because fuel consumption is slightly higher, you can count on no more than a week's worth of fuel from any 22-ounce container. In the summer, one container may last as long as two weeks.

Fuel bottles can be purchased in a variety of sizes from half a liter to 48 ounces. Non-corrosive aluminum is the most popular material for fuel bottles, but the nylon (Nalgene) fuel bottles are also available. Fuel faucets are available for most fuel bottles, as well. These screw-on caps allow you to turn the top to pour and turn again to seal without a leak.

Not all fuel bottles fit all stoves. Check with the manufacturer's instructions before purchasing. For example, Nalgene bottles do not fit MSR stoves or the Coleman Apex.

The following stoves are among the favorites because of the availability of fuel and their versatility in hot and cold weather:

MSR Whisperlite 600 Internationale
This stove has become a standard among backpackers. It is light (14 ounces without the fuel bottle), compact, fast and durable. It burns white gas, operates right out of fuel bottles of 11 ounces or more, and boils a liter of water in about four-and-a-half minutes. The chief complaint about Whisperlites was that they clogged easily and required frequent cleaning. Although the cleaning procedure was always simple, MSR

has corrected this flaw; they made it effortless to clean the 600 model by building a weighted cleaning tip into the stove. The jet is cleaned out every time the stove is turned upside down and righted again (which often happens in normal packing and handling).

The other concern mentioned about Whisperlites is that they won't simmer. They will, if you know the trick. Instead of pumping the stove up 15 to 20 times to get the gas in the bottle pressurized, use just 8 pumps. With the reduced pressure in the bottle, light the stove and bring to a boil as usual. When you are ready for a simmer, turn the control valve down until the stove sputters, then give it more gas until the flame just starts to stabilize. This will keep the stove at a simmer for quite a while. If the stove begins to sputter again, give it a few more pumps to increase pressure in the bottle.

The Internationale can burn either white gas or unleaded auto fuel with the G-jet that comes installed in the stove. The auto fuel, however, is not only more volatile, but it has additives that will leave deposits in the fuel line. It is best to use white gas whenever possible. A K-jet is also supplied with the stove and can be used to burn kerosene or jet fuel. This is a nice addition if you plan to travel overseas where kerosene is often the fuel of choice. At about $60, this is a great stove for backpackers, bikers and canoeists.

Other popular MSR stoves are the regular Whisperlite and the XGK, which is a high-output mountaineering stove that burns nine types of fuel. They cost about $50 and $85, respectively, and weigh in at 14 and 15.5 ounces without the fuel bottle.

>>Camping Tip<<
Lids used on your cook pots will decrease the cooking time.

Coleman Peak 1 Apex II

With its detached burner, this stove looks like a fusion of Peak 1's multi-fuel stove with an MSR Whisperlite. As you would expect from such a combination, it is a great stove. At 18.6 ounces (including an empty fuel bottle), it is negligibly heavier and only slightly bulkier than the Whisperlite. Apex stoves boil a liter of water in four-and-a-half minutes. The Apex II burns white gas and, by exchanging the generator, kerosene. With the Apex II, the manufacturer warns that the fuel bottle can be filled only to the two-thirds mark on the side of the tank.

The big advantage that the Apex II has over the rest of the smaller stoves is that it has a low flame setting and can effortlessly hold a simmer with no special tricks. We have particularly enjoyed this feature when using an Outback Oven (mentioned in detail below), which bakes on simmer. Turning the flame adjuster back and forth several times has the added benefit of cleaning the generator tip. Another advantage to Apex stoves: the fuel-feed system mixes fuel and air to eliminate the need for priming.

The Apex II is similar in all aspects to the Apex, but it has the added benefit of being able to burn unleaded auto fuel. This $60 stove system is another top choice for campers who have to consider the weight and bulk of their equipment.

Other Peak 1 stoves to consider are the Feather 440 and 442 or the Multi-fuel. These stoves cost $40 to $60 and all weigh about 22 ounces.

Outback Oven

Baking in the backcountry is something that often feels a little too good to be true. But the Outback Oven fits most any backpacking stove and makes baking easy. Many recipes take thirty to forty-five minutes to bake, but since the Outback Oven works on a simmering stove, it uses little fuel.

The Oven can be bought four ways: the Ultralight, the Outback Oven Plus 8, the Outback Oven Plus 10 and the Plus 10 Plus. The Ultralight (nine ounces) uses your cook pot and comes just with the convection dome, thermometer, diffuser plate and reflector collar. With the Plus 8, you also get an 8" Teflon Pan and cover (the Plus 10 comes with a 10" Teflon pan and cover). This is a very handy pan that you can use even if you aren't baking. The Plus 10 Plus also comes with a cutting board, pot lifter, spatula and stuff sack.

Though I have a number of baking recipes for camping that I like, I also use the baking mixes sold by Traveling Light. The pizza, brownies, carrot cake, banana nut bread, foccacia and quiche are all easy to make and very tasty.

The Outback Oven costs about $30 for the Ultralight, $40 for the Plus 8, $45 for the Plus 10 and $55 for the Plus 10 Plus. The mixes cost $3.50 to $7.

Butane Stoves

For short, warm-weather camping trips, butane stoves are the easiest to use and maintain. But depending on the type of trip you are planning, a butane stove's disadvantages may outweigh the advantages. The advantages are inexpensive stoves, no fuel spills, no priming required, immediate maximum heat output and ease of use. The disadvantages include more expensive fuel, low heat output (boil times are double those for white gas stoves), and fuel cartridges that must be kept above freezing to work effectively. A foam beverage container slipped around the cartridge can help keep it warm in cold weather. Manufacturers of butane stoves are beginning to use a mix of butane and propane fuel, which allows the stoves to perform better in cold weather.

Three popular butane stoves are the Camping Gaz Bleuet 206, Olicamp's Scorpion II, and the MSR Rapidfire. They cost $30 to $50 and weigh between 12 and 15 ounces.

Operating and Maintaining Your Stove

No matter what type of stove you choose, these tips will help you make the most of it.

- Use your stove at home, before you take it on a camping trip for the first time.
- If the manufacturer offers a repair kit, buy one and keep it with the stove at all times.
- Use the stove's heat deflector and wind screens to reduce fuel consumption.
- After each trip, empty any white gas, auto fuel or kerosene from your stove. Burn what you can't pour out. Fuel left in stoves leaves residue that will clog your fuel jets and filters.
- Burning a cap of Gumout Carburetor Cleaner along with a half pint of gas will help dissolve residue. Doing this annually will keep your stove clean.
- Residue builds up in the fuel source (such as a can of Coleman fuel) if you don't use it quickly enough. If your fuel is over a year old, get rid of it.
- Keep your stove in a dust-free environment (such as a fabric sack) when not in use.
- Pre-filter any low grade fuel to avoid clogs and repairs. A filtering funnel will add to the life of your stove. Use it at home to filter fuel into the bottle, and you'll have once less thing to misplace in camp.
- Pack out any used fuel cartridges.

Stove Safety

For safe and efficient use of your fuel, follow these few tips:

- Make sure that air can circulate even with the wind screen in place. If the cook pot fills up the space left by the windscreen, an explosion could occur.

- Don't fill white gas stoves more than three-fourths full (no more than two-thirds full for the Apex stoves). The extra air space is needed to safely generate pressure.
- Warm fuel cartridges in your sleeping bag overnight or by rubbing them with your hands. Never warm a fuel cartridge with a candle or lighter.
- Unless the fuel cartridge is self-sealing, never remove it from your stove inside the tent. The fumes can be deadly.
- Never light a stove in your tent. The fumes are dangerous, flare ups are common, and, once the stove is successfully lit, the fire hazard is great on the floor of the tent as your stove heats up. If you don't want to get out of your tent, you can try cooking in a vestibule.

Cooking on a Fire

Cooking over a fire is tricky when compared to using a camp stove. But even in the environmentally-conscious 90s, it is hard to completely avoid the appeal of flames licking at a pot of camp coffee or fresh fish grilling on an open fire.

You will want to build your fire in an established fire ring when possible. If a fire ring isn't already available, really consider not building a fire. If you must, clear vegetation from an area at least a foot wider than your planned ring. This will keep leaves underlying the rocks of your fire ring from spreading the fire to the surrounding woods. A ring of rocks around the fire is an absolute necessity, as it will contain the

---

>>Camping Tip<<

Surefire firestarter: Use a cotton ball smeared with petroleum jelly to help start your campfire. Pull one to two cotton balls into a web, place them under your kindling and light. Store the balls in a film canister, which can hold more than thirty cotton balls if packed tightly. The lint from your clothes dryer also makes a good fire starter.

flames. Don't choose river rocks as they sometimes explode when the water trapped inside the rock is heated past the boiling point and tries to escape as steam.

Once the fire has burned long enough to establish a good bed of coals, you are ready to cook. A portable grill can be placed over the coals, or you can form a trough in the fire ring between two large, dry rocks. Rake the coals into the trough and balance your cooking pot on the stones.

Never count on a fire as your only means of cooking. Fires are not allowed in some parks or forests at all, and many areas are closed to fires when fire danger is great. And inclement weather makes wood nearly impossible to start.

Fire Safety

- Do not build your fire in an area with low overhanging branches. Even though they probably won't catch on fire, the heat from the fire could kill the branch.
- Never leave your fire unattended, even for a moment. If someone can't watch the fire while you collect more wood, stockpile all the wood you will need before igniting the fire.
- If it is very windy, or the area you are camping in is under a fire hazard, do not build a fire.
- Keep a canteen filled with water nearby in case sparks from the fire ignite a blaze outside the ring.
- Never build a fire against a large rock because the black scar the fire leaves will last for decades.
- When finished with the fire for the night, or before breaking camp, make sure that your fire is completely out. Stir the ashes to make sure no hot coals are left, then drown the fire with water and cover the area with a layer of dirt.
- If no fire ring existed before your camp, wait till the rocks have cooled and then scatter them in the woods again.

Cooking Pots and Utensils

What you carry in the way of cooking and eating gear will depend heavily on how many people are in your group and how elaborate your cooking setup will be. As a minimum, a solo camper needs one 2-quart pot with a lid and handle to cook in and a cup, bowl, spoon and knife to eat with. The 2-quart pot will be a breeze to cook in and clean up compared to the 1-quart pots many solo campers choose, and it doesn't add significantly to the bulk or weight of your gear. A second pot would be the next piece of equipment to add. Nesting pots make carrying two pots and a lid easy, and they give you one pot for your meal with a second pot to boil the water for a hot drink or for washing dishes. Some smaller stoves, such as the MSR Whisperlite, even fit inside nesting pots for protection and ease of packing.

Two campers will be served well by a set of nesting pots with 1.5- and 2-quart pots, a lid and pot holder. Carrying a griddle or 10" Teflon frying pan and a spatula will add new possibilities to the menu. The griddle or frying pan will make it easier to cook French toast or pancakes for breakfast, to grill sandwiches for lunch and to brown beef for spaghetti at dinnertime. A fork and plate in addition to the bowl, knife, cup and spoon mentioned above can round out the minimum cooking and eating gear. Some of the group gear below might make cooking in camp easier as well.

Groups of four or more will need a 4-quart cooking pot and a hefty wooden stirring spoon. If weight and space are not an issue, groups may want to carry some or all of these items as well: A mixing bowl, cutting board, grater, measuring cup,

---

>>Camping Tip<<

If weight or bulk is an object, carry a Frisbee. It can be cleaned off and used as a plate when you're not tossing it around.

pot holders, long-handled tongs, coffee pot, cast iron Dutch oven, steak knives and strainer.

No matter how many pots, pans and utensils you pack, always plan out at home a routine for cleaning up after meals. You will need to bring a non-abrasive pot scrubber or steel wool and some biodegradable soap. Cleaning up is covered in detail in Chapter 1.

Kitchen Gear
If you are going to cook complicated meals with fresh foods, you will need most of the same pots and utensils you need in your kitchen at home. If, however, you are cooking only one-pot meals, your needs will be few. What follows is a list of many of the items you may need to fill out your kitchen equipment list. It is doubtful that you will need every item listed on any one trip.

Two or more pots (from one to eight quarts based on need)
Frying pan or griddle
Portable grill (with charcoal)
Coffee pot
Mixing bowl(s)
Knife, fork and spoon for each person
Steak knives
Paring knife
Cutting board
Plate and bowl for each person
Hot (and/or cold) drink cups for each person
Spatula
Mixing spoons
Ladle
Tongs
Can opener
Corkscrew

Matches and/or lighter
Large sponge
Pot scrubber
Paper towels
Cooler
Thermos
Citronella and/or bug spray

No-Cook Camping

For the ultimate in simplicity, you can leave your stove and other cooking gear at home. Though you will have to live without a morning cup of coffee (or buy your coffee at the trading post), you will have a lot less gear to keep up with. This really works only for an overnight camping trip when you can prepare everything ahead at home as if going on a picnic. All of your food can be packed into a big cooler and/or grocery bags to be eaten with little in-camp preparation. Possible meals are toaster pastries for breakfast, peanut butter and jelly or other sandwich for lunch, and fried chicken and potato salad for dinner.

Why bother? Because this stoveless option can simplify difficult trips, such as when you are bringing an infant along on her first campout.

· 3 ·
Essentials

We had had twenty-seven days of rain in twenty-nine. We had lost our boat, much of our equipment, and—as it turned out later—part of our pictures. . . for a purely good time, it would be hard to beat our four weeks' adventure in unexplored wilderness.

—Bob Marshall
Alaska Wilderness

Packing for a car camping trip seems easy. There's lots of room in the trunk (or even backseat), so you just toss in what you need and hit the road, right? Not exactly. This lesson really hit home for my husband Frank and me the year after we backpacked the length of the Appalachian Trail. We planned a car camping trip with my twin brothers, Tom and Ben. We would drive from Georgia to New Hampshire and back, camping along the way. Our small, two-door car was filled up with the then twelve-year-old boys and the two of us. To fit everything we needed in the trunk for the long trip meant that we had less room for each persons gear than Frank and I had had in our backpacks the year before. Car camping was supposed to make it possible to carry more gear, but we had to look at what we packed even closer as we planned for this trip. Other than the basics, everything you bring will have to find a place in your car, RV, canoe or wherever you pack. Paring down your list of gear will make for a simple and enjoyable trip, but forgetting to bring a can opener or toilet paper can ruin even the best of trips.

Toiletries

Depending on the length of your camping trip, you may want to consider bringing along items such as toilet paper, towels, shampoo/soap, deodorant, razors/shaving cream, toothbrush/ toothpaste and eyecare items. Because perfumes and aftershaves attract some insects, they are not recommended in the outdoors. You also risk not seeing the many animals who were warned off by your overly-scented body.

Toilet Paper

Of course you know you need to bring toilet paper if you are camping in an area without bathhouses or latrines. Even day hikers need to carry toilet paper.

And while we're on the subject, one of the worst sights you'll see when camping is wads of toilet paper scattered throughout the woods. If there is no established latrine, please take the time to dig yourself a cat hole for your feces and toilet paper. A plastic trowel made just for this purpose can be found at most outdoors stores and costs less than $2. That's well worth the "trouble" when you consider how much it will lessen your environmental impact.

Never relieve yourself near a water source. Always find a site at least fifty yards downhill or to the side of a water source. This is for the protection of wildlife as well as other

>>Camping Tip<<

Baking soda is a multi-purpose camping item. It can be used for toothpaste, boot and sleeping bag deodorizer, foot soak, deodorant and fire extinguisher (if your stove catches fire when or where it shouldn't). Mixed with a bit of water, it forms a paste to take the ouch out of insect bites and stings and poison ivy.

campers. According to the Centers for Disease Control, beavers living downstream from national parks and forests contract giardiasis (caused by humans) more often than humans pick up the notorious stomach ailment.

Note to Women

Urination for male campers in the outdoors is as easy, if not easier as it is in the real world—because there is no seat to lift. Female campers don't have it so easy. Although some places offer the occasional latrine, you cannot count on it.

There are a number of ways to urinate outdoors without getting your boots wet. One method is to drop your drawers to your knees, bend your knees a bit, lean forward with your hands on your knees for support, relax and go.

Another option is to find what Kathleen Meyer, author of *How to Shit in the Woods*, calls the perfect pose. Find two rocks, a rock and a log, two logs, or if necessary, a steep slope and a log or rock. Sitting on one, you balance your feet on the other, once again avoiding splashed boots.

A third option is the funnel, but make sure you purchase one with a long hose. The funnels, available at outdoors stores and through some camping catalogs, are designed to slip easily into your pants and transport your urine outside.

Menstruation is another problem women face in the outdoors when not in the presence of a bathhouse. On backcountry trips, it's going to be "pack it in, pack it out," so make sure you bring along enough resealable bags to hold your used tampons or napkins. Burning is not really an option because the fire must be very hot to completely burn a tampon or napkin, and plastic applicators shouldn't be burned because they release poisons into the air.

Your best choice is going to be an applicatorless tampon such as OBs or applicators made of paper products. OBs are compact and produce the least amount of waste all the way around. Once used, wrap them in a bit of toilet paper and seal in a plastic bag until you reach a suitable dumping station. Never throw tampons or napkins in a latrine, nor bury them because it will take them years to disintegrate, if animals don't dig them up first.

Towel

For most camping trips, it is appropriate to bring a towel because you will be using the showers in a bathhouse. But what if you are camping at a primitive site or in the backcountry? Do you intend to swim or rinse off in a river, lake, etc.? If so, by all means throw a towel in with your other gear.

A lightweight Pack Towl absorbs ten times its weight in water and dries quickly. Most outdoor stores sell this brand or a similar product.

Shampoo/soap

Never, ever, wash yourself or your hair in a stream, pond, or other body of water. Stand on dry ground and use a biodegradable soap and a pot of water to wash yourself. A lot of water sources provide drinking water for campers as well as animals. Would you want to drink water that somebody had rinsed their soapy body in?

Before depending on a biodegradable soap as an all-round cleaner, I would suggest testing it on various things you plan to use it for—hair, body, clothes, pots and pans—before leaving home. This way you can find out if it works for you while you have backup soaps and cleaners on hand. There are a number of biodegradable soaps available from outdoors stores, including Mountain Suds, Bio-suds and Sunshower Soap. These soaps average about $3 for a 4-ounce bottle.

There are two products on the market called NO-Rinse that require no water for a shampoo and only one quart of water to bathe. N/R Laboratories claim that you simply massage NO-Rinse in and towel dry it out. NO-Rinse Body Bath and NO-Rinse Shampoo are available from Goodman Marketing (P.O. Box 5459, Dept. S, Fresno, CA 93755-5459). The cost is $14.95 plus $4 shipping and handling for an 8-ounce bottle of each.

If your soap doesn't work as a shampoo, most discount department stores and drug stores offer trial or sample size products that are great for camping trips. Shampoos are commonly available in sample sizes as are toothpastes and lotions. I've used a variety of shampoos while camping, but if you can find a biodegradable shampoo you'll lessen your detrimental effect on the environment. Some products for use at home, such as Ivory, are more earth-friendly than others. The fewer dyes and other additives, the easier the shampoo or soap will biodegrade. As with soaps, though, never wash your hair with shampoo in or near a water source.

If you are camping in a developed campground with a fully-equipped bathhouse, the type of soap or shampoo you use is less of an issue. But if you are trying to keep down the mass of your gear, sample sizes are great for this type of camping too.

>>Camping Tip<<

Is it impossible to bathe or shower? Try baby wipes. Sold in a variety of sizes, they clean, deodorize and moisturize and all in the privacy of your own tent. Remember to pack them out!

Deodorant

Unless you're spending a week in the backcountry, deodorant is probably a necessity. The most natural way to deodorize yourself is by using what is known as a deodorant rock. Composed of natural mineral salts, this crystal-like deodorant supposedly lasts a full year with normal use. My husband and I tried one at home and found that unless we thoroughly cleansed our underarms before each application, our underarm odor built up very quickly. However, this deodorant might be perfect for someone else. Deodorant rocks are available at health food stores and through some catalogs. Two of the more popular brands are NATURE'S Pure Crystal Deodorant and Le Crystal Naturel. Deodorant rocks cost approximately $16.

Another relatively natural way to deodorize yourself is to use a baking-soda based powder such as Shower-to-Shower. If you're not interested in this natural methods of stopping perspiration odor, you can always carry your favorite deodorant in its sample or regular size.

Razors/Shaving Cream

When camping, whether to go through the extra bother of shaving is primarily a matter of preference. Many men opt to grow a beard while women prefer to continue shaving. If you have a bathhouse at your disposal, it will be much easier to shave than in the backcountry. Remember to shave away from water sources.

Toothbrush/Toothpaste

Don't brush your teeth near a water source, either. Rather, dig a small hole to spit into and then cover your spit. As at home, you should brush after every meal (and floss, too!).

As for toothcare products, there are variety of options on the market. If you worry about how much you're bringing, try using a child's toothbrush while camping. They are both small and lightweight. Toothpaste can easily be purchased in sample sizes, or you might want to try using baking soda that you can transfer to a small bottle for convenience.

Eyecare

Don't be afraid to wear your contact lenses while camping, although you might want to carry along a pair of glasses just in case. The new, daily, extended-wear and disposable lenses are easy to care for, and the cleaning fluid does not add too much bulk to your toiletries kit.

Lighting

Very simply put, it is a good idea to bring along some source of light for evenings at camp. Sitting outdoors before you retire for the night is one of the most relaxing and peaceful times during your camping trip. Lanterns and flashlights are among the types of lighting you might need for camping.

Lanterns

The big, white gas lanterns are perfect for car camping. They are both bright and efficient and relatively easy to light. Coleman is a major manufacturer of lanterns and makes everything from dual-fuel (unleaded gasoline or standard camping fuel) lanterns to propane and fluorescent lanterns. Gas lanterns range in price from $10 to $50 but also require the purchase of fuel and mantles to keep them running. Because most of these lights are adjustable, they can burn for as little as three hours and as much as eighteen.

Burning a lantern late into the night in a campground is a sure way to disturb your neighbors. The bright light can shine into other campers' tents and make it hard for them to get to sleep. When everyone else is settled down in the campground (usually by 11 P.M.), it is time to put out your lantern and revert to a flashlight or smaller candle lantern.

Smaller and lighter than a gas lantern, but not providing as much light is the candle lantern. Some of these small lanterns can be equipped to use gas, as well. They weigh as little as 6 ounces (sold by Limelight Productions, REI, Early Winters, and at some outdoors stores under the generic— Candle Lantern). One candle will give you as much as eight hours of illumination. As I said, the candle lantern does not produce as much light as the bigger gas lanterns, but it does work better than a flashlight when it comes to cleaning, reading and writing after dark.

The candle lantern is better than a candle alone because it is safer. It is housed in metal and glass, so you are less likely to start an unwanted fire if it tips over. It is also more economical because it is protected from the wind and, thus, does not burn up as quickly as an exposed candle. You can purchase a candle lantern for $10 to $20 and refills for about 50¢ a piece.

Small oil and gas lanterns burn for up to twenty hours per fill-up and cost about $20 to $30. They weigh the same as candle lanterns, and some can take different grades of lamp oil, including citronella (an insect repellent).

All small lanterns are equipped with a hanger and can often be rigged to hang from the apex of your tent by an attached nylon cord. Many tents have loops in the apex that will allow you to fasten a cord. If your tent does not have a loop at its apex, it may be possible to add a loop of Velcro or to sew on one yourself. Some tents have loops in the corners designed to hold gear lofts from which you can rig a line to hold a lantern. Remember to keep the lantern a safe distance from the material of the tent so you won't burn holes in the tent or set it afire. Not a single manufacturer of lanterns recommends they be used in tent; do so at your own risk. With a four-year-old daughter sharing my tent, I use a flashlight.

Flashlights

On my first camping trip as an adult, I didn't think I would need a flashlight because I was carrying a candle lantern. I soon learned differently. Even if you're carrying a lantern, you will probably also want to carry a flashlight. It can come in very handy.

First of all, it's not easy to wake up in the middle of the night and light a candle lantern just so you won't walk into briars (or worse!) when looking for a spot to relieve yourself. Even the trip from the tent to the bathhouse sometimes needs illuminating. Flashlights are great inside a tent because the light can be directed, and you don't risk waking up nearby campers with a suddenly bright light.

A spectacular flashlight, manufactured by Eveready, is a dual flashlight/lantern. By sliding back the battery cylinder and setting the flashlight upright, you get a soft and diffused area light. Time for a trek to the bathhouse or woods? Transform the lantern back into a flashlight. The krypton lamp uses four AA batteries and costs about $12.

The flashlight you take camping will depend on your preference. From mini-mags that run on two AAs to the super heavy flashlights that require two D cell batteries, you have quite a variety to choose from. For most camping trips (unless you do not have a lantern), the heavier flashlights are overkill. Surprisingly, the mini-mags provide a lot of output for very little weight.

Flashlights range in price from less than $5 to more than $30, and can be purchased at nearly any store. Remember

---

>>Camping Tip<<

Your flashlight can do occasional double-duty as a lantern. Place a Nalgene brand or other translucent bottle over the end of the flashlight to disperse light. Stand the bottle up on the open end and you have a serviceable lantern.

though, if you decide to depend solely on a flashlight for your light, you will need a steady supply of batteries.

Batteries

When it comes to camping, there are only two types of batteries that are worth considering—alkaline and lithium.

Alkaline: These batteries are far more efficient and longer-lasting than standard and heavy duty batteries. They offer as much as double the life of standard batteries, yet weigh and cost just a bit more. Unlike carbon-zinc cells, the alkaline battery dies suddenly rather than fading out—a minor disadvantage. Alkaline batteries do recharge themselves a bit and will last for another twenty minutes or so if left to recharge for half a day, unlike standard batteries that recharge only enough to put out a dim light for another five minutes. Alkalines cost about $2.50 for two AA batteries, $3 for two C batteries, and $3 for two D batteries.

Lithium: Extremely light and efficient, lithium batteries are also expensive (though in ratio to their effectiveness and weight not inordinately so). Unlike alkaline batteries, lithium will work in cold temperatures. Lithium batteries also have a much longer shelf life than alkaline batteries.

As for drawbacks, lithium batteries are still not widely available. Alkaline batteries can be purchased in almost every supermarket, drug store, convenience store and discount store in the United States. Lithiums are much harder to find but are usually stocked by good outdoors stores. They also require special bulbs, and there are restrictions about carrying them on aircraft. It is said that under certain conditions (intense heat or prolonged shorting) lithium cells may explode, although it is more likely that they will release a small bit of sulfur-dioxide gas than explode. Lithiums range in price from $8 for AA to $15 for a C to $20 for D cell.

Rope

Rope will definitely prove its usefulness on most camping trips. A length of rope, at least ten feet long and approximately three-sixteenths of an inch in diameter, is absolutely necessary for camping. As a matter of fact, it would be wise to carry several lengths of rope, ranging from a few feet to twenty feet in length.

For instance, many camping areas are located in bear country. Whether protected or hunted, bears love human food. Some national parks provide poles on which you can hang your food. In other areas, rope can be used to suspend a bag containing your food and other smellables from a tree to keep them out of reach of bears.

Rope can also be used for hanging your sleeping bags to air and hanging your wet clothes, rigging tents and tarps, making a belt, replacing frayed straps on gaiters or laces on boots, or for tying to a water bottle when it must be used as a dipper.

Keep in mind that if you intend to use a tarp on your camping trips, you will probably need at least fifty feet of rope, because you never know how far apart the trees, rocks or shrubs will be that you will use to set it up. (Remember, too, that you can tie two lengths of rope together, if necessary.) Most outdoors stores offer several types of rope, but the best for general camping is heavy-duty twisted or braided nylon rope ranging in width from one-eighth of an inch to one-quarter of an inch (or three to eight mm). Before using nylon rope, always burn the ends into hard knobs so that the rope does not unravel.

Knots

There are dozens of knots that can be learned, but fortunately only a few you'll need to know for camping. When tying knots, make sure the tail of each knot is at least a couple of inches long to insure that the knot won't slip.

Double fisherman's knot: This is the most common camping, backpacking and climbing knot because it can be used to tie two pieces of rope together. It is the safest and easiest to tie:

Sheet-bend: This is the simplest way to tie two unequal sizes of rope together and is very strong, but the double fisherman is still recommended for climbing ropes.

Tautline hitch: This knot can be used for securing lines from a grommet to a stake or tree.

Clove hitch: You might use this knot when hanging your food for the night or securing your tarp to a tree.

Repair Equipment
Even if you're just going on an overnight camping trip, it is wise to carry along a few small items to help you out in a pinch. Most problems can be taken care of with these miniature repair kits.

Tent Repair
We always carry a tent repair kit, and, boy, has it come in handy—and not just for our tent. I've used it to repair my sleeping bag stuff sack and Frank's rain pants, as well as our tent.

❦ *Camping Secret* ❦

For a rough estimate of how long you have until sunset, hold you hand out at arm's length and line your fingers up with the horizon. Each finger that you can fit between the horizon and the bottom of the sun represents about fifteen minutes. If six fingers separate the sun and land, the should set in about one and a half hours.

Tent repair kits usually include tent fabric tape (adhesive-backed, waterproof ripstop nylon of two types), a small amount of duct tape, a needle and thread, a short length of cord, an aluminum splint for tent poles, and no-see-um netting. A good kit, manufactured by Outdoor Research, costs $5 and weighs only 2.5 ounces.

If you're going on a long-term camping trip (more than a week), you'll probably want to bring along some seam sealer as well. Extensive use is hard on a tent, and you'll need to reseal the seams every week or two, depending on how much it rains and how much you're inside the tent.

Stove Repair

Carry a stove repair kit or learn how to build fires. Stoves will break or have problems when you least expect it or desire it. If the manufacturer of your stove offers a kit, it is wise to purchase one. Packing the kit is well worth the peace of mind. We use ours, and everyone else we know uses theirs.

Repair kits cost about $5 to $10 and weigh approximately 2 ounces. Not all stove manufacturers offer repair kits for their stoves; some stoves are not designed for field repair.

Clothing Repair

You can purchase a miniature sewing kit, complete with a number of different colored threads, needle, thimble, scissors, needle threader, snaps and buttons, at almost any drug, discount, grocery or outfitter store. For overnight camping trips, a sewing kit is probably not necessary. If you don't feel you need all the accessories, put a needle and some thread into your tent repair kit instead.

I carry an entire sewing kit (approximately 2" by 3") that weighs about an ounce, and I have used it innumerable times. Dental floss is a high-strength sewing material if an emergency should strike.

> ## >>Camping Tip<<
>
> Looking for a little solitude? By camping in little-used areas, you'll not only find peace and quiet, you'll spread out the impact humans make in a given area. Ask park rangers and others familiar with the area if they know of any infrequently used campsites.

Fanny Packs

One way of keeping things handy while day hiking is by using a fanny pack. Many hikers use these miniature packs in reverse, snug across their bellies with the strap fastened in the small of the back. Cameras, water, snacks, guide books, or whatever you need quick access to can be carried in this way.

Fanny packs, though useful, are not as comfortable as daypacks because they do not distribute the weight as well and often cannot carry as much as you might like to bring. They can be used along with a daypack or alone (if you have a partner carrying a daypack).

When purchasing a fanny pack, make sure the belt is well padded for comfort and the sack is sturdy enough to carry the load you intend for it. Some fanny packs are designed to carry only very light loads and will sag if heavy objects are placed in them. Also, if the fabric is thin, you may get poked and prodded by the objects inside.

Daypacks

Most daypacks are made in the same teardrop style, so the important thing to look at is how well the pack is made. Inexpensive daypacks can be purchased at any discount store, but if they are poorly padded and have little support, you won't have hiked a mile before you regret the purchase.

Leather-bottomed packs are the most durable and carry the load better by supporting the weight rather than collapsing beneath it. Make sure the shoulder straps on your daypack are very secure because this is the first place that such packs fall apart. This occurs because you are carrying the weight on your shoulders as opposed to your hips (as with backpacks). To prevent ripping, a number of daypacks have extra reinforcement where the shoulder straps connect to the sack. Another feature to look for is padding at the back of the pack. The more reinforced this section, the less likely you'll be poked by objects inside the pack.

Features to look for in daypacks include:

- Convenient loading through top or front panel.
- Pockets for smaller items (some daypacks feature a special loop to hold keys).
- A waist strap to keep the pack from bouncing against your back.
- Padded shoulder straps.
- Lash points for extra gear.

Daypacks are usually less than $100, and most manufacturers feature a variety to choose from.

First Aid Kit

It is next to impossible to create a perfect first aid kit. You can never be sure what type of emergency you will encounter. But it is easy to create a kit that will cover most of the problems you are likely to encounter.

Do not carry anything in your kit that you do not know how to use. For example, a suture kit will be useless to you unless you have been trained in suturing wounds. Don't carry prescription medicines unless you are fully aware of how to use them and their side effects. Proper training in a wilderness first aid or Red Cross standard first aid course will heighten your awareness of emergencies and prepare you to deal with them properly.

Depending on how safety-conscious you are, there are all sorts of items available to ease your mind while camping. Everything from dental emergency kits to accident report forms can be purchased for your first aid kit. Hard plastic containers (Rubbermaid and Tupperware brands are good examples) make durable, waterproof containers for first aid kits.

The following is a list of what makes up a close-to-perfect kit:

- A Ziploc or other brand zipper-lock plastic bag to hold the items in your first aid kit.
- Approximately six 1" x 3" band-aids. These can be used to cover most scratches, cuts and scrapes.
- Two 4" x 4" sterile gauze pads. These can be cut down or doubled up, depending on the size of the wound.
- A roll of 1" athletic tape ten yards long. It has a variety of uses, from holding on the sterile gauze to wrapping ankles.
- A 6"-wide elastic wrap (such as made by Ace). These can be used to wrap strains and sprains as well as to hold

bandages in place, constrict snake bites, compress heavy bleeding or splint a broken bone.

- **Tincture of benzoin.** Not only does this liquid toughen feet, but it helps tape stick better when rubbed on the skin.
- A couple of butterfly band-aids for closing small, gaping wounds.
- A sanitary napkin is great for stanching heavily bleeding wounds.
- Povidone-iodine ointment has a number of uses—disinfects wounds (straight from the tube), dissolves in water for a wash for larger scrapes, and can even be used as a lubricant or to treat water in an emergency. Betadine may also be used.
- Large triangular bandage or extra bandana for immobilizing breaks.
- Moleskin to treat hot spots and blisters.
- A few safety pins always come in handy. They can be used to hold the Ace bandage, drain blisters, repair clothing, etc.
- Your favorite painkiller for aches, pains, fever, etc.
- A few antihistamine tablets such as Benadryl to combat insect bites and poison ivy.
- Pepto-Bismol or some similar tablets for upset stomachs.
- Scissors and tweezers. (You may be able to find a pocket knife with these items. My tiny Victorinox has both, and they have come in handy many times.)
- Surgical gloves to protect you from a risk of contracting HIV. Paramedics and other health care workers also wear a face mask, to reduce the chance of infection from a variety of diseases.

Other items to consider, depending on the time of year and where you are camping, include meat tenderizer or Sting-eze for insect bites, sunscreen, alcohol to help remove ticks, lip

---

>>Camping Tip<<

Use duct tape to prevent blisters if you are out of moleskin. Wrap a bit of duct tape around your Nalgene bottle (or other canteen). It will also come in handy to repair equipment in emergencies.

---

balm, lotion, prescription drugs if you need them, a bee sting kit if you are allergic to insect stings, and DEET repellent for mosquitos and other insects (see Chapter 13). Remember that a first aid kit is a very personal item. For example, if you are allergic to insects, have heart problems, have trouble with constipation, hemorrhoids or are prone to sinus headaches, make sure your first aid kit has the medicine, laxative or ointment you may need. If you are a diabetic, heart patient or have other special health concerns, be sure that someone in your group is prepared to help you in an emergency.

I use lip balm (Chap Stick works best for me) constantly both at home and away from home. I can't abide the feeling of chapped lips and always carry several tubes of Chap Stick with me wherever I go. Other good lip balms are Blistex, Carmex and Labiosin. Petroleum jelly works well too. You can find many options both at drugstores and outdoors stores.

Always carry an SPF15 sunscreen. It will give you enough coverage to protect you from the sun without overdoing it. Some people are allergic to the stronger SPF factor sunscreens, and tests show that they do not help significantly better than SPF15. As with lip balms, you can find a wide range of sunscreens to choose from at your local drug, discount and outdoors stores.

Lotion is another product you may wish to add to your kit if you intend to be camping in hot, dry weather. Some sunscreens combine lotion with the screen, or you may wish to carry a sample size of your favorite brand. Remember, though, that baby oil acts as a sun tan lotion as well as a skin softener and could be potentially dangerous if you intend to use it as a lotion. If you will be doing some desert camping, you may want to carry along a lotion with aloe vera that will help soothe any sunburn you might experience. If your skin is very sensitive to the sun, a sunburn therapy such as Solarcaine or Ahhh might be worth the space in your first aid kit.

Although I've never known any one to use one, some people feel safer if they carry along a snake-bite kit. There are several kits on the market ranging from $5 to $15. The simplest kit contains two big suction cups plus a smaller cup for bites on small surfaces such as fingers. The kit also includes a lymph constrictor, scalpel, antiseptic vial and instructions. The $10 Extractor is a double-chamber vacuum pump with four cup sizes, antiseptic, band-aids, a safety razor, instructions and a carrying case. The Extractor is the only recommended first aid for snake bites these days, and it is said even it does little to help.

Unless you have a special need or problem, do not carry too many specific items in your first aid kit. The kit and its contents should be as versatile as possible. It won't matter that you have to cover a 2"-wide wound with a 4"-wide bandage, for example. Space for your first aid kit will only be a problem when hiking, biking or canoeing. You don't want to overdo it but remain prepared.

Also, remember to repack your first aid kit seasonally or yearly. Medicines expire and may need to be replaced, so always check the expiration dates before heading out on any trip. And there is no use carrying insect repellent on a winter trip when there are no bugs around. Your first aid kit should reflect your personal needs as well as the season and geographic area in which you're camping.

Another option is to buy a preassembled first aid kit. Outdoors stores offer a variety of kits ranging in price from $8 to $80. Outdoor Research, Adventure Medical Kits and REI are some of the major manufacturers of first aid kits for hikers and campers.

Items for Emergencies

When it comes to emergencies, what you bring with you will depend very much upon where you are camping. In developed parks, there is usually a ranger, host, or manager nearby who is either capable of administering first aid or can summon someone who can.

If you are camping in a backcountry site, there probably won't be an emergency, but some people like to bring a mirror, flares and a whistle just in case. Most campers carry mirrors, anyway, to help with shaving, contact lenses, brushing hair, etc. A mirror can help signal someone above or below you. Some watches have reflective surfaces, and some compasses have sighting mirrors that can be used for signaling. Foil, your stove's windscreen (if it reflects) or even your sunglasses can also be used to signal. Signal mirrors, on the other hand, are heavy and an extra item to keep track of.

I've never taken one camping, but some campers feel safer if they bring a flare or smoke bomb for emergencies. The bomb emits clouds of orange or red smoke that can be seen from both the ground and the air. Flares can be shot up into the air and usually burn for an average of seven seconds. I have seen both smoke bombs and flares available through catalogs—$8 for the bomb, $16 for three flares—and most outdoors stores keep them in stock as well.

>>Camping Tip<<

In emergency situations that require the use of distress signals, try using a space blanket as an emergency flag. The reflector-like silver coating of the lightweight blanket will be highly visible to aircraft when attached to a tall tree.

For use in both an emergency and as a warning to bears, you can also carry a whistle in your emergency kit. Just make sure you use the whistle only in emergency situations, because in addition to crying "wolf," you'll also be disturbing the other people out there who are seeking peace and quiet. If you purchase a whistle, make sure the balls inside are made of metal or plastic. Survival whistles can be purchased for under $3.

There is a gadget on the market called the Survivo II that includes an accurate compass, waterproof matchcase, whistle, striking flint and signal mirror. It is packed in a 4.5" x 1.25" case, weighs a mere ounce and costs only $4.

Sunglasses
There are so many options when it comes to sunglasses that I cannot begin to recommend any one particular brand. If you do carry sunglasses, and I recommend that you do, make sure that the lenses are designed to filter out the sun's harmful rays—both ultraviolet and infrared. Sunglasses are especially essential for desert and snow camping where the sun reflects off the ground and into your eyes and on boating trips.

Sunglasses can be purchased from $5 to $75 and up. Quality sunglasses are also manufactured for children, including glasses that filter out ultraviolet and infrared rays. Straps to hold your sunglasses around your neck—Chums, Croakies and others—are worth the extra $5 because they keep you from losing sunglasses. This is especially beneficial if you just paid $40 for your shades. There are also a number of other gadgets that can be purchased for sunglasses (and glasses, if you wear them) including defoggers and lens cleaners, cases, windguard and clip-on sun shades for eyeglass wearers.

Binoculars

Carrying binoculars is a matter of preference, but modern technology has made them both lightweight and tough so the heavy, bulky binoculars of yore are no longer an excuse not to bother.

When purchasing binoculars, there are two things to keep in mind besides weight and durability: magnification and lens size. These traits are identified by two numbers (for example, 10 X 25). It is these two numbers that determine the quality of your binoculars. The higher the magnification number and the larger the lens, the more expensive your binoculars will be.

Magnification—the larger the number, the greater the magnifying power. Numbers greater than 10, though, mean you will have a hard time keeping your hand steady enough to focus on whatever object you've sighted.

Lens size—the second number identifies the diameter, in millimeters, of the objective lens (the objective lens is the lens farthest away from your eye). The larger the objective lens, the more light reaches your eye and the brighter the image you see.

There are a number of binocular manufacturers including, Brunton, Leica, Nikon, Minolta, Swarovski, Pentax, Steiner and Bushnell. The staff at your local outdoors store or camera shop should be able to help you choose your binoculars.

Guns

Some campers consider guns essential, but carrying weapons into a national park is a federal offense, and firearms are outlawed in many other areas as well. The real question is, are they necessary? Firearms are a controversial subject among campers. Most feel that guns are unnecessary, but a few do carry them along on camping trips. Sitting around a communal campfire in a south Georgia state park, the talk turned to firearms with several RVers claiming to have guns in their trailers and motorhomes to protect themselves from break-ins. Many of the non-guntoting crowd seemed a little edgy that the subject had even come up. After a lengthy exchange of gun-related anecdotes, it became clear that although many campers had heard of the occasional theft, nobody knew of a case where a gun had been used, success- fully or otherwise, to protect a camper.

Guns are only necessary if you're camping trip is part of a legitimate hunting trip. Frank and I have talked to people who have camped from coast to coast in the United States as well as some who have camped in Europe, New Zealand and elsewhere throughout the world. The bottom line was this: there was neither a single instance where a firearm was used to threaten one of these hikers nor a case of a firearm helping a camper out of a jam. No one felt a gun was necessary either for protection from animals or protection from humans.

What Else?
There are a number of other items you may want to take along on a camping trip, including books, radios, **lawn chairs**, maps and compass (if you intend to do some bushwhacking), etc. It all depends on your personal needs and the room you have in your canoe, car, RV or whatever, to get your equip- ment to camp.

· 4 ·
Clothes

A Scout's clothing should be of wool as much as possible, because it dries easily. Cotton next to the skin is not good unless you change it as soon as it gets wet.

—*Lord Baden-Powell*
Scouting for Boys

In 1907, clothing for campers could be summed up in the above lines. There weren't any high-tech choices on the market. Wool, silk and cotton were the only options, and dealing with wool up against your skin was the only trick. Today an array of engineered fabrics, including Synchilla, Lycra spandex, Thermax, Polypropylene and Gore-Tex, elbow one another (and the old standbys, wool and silk) for shelf space in the stores and ultimately a place in your camping wardrobe.

The type of clothing you wear will virtually determine the comfort of your camping trip. Just because you plan a camping trip to the beach does not mean your suitcase or duffel bag should contain only shorts, T-shirts and bathing suits. I have worn long johns and a wool sweater when camping on a barrier island off the coast of Florida during the month of May. Clothing is undoubtedly a matter of personal preference, but there are some tips that could save you a lot of frustration. The most important tip is the famous Boy Scout creed—"Be prepared."

You do not have to carry a suitcase for every season to be prepared for all types of weather. Shorts, T-shirt, long johns, wool sweater and rain gear can all be layered to add warmth. Camping in the low desert of southern California can be akin to a day in Dante's inferno. During the day it is hard to stay cool in the lightest of T-shirts and shorts. But when the sun drops below the horizon, it doesn't take long for things to cool off, and you will actually relish the warmth of your sleeping bag. You may also find yourself adding pants or long johns as the moon rises. There are even nights when a wool sweater would be in order.

Layering
Take the time to select your clothes carefully and think about layering. Layering has two benefits—extra insulation and adaptability. The air trapped between layers of clothes adds to the insulation value of the clothes themselves. Also, by adding or removing a layer, you can easily adapt your wardrobe to suit changes in the weather or different amounts of activity.

Buy an ensemble that can be adjusted to fit the circumstances. Consider your clothing options if you awake to a warm but rainy morning—long johns, pants or shorts, a shirt, sweater or fleece jacket, and rain gear. The rain gear applies only if you intend to be out and about in the rain. If you intend to stay in your tent, tarp or camper, your options will vary. Because it is warm but rainy, you will probably

>>Camping Tip<<

To keep your child warmer when packing her in cold weather, pull your wool socks over her shoes and legs. If the socks threaten to fall off, pin them to her pants. Whether hot or cold, keep a continual watch on your child to make sure the temperature does not affect them excessively.

want to wear only shorts and a T-shirt, and don the rain gear when you step outside. If your time outside your shelter is short or if you plan on hiking or some other physical activity, you may want to drop the rain gear all together and just get wet. Still, even if you intend to be moving around (hiking, jogging, etc.), make sure rain gear or a sweater or jacket is available to you when you stop moving. Your body in motion will keep you warm but once you stop moving, you can easily catch a chill.

Come evening, the temperature is bound to fall, and you may want to add a layer or two to keep you warm. On the other hand, if the morning had been rainy and cold, you could have layered your long johns or tights under your shorts and added sweater, rain gear and hat depending on just how cold it was outside. In the fall and winter particularly, a loose pair of pants or a pair of tights might work out better than shorts.

Layering allows you numerous options, and the clothes involved in layering are lighter, more durable, and allow you greater physical flexibility. The layering system works better than other methods (such as a separate outfit for each weather condition), especially when you get wet or sweat. It is important to layer with the right pieces—long johns or tights, pants or shorts, a wool or pile garment and a waterproof shell. As a general rule, you can wear just about whatever you want when camping, because in most cases you have transportation nearby (if you're not living in it) and can

head for home if you are really miserable. Even so, why get to the point that you're miserable? For example, layering cotton long johns under blue jeans may keep you warm at first, but as soon as the garments are wet with rain or sweat, you'll feel wretched.

When you are layered correctly, you can open up easily in response to the warmth. If you are sweating, take off your hat first. Because you lose most of your heat through your head, removing your hat or hood will act as a kind of air conditioning. If you're still hot, unzip your rain jacket a bit and loosen the sleeves (buy rain gear that allows the sleeves to be cinched tight) to let the air circulate.

Layering properly can be your best defense against hypothermia (discussed in detail in Chapter 12). It doesn't have to be freezing or even near it for you to become hypothermic. Getting wet in clothes that don't insulate when wet (such as cotton) can increase your danger of hypothermia. Allowing yourself to overheat and sweat can also prove dangerous. When you stop to rest or make camp, the sweat will evaporate and lower your body temperature. Remove and add layers as you get warm or cold. It may seem tiresome and time-consuming at the time, but it is the best way to regulate your body temperature.

Layering is appropriate anytime the weather gets cool. Even in the late spring and early fall, layering pile pants and a jacket over shorts and a T-shirt at dark will keep you warm into the night without your having to change clothes.

Fabrics

Choosing the fabric of your clothes is as important a decision as choosing what clothes you will bring on a camping trip. But glancing through the pages of an outdoors catalog is a mind-boggling experience! Synthetics with names such as Supplex nylon, Polartek polyester, Thinsulate and PolarGuard polyesters, Taslan nylon, Lycra spandex, Cordura nylon, Tactel nylon, Orlon acrylic, Hydrofil nylon, Capilene polyester and Ultrx nylon make you feel as if you need a degree in chemistry to purchase your outdoors clothes. Fortunately, it is not all as overwhelming as it seems.

Cotton

Beginning with the basics, cotton is inefficient in the outdoors. It doesn't keep you warm when it's wet, and it takes a long time to dry. For these reasons, clothes that might serve you well at home will not do as well on a camping trip.

The best example is blue jeans. Not only are they constricting, but when they get wet, they double or triple in weight. They also take forever to dry. Other cotton clothing to avoid includes long johns, socks, sweaters, and 100 percent cotton T-shirts. However, as I have said before, if your camping trip involves nothing more than a pleasant day's rest and relaxation at your campsite, you can wear whatever you feel most comfortable in—cotton, tapa or fig leaves.

An alternative to 100 percent cotton clothing is a cotton blend. For instance, Patagonia Baggies (shorts) are made of a nylon-cotton blend and are favored by many outdoorsmen (and women!) because they are lightweight, roomy and water-resistant. Many manufacturers make pants and shorts of nylon-cotton blends. T-shirts made of cotton and a synthetic are popular, especially when hiking, because they allow freedom of movement and because they dry more quickly than all-cotton T-shirts. For camping trips or day hikes in pleasant weather and moderate altitudes, a blended cotton T-shirt is a good choice.

Wool

Wool is your best bet for winter wear, and when it is blended with polypropylene or other synthetics, it makes excellent socks. Wool keeps you warm when it's wet, and a wool sweater can be a lifesaver on cold and/or wet days. Temperatures at high altitudes can drop below freezing even in the summer. I have never been on a camping trip that I wasn't glad that I had brought something warm along (almost always a wool sweater). Even if you are packing lightly for a summer camping trip, carry along something warm and wooly (coat or sweater); it may be worth the peace of mind. New synthetics—the "Polars" and Synchilla—are giving wool a run for the money, and unlike wool, are never itchy. Unlike wool clothing, which can sometimes be found in thrift shops, new outdoor wear is expensive.

Silk
Silk is one of the lightest fabrics and is often used in long underwear. Although silk is a strong, flexible fabric, it tends to be less sturdy than synthetics, giving way at the seams more quickly. Silk must also be hand-washed and line-dried. The benefit of silk is that it gives you warmth without bulk, provides an effective first layer, and is wonderfully comfortable.

Polypropylene
This petroleum-based material forms a lightweight fabric that keeps you warm when it is wet. Polypropylene dries more quickly than wool and does not retain moisture, wicking it away immediately. When used as a first layer of clothing, it keeps your skin dry by transferring moisture to the next layer. Polypropylene is primarily used in long johns and socks. One drawback to polypropylene is that it absorbs the scent of perspiration and must be washed in a special detergent to remove the odor. It is also renowned for its pilling, which can be annoying, especially to the fashion conscious. Polypropylene must be line-dried to prevent shrinkage.

Thermax, CoolMax, Capilene and M.T.S.
Thermax is another synthetic used in garments designed to keep you warm. Like polypropylene, it draws moisture away from your body, and its hollow-core fibers trap air to provide insulation. Thermax can be machine-washed and tumbled dry, and it does not retain the odors of perspiration.

Du Pont's CoolMax has a modified rib base that has been manufactured for activities where you need lightweight clothing and a maximum of wicking away of perspiration. CoolMax has a four-channel construction that transports moisture away from your skin. It also has a twenty percent larger surface area than most fabrics, which contributes to quicker evaporation and therefore, dryer skin.

Capilene is a polyester fiber and is similar to Thermax in its attributes—it is odor resistant and can be machine-washed and dried. Both Capilene and Thermax are said to be softer than polypropylene and provide a lot of warmth for their weight.

M.T.S. or Moisture Transport System is a fabric sold by R.E.I., and like those above, was manufactured to move perspiration away from your skin as quickly as possible. It also boasts an extra-sturdy construction and an "active" fit, which basically means that it does not constrain your movements. M.T.S. comes in a variety of weights from 100 percent or expedition weight M.T.S. to the lighter M.T.S. fabrics, which are usually blended with polyester and Lycra.

Nylon
Because it is one of the easiest synthetics to manufacture, you will find many nylons on the market. Nylon is inexpensive, durable, abrasion-resistant, strong, and quick-drying. There are hundreds of types of nylon, from the rough-textured Taslan and the super-tough Cordura to the supple, softer nylons such as Supplex and ripstop.

The best purchase I have ever made was my nylon jogging shorts. Not only do they have a built-in liner (making underwear unnecessary), but they dry very quickly. And, if you're into backpacking, they are a lifesaver when it comes to keeping your hip belt from rubbing your hips raw.

Polarplus, Polarlite, Polartec,
Patagonia Synchilla and PCR Synchilla
These bunting, pile or fleece materials are good insulators. Comfortable jackets and pants can be purchased in Polarplus, a double-faced pile of fine-denier Dacron polyester (denier is a unit of measure for textile fibers); Polarlite, a lighter and stretchier version of Polarplus; Polartec polyester fleece, a

fabric constructed of fifty percent post-consumer recycled polyester; and Synchilla, Patagonia's well-known, double-faced synthetic pile, which now comes in a PCR version (post-consumer recycled) with eighty percent of the polyester manufactured from such things as plastic soda bottles.

These fabrics are bulky and heavy but heavenly soft and warm and worth their weight and bulk on a cold night. When hiking, the insulation these materials provide offers good protection from wind and cold, particularly at high altitudes or when taking a break. Though generally far too warm to hike in, they are still warmer per pound than wool and also dry more quickly than the natural fabric.

Although Polarlite is supposed to be lighter than Polarplus and Synchilla, it appears to weigh approximately the same, if not more, when used to fabricate similar garments. As with food, you may want to inspect a little more closely anything termed "lite."

Others
Lycra spandex is a very stretchy, strong synthetic used extensively in clothing—from cuffs and waistbands on jackets, to bras, socks, running tights and shorts. Tights made of a blend of polypropylene and lycra are especially popular because they keep you warm and conform to your body, allowing you a lot of freedom of movement.

Fibers polymerized from acrylonitrile are called acrylics and are rarely used in their "pure" form in clothing except maybe in underwear. Acrylics such as Orlon are often found as a blend, especially in socks.

There are actually of dozens of specialized fabrics used in outdoors clothes these days, but some of the worthier of note are used by Columbia Sportswear, a major manufacturer of outdoor clothing among the ranks of Patagonia, North Face and Woolrich.

Bergundtäl cloth, used by Columbia Sportswear in its parkas and other cold-weather clothing, is Columbia's version of Gore-Tex, a water-repellent but breathable fabric. The texturized nylon is treated with a special process to make it water repellent and virtually windproof. Columbia uses Omni-TechST, another waterproof, breathable fabric, in its Hammerhead Oxford to construct a virtually indestructible fabric. Hammerhead Oxford consists of extra-heavy polyester yarns, which creates an abrasion-resistant fabric; it is coated with polyurethane to help waterproof the fabric. Other fabrics include Harrier Pile, Columbia's 100 percent polyester pile; Rhino Skin, a 100 percent heavy-duty nylon oxford canvas that is sanded down to a cotton-like softness; Thermoloft, DuPont's combination of Dacron solid-core polyester fibers and hollow Quallofil fibers; Hydro Plus, woven from soft, drapable 100 percent nylon taffeta and coated for breathability and water repellency; Technicloth II, woven from high denier 100 percent nylon yarns and coated with polyurethane; and Alpen Plus Fleece, made of 100 percent polyester that is fleeced twice.

Rain Gear

The type of camping you plan to do will determine what type of rain gear you need to purchase. If you intend to spend a lot of time outdoors (as opposed to inside your tent or camper), you will want to purchase a good set of rain gear—pants and jacket. Whether canoeing or hiking, you'll want something that will keep you both warm and dry. If you intend to stay in your tent except for quick trips to the bathhouse or the woods, an umbrella will suffice.

In warm weather, if you choose to keep active, you can probably survive the rain in just shorts and a T-shirt. Truthfully, many outdoorsmen refuse to fight the battle, opting to get wet. The more you move, the more likely you are to get wet even if you are wearing state-of-the-art rain gear. But the risk to your health when it is steamy outside is negligible. What about when it is cold or even just a bit chilly?

Wet clothes can lower your body temperature to the danger point. People die of hypothermia every year when they ignore their wet clothes on cool days, making rain gear one of the most essential items on your clothing checklist.

Ponchos

The least effective of all rain gear options, most rain ponchos are designed to cover you, and if you're backpacking, a pack. Ponchos do shield you from a lot of rain under ideal conditions, but in the wind they are practically useless.

While a number of people find that ponchos meet their needs, most outdoorsmen who have tried ponchos dispose of them shortly after their first rain. Ponchos cost from $3 for a vinyl poncho to $30 for a coated nylon backpacker's poncho.

Rain Suits

Rain Suits (a jacket and pants), although usually designed in sets, can also be purchased as separates. They afford the best protection against the cold and rain. When purchasing a rain suit, remember to consider whether you want a suit in Gore-Tex or coated nylon.

Gore-Tex: This fabric, developed by W.L. Gore, has been adopted by a number of manufacturers of rainwear as well as many other clothing manufacturers. The fabric has also been copied as closely as possible. Gore-Tex is a hotly debated subject: campers either swear by it or at it; it is everything it claims to be or too expensive for the little it does.

Clothing made with Gore-Tex promises to be both water repellent and breathable. The key to its properties is an extremely thin and very lightweight membrane patented by

>>Camping Tip<<

If your sleeping bag isn't warm enough, try wearing your raingear over your long johns as an improvised vapor barrier. Plastic bags or stuff sacks can be tied over your feet to keep them warmer.

the W.L. Gore Company. Made up of two different substances, the Gore-Tex membrane keeps out the water while allowing moisture vapor to escape. The component that repels water is pure expanded polytetrafluoroethylene (ePTFE), which is similar to Teflon polymers and contains nine billion microscopic pores per square inch. Because the pores are smaller than a droplet of a water but much larger than a molecule of water vapor, water (in its liquid form) cannot penetrate the membrane. On the other hand, vapor released from your body can escape through the membrane to the outside.

The second part of the membrane consists of an oleophobic or oil repellent substance that allows water vapor to pass through but keeps oil-based contaminants from penetrating the membrane. Oils, cosmetics, insect repellents and food substances would otherwise affect the breathability of the article of clothing. The oleophobic substance is also impenetrable to wind. This is said to make Gore-Tex both warm and water repellent.

The Gore-Tex membrane is found between the outer layer and inner lining of the garment. Depending on the piece of outerwear you purchase, the membrane will be laminated or bonded to the outer fabric or hang freely between the two layers.

The argument over whether or not Gore-Tex works centers around whether it is truly breathable and waterproof. I have spent thousands of hours in the outdoors in my Gore-Tex rain jacket (many of those when it was only cold and not raining). On separate occasions, the jacket has left me either wet or dry and hot. The wet, though, was caused by perspiration and not by the rain, except in cases when it was raining so hard that raindrops dripped off my hood and along my face and neck and thus inside my jacket. The fabric is sufficiently waterproof against light and/or brief rain showers. Downpours or all-day rains can be a problem, but if you are camping and not forced into an all-day ramble as you might be with backpacking, set up camp or remain in camp, and you eliminate this problem. Now, the wetness caused by sweating should be eliminated by the fabric's "breathability." If you perspire heavily, and lots of people do, it is my experience that the fabric seems incapable of keeping up with the water vapor escaping your body when you are physically active—canoeing, hiking, climbing, etc. Regardless, Gore-Tex is still the best fabric when it comes to rain gear because it keeps you as dry as coated nylon but offers a lot more breathability.

Gore-Tex rain suits can be purchased from $200 to $500; most cost approximately $300. You can also purchase suits in a variety of weights—some with extra protection, some with liners for added warmth. Among the designers of Gore-Tex rain wear are Campmor, L.L. Bean, Marmot, Montbell, Moonstone, Nike, The North Face, REI, Sierra Designs, Solstice and VauDe.

Nylon: As with Gore-Tex, coated nylon rain suits can be found in a variety of styles. Because coated nylon makes no effort to be breathable, it doesn't keep you as cool as Gore-Tex, but it is also less expensive.

Coated nylon rain suits must have the seams sealed to be effective. Seam sealer can be purchased through outfitters and mail order houses. Following the directions carefully and resealing the seams occasionally will ensure proper waterproofing. Nylon rain suits range from $50 to $150.

Hats

Hats are an indispensable part of a camping outfit, especially if you intend to spend a lot of time in the elements (sun, wind, cold, rain and so on). If your feet are cold, putting on a hat will warm them up, because much of the body's heat is lost through your head. As a matter of fact, warming your head will do more toward warming your feet than adding an extra pair of socks. Another pair of socks might actually make your feet colder by making your shoes too tight and constricting the circulation in your feet.

A wool cap with a polypropylene liner will keep your head warm while wicking away perspiration. Thermax hats are also good for the same reason. If you will be doing a lot of cold weather camping (winter is a great time for a solitary camping experience), you may want to invest in a balaclava. This hat covers your head and neck and most of your face and is much lighter to carry than an extra shirt or sweater!

While not as warm, baseball-style caps are great worn under your rain jacket hood to keep the hood from dripping rain on your nose and to help the hood move with your head. All types of baseball caps are available, including those that offer a neck flap for extra protection against the sun.

For those of you who go for the high-tech products, Sequel offers the Desert Rhat Hat. An adjustable chin strap keeps

---

>>Camping Tip<<

Being attacked by mosquitos? Use your DEET repellent on the brim of your hat and coat your bandana with it. By knotting the bandana at the back of your neck with the point hanging down your chest, you will keep most of the mosquitos away from your face and neck. If you are going to be out for several days or more, add less DEET each day because it will not evaporate completely with each use.

the hat on your head even in high winds, a large bill with a black underbrim provides sun protection for your eyes and face, a breathable lining of Tex-O-Lite metallic film shields the top of your head from the sun's intensity, a removable white cape reflects the sun, and a terrycloth headband absorbs the sweat—all for under $30.

Socks

Unless you intend to do some hiking or if the weather is especially cold, it really doesn't matter what type of sock, if any, you wear when camping. And, even if you intend to do some hiking, there are so many options that a discussion is relatively moot. There was a time when there was only one type of sock to wear with your hiking boots—it was wool or nothing. Now, it's hard to decide. While wool socks are still very present in the sock market, they are giving way to synthetic blends designed especially for backpacking.

Wool, cotton/wool blends and cotton socks are not as good for backpacking compared to the wool/polypropylene or nylon blends and the Orlon acrylic/nylon blend of Thor-Lo socks. If you prefer natural fibers, you will have to choose your disadvantage: wool socks retain much foot odor, and cotton socks tend to lose their shape. The Thor-Los were designed specifically for sports and include designs for running, hiking, climbing and backpacking. The hiking socks average about $7 a pair.

Gloves

My hands get cold easily, but I find that when camping, I rarely need gloves except on especially cold and wet days. This is good; otherwise, it would be hard to set up camp with bulky gloves restricting the movement of my fingers. I tend to use glove liners instead whenever possible, especially for tricky operations—clipping tent poles, firing the camp stove, etc. The liners are easier to maneuver your fingers in because they don't have the bulk of leather or wool gloves. Another option is to wear fingerless gloves while working with a stove or setting up a tent, or other times when your full-fingered gloves are too bulky.

But, once you have made camp and are no longer active, your body begins to cool down, and if you are anything like me, the first things to turn into blocks of ice are my hands and feet. Fortunately, there are a number of options in both gloves and mittens. From Gore-Tex shell and wool mittens to gloves of wool, wool-blends, Thinsulate, pile and other synthetics, you should be able to find a pair of hand warmers that fit your needs.

Keep in mind that you can also purchase glove and mitten liners (usually very lightweight and made of silk or synthetics used in the manufacture of thermal underwear) for extra cold days. If you're desperate, use plastic bags as vapor barrier-style gloves. Your hands might sweat but at least they'll be warm.

Bandanas
In the outdoors world, you're not a true camper (hiker, angler, etc.) unless you have at least one bandana on your person. Bandanas are wonderfully versatile. They can be used as headbands, hats and handkerchiefs. They can also be used to strain water before filtering and to cool hot necks (dipping the bandana in water and loosely tying about your throat). Similarly, they can be used as a cloth for washing and a towel for drying (your body or your dishes). I always carry several with me when I am camping.

Taking Care of Clothing
Caring for your clothing will only be a concern if your camping trip takes you into the wilderness for more than a few days. Most campgrounds, public and private, offer laundry facili-

ties. Most of the time, unless your clothes are just unbearably filthy, you can wait until you're in the comfort of your home (or the local laundromat) to wash them.

As with most clothing items, it is wisest to follow the washing instructions on the clothing labels. If you limit your wardrobe when camping, as I do, you might find it convenient to carry clothing that will wash and dry easily in the outdoors. Nylon shorts are perfect summertime camping wear because they can be rinsed out every day or so and unless it rains, will dry overnight. On wet nights, I have been known to pack my rinsed and wrung shorts at the end of my sleeping bag where they dry out from the heat of my body. If they are still damp in the morning, I can slip them on and though briefly uncomfortable, it is usually not long before my body's heat finishes the job of drying, that is, if my sweat doesn't soak the shorts first. (I do a lot of hiking on camping trips!)

T-shirts and socks can also be rinsed out and even washed occasionally by using a biodegradable soap. Remember that some synthetics require a special detergent to rid them of perspiration odors. Read the labels and know before you go. Never, never wash your clothes near a water source—even biodegradable soap leaves suds and a bad taste. Always dump dirty wash water far from any water source. If you are on a lengthy camping trip, you may want to make an occasional trip to the closest town where you can wash your clothes at a laundromat. Camping trips of this length that are confined to the wilderness are rare unless they involve backpacking as well. Some long-distance canoe trips may force you into an occasional town for resupply as well as washing. Canoeing is as hard on clothes (because of the physical exertion) as backpacking, but since you tend to be confined to the backcountry (ie., away from the general public), body odor and dirty clothes are not usually a high priority concern.

As for drying clothes, if you have a base camp or will be

camping in one area for any length of time on any given day, you may want to try making your own clothesline. Light-weight clothespins are available at most outdoors stores, or you can center your rope around a tree, twist it tightly, tie it to another tree, and then pull apart a twist to hold your clothes. You may want to carry a thin, lightweight line just for this purpose.

Vapor Barrier System
The vapor barrier system is a way to get warm as quickly as possible when you are really cold. It involves using an impermeable barrier such as a plastic bag to retain both your body's heat and moisture. Although not exactly comfortable because you stay wet, it is extremely effective.

Vapor barriers can be used in sleeping bag liners and in clothes such as pants, shirts, socks and gloves. I am from the school that believes vapor barriers are just fine when it's freezing cold outside and there is no other way to get warm. Some people believe in using vapor barriers in all cold-weather situations while others would rather die than submit themselves to the agony of a vapor barrier.

Try this method before you decide. Use plastic bags as a makeshift vapor barrier and see if you like the way they work. I have used plastic bags a number of times to warm up my feet, especially when my boots have failed to dry from the previous day's rain and it is raining again.

If you get really chilled, you will need to use every trick in the book to get warm. Even if you don't like the feel of the hot moisture trapped by a plastic bag around you feet or hands,

---

>>Camping Tip<<

When hiking in desert heat, dowse your clothes with water every chance you get. The continual evaporation will keep your body cooler.

use a vapor barrier when nothing else will work. Don't let yourself succumb to hypothermia.

Heat Loss

When recreating in the outdoors, you expose your body to four types of heat loss. Keep these in mind when purchasing and packing clothes for your camping trip. Always ask yourself if the clothes you are buying and/or bringing prevent or produce this heat loss?

Convective Heat Loss: This most common form of heat loss occurs when air and water come into contact, or near-contact, with your body and carry heat away with them. Materials such as pile, down, wool, PolarGuard, Hollofil, and Thinsulate work as a barrier against convective loss helping to retain most of your body's heat.

Evaporative Heat Loss: When you sweat, you lose heat through the evaporation of the liquid. This is great in warm weather because it cools the body; but when it's cold and you haved stopped moving, your clothes remain wet and so do you. This can lead to hypothermia. Fortunately for outdoorsmen, materials such as polypropylene have been designated to wick away the moisture or sweat. These materials work by removing the moisture from the skin before it evaporates.

Conductive Heat Loss: Although this is usually a relatively minor way to lose heat, it can be dangerous in certain circumstances. Conductive heat loss occurs when the body loses heat to the air, water or fabric that is in contact with the body at a lower temperature. Falling into cold water, for example, can cause you to lose all your body heat to the water, a potentially fatal situation.

Radiant Heat Loss: Another usually minor method of heat loss is when heat radiates out from your body into your clothes. Unless the fabric you are wearing reflects the heat back to you, the heat is lost to the air. Vapor barriers reflect the heat back to your body.

· 5 ·
Footwear

Today I have grown taller from walking with the trees.
—Karle Wilson Baker
Good Company

The main thing to keep in mind when selecting shoes for camping is comfort. Among the more popular choices for camp wear are hiking boots, river sandals, tennis shoes and aqua socks. While a few years ago sports sandals were the most common footwear to be seen around camp, today lightweight hiking boots have superceded the sandals as the most popular camp shoe.

Boots
Twenty years ago three types of boots were available to campers—work boots, alpine-style (heavy) hiking boots and combat boots. Today, hiking boots are one of the fastest growing markets in the outdoors business. Not only is there a variety of styles to choose from, but hiking boots can even

make a fashion statement. They are made for babies, children and adults. Teenagers wear them to school, and a recent article in Newsweek pointed out hiking boots' popularity for aerobic and workout wear.

Hiking boots are not the prerequisite footwear for camping that they are for backpacking, but if you intend to do any day hiking, purchasing a pair of boots is definitely a good idea. They offer more support than tennis shoes (even hi-tops) because they are built for hiking. The thick soles help protect the bottom of your feet from rocks and roots. Some hiking boots are offered in a below-the-ankle style, but I highly recommend the ankle support of regular boots. I have been hiking for years, and I have seen people hiking in some pretty idiotic footgear (including high heels) over incredibly rough terrain, including lava rocks. Sandals and high heels are really never appropriate for hiking, not even on the beach.

But boots can also destroy your feet, particularly if they are not well-fitted. They can cause everything from mild to ulcerous blisters and even swamp rot, depending on where and when you hike. Therefore, well-suited boots will be one of your most important gear acquisitions if you intend to do a lot of walking when you're on a camping trip.

Boot Weight

Your selection of boots will depend on where and when you want to hike, and how often. For day hikes, lightweight boots are ideal. Most of the trails on the east coast can be hiked in lightweight boots. Rougher terrain and rock scrambling, often found out west, call for mediumweight boots, which are better suited to that kind of stress.

Lightweight Boots

Lightweight boots usually weigh less than 2.5 pounds per pair and are generally made of a combination of leather and

> ## >>Camping Tip<<
>
> Try this technique for selecting the proper boot size. With the boot unlaced, slide your foot to the front of the boot. If you can just slide two fingers in between your heel and the boot the fit should be right. It will allow the little extra room you need without giving too much play.

a breathable fabric. Lightweights have been around for only a decade or so, but it would be impossible to hike along any trail without running across someone wearing a pair. Beyond the fact that they don't weigh your feet down, lightweights rarely require a breaking-in period. If they do, you're probably wearing a mediumweight boot, or you've purchased the wrong size or brand. This type of boot is more flexible than the mediumweight, and it has shallower lug outsoles. And, they usually cost a lot less than heavier boots.

There are disadvantages to lightweights to keep in mind. Your feet will get wet more quickly if it starts raining or when you're walking through dew-soaked grass or leaves. On the other hand, they dry out more quickly than other types of boots. They offer less support than heavier boots, particularly in the ankles, and they don't last as long.

For all their disadvantages, lightweight boots are still the best choice for day hikes and light hiking. Be sure to look for a fully gussetted tongue when purchasing a pair of lightweights. This extra material sewn between the upper and the tongue will help the boots shed both moisture and trail debris (dust, leaves, twigs, etc.).

Although Frank has lost the soles of a pair of lightweights, it is usually the seams that begin to fall apart first. On the other hand, I have put more than a thousand miles on a pair of lightweights. If the boots fall apart early, most manufacturers will repair or replace the boots.

Mediumweight Boots

For most hiking conditions, mediumweight boots have replaced the heavy boots of yesteryear. Weighing between 2.5 and 4 pounds, mediumweights are almost entirely, if not all, leather, although you will see some stronger fabric/leather combinations in this category. Compared to lightweight boots, mediumweight boots have higher uppers, which offer better ankle support and more protection in snow and on rocky terrain. Wider outsoles and heavy-duty midsoles, combined with a half-length to three-quarter-length steel shank to strengthen the sole, help to protect your feet from bruising stones. Unlike lightweights, it usually takes mediumweights longer to get wet and, conversely, longer to dry out.

Top priority for mediumweights boots is fit. You must try them on before you buy them,or purchase them through a mail-order house with a liberal return policy.

Fit

Hiking is an activity that puts a lot of pressure on your feet. Select your boots carefully. The strongest welt, toughest leather and super-traction soles will mean little if every step is agonizing because of improper fit. You may be proud of your small, shapely feet, but buying a boot because it enhances your appearance is foolish and may amount to a face lined with anguish by hike's end.

Boot sizing is notorious for its inconsistency. You might normally wear a size 6 in a tennis shoe but a 5 or 7 in a boot. Make sure that the boots are not only long enough for you but wide enough as well. A number of brands come in several widths: find the one that's right for you.

The most important thing when purchasing a boot is whether or not it's comfortable. When trying on the boot, wear hiking socks. A boot might feel comfy over a thin cotton crew, but slip it over a thick polypropylene sock and suddenly

>>Camping Tip<<

Spray the inside of your boots with a fungicide to prevent boot rot and bad odor.

your foot feels like a sardine. Also, if you intend to wear insoles to give you extra cushioning and arch support, bring them along when you are trying on boots, because insoles also affect the way a boot fits.

While my first pair of boots didn't give me blisters, they were too short. On the downhill, my feet jammed into the toe of the boot, resulting in painfully numb toes that throbbed all night long; not even aspirin could dim that pain. A boot that is long enough will help alleviate that problem. On the other hand, make sure your heel doesn't slip. This could lead to blisters. The heel should be snug but it shouldn't pinch you.

When trying on boots, lace them up securely. Is there any part of the boot that is uncomfortable? Pressure should be even all over your foot, which contains more than twenty six functional bones. Tell the salesperson what you feel. Is there unusual pressure at the instep? Let him or her know. They'll probably suggest a boot that will suit you better.

Finally, don't be surprised if you can't find a perfect fit. With more than 132 potential foot shapes, no manufacturer can fit everyone. Once you've found the next best thing to perfect, the boot can probably be altered with orthotics and broken in to fit. Custom-made boots are another option.

Waterproofing
If your boots have any leather in their construction, they need waterproofing. Sno-Seal, and the newer Aquaseal, are two popular brands of sealant, although there are a number of others. Devoutly follow directions for the waterproofer you purchase. It really does help to have dry feet! Unfortunately,

sealing your boots is not a one-time deal. It must be done periodically, and the more you use your boots, the more often you must seal them.

Taking care of your boots will ensure a longer lifespan (for your boots, that is). After every hiking trip, brush off dirt and debris before storing. If your boots are wet, try stuffing them with newspaper to soak up the inside moisture and let them dry in a cool, dry place. Don't try to dry them quickly by setting them near a heater, oven or open flame. It could mean the death of your boots. Once they are dry, reseal them with waterproofer. Seams and welts and the leather used in lightweight boots require a special sealant. The welt seal works better if applied before waterproofing the boots. All boot sealants can be purchased in outdoors stores.

Breaking in Your Boots

The single most important advice when it comes to boots is "break them in." Any experienced hiker will tell you (and it certainly cannot be stressed enough) that boots must be broken in if you intend to hike more than a mile or two in them.

Once you find a pair of boots that fit comfortably and have sealed them properly, it's time to break them in. Start by walking around your neighborhood. Wear them to the store and on short errands. If you start to get a blister, put moleskin

---

>>Camping Tip<<

Placing muddy or dirty boots in your tent can be down right messy. If you do not have a vestibule to leave them in, take several plastic bags with you. Slip your feet into the bags before pulling your legs into the tent. Then, when you take off your boots (still in the bags), you don't get your tent muddy, wet or dusty and you prolong the life of the floor of your tent.

on it immediately—don't wait. If you catch a hot spot before it becomes a blister, you'll save yourself a lot of pain.

The next step is to take a day hike or at least to try wearing your boots for an entire day. Once they feel comfortable, take a day hike wearing a day pack to make sure the boots still feel comfortable with a little extra weight on your back.

Inserts

Some people find they can make their boots more comfortable, and more supportive, by adding special insoles (sometimes insoles come with boots). Insoles provide additional arch support and can extend the life (and comfort) of your boots. They can also provide extra warmth and insulation. Insoles and arch supports wear down after a while and should be replaced. They can be purchased at most outfitters or department, discount, and drug stores.

Laces and Lacing

While leather laces used to be popular, their tendency to stretch when wet has been their demise; and nylon has replaced them as the standard lace for hiking boots. The durable, soft, woven, unwaxed nylon laces also hold knots best.

Hiking boots usually feature three different methods of closure—grommets, D-rings or hooks. Lacing using only grommets is probably the sturdiest, and grommets usually last well past the lifetime of the boot. The only problem with an all-grommet boot is that it can be difficult to lace, particularly when your hands feel like blocks of ice. Many boots have grommets in the lower half of the boot and hooks at the top.

My boots have D-rings on the lower half and hooks above. They are very easy to lace, even with numb fingers (it's the knot I have trouble with when I can't even feel the laces).

There are a couple of tips to keep in mind when lacing your boots. If the upper knot of your laces rubs against your shin, lace the boots to the top, then back down a few notches and tie the knot midway down your boot to prevent a painful bruise. Another advantage of this method is that it keeps the knot from loosening under the pressure of your constantly-bending ankle. If your toes are feeling cramped, try loosening up the lower laces a bit, tie a knot, and continue lacing the boot tightly. This won't work on the downhill because loose laces will cause your toes to slide painfully into the front of your boot. In this case, you might want to try the opposite approach.

Boot Maintenance
Boot leather needs periodic waterproofing. Trips of a week or more, particularly in wet seasons, will wear the waterproofing off your boots. If you intend to be out for more than a week, you need to carry along Sno-Seal (or whatever you use to waterproof your boots—Silicone Water Guard, Biwell Waterproofing, Aquaseal). If the trip is about a week long, you may want to waterproof your boots as soon as you return home. Waterproofers for boots cost from $3 to $8.

Socks
It used to be that you needed to wear several pairs of socks with your hiking boots just to be comfortable. Fortunately, the way boots are made these days, all you really need is a pair of liner socks and a pair of hiking socks.

Liners made of silk, nylon, polypropylene, Thermax or Orlon are important. They wick away the perspiration and help keep your feet dry. Keep your liners clean; otherwise they will clog up and block the flow of perspiration.

Choose your outer pair of socks wisely. Most experts suggest a blend of wool and nylon or wool and polypropylene. Cotton is never recommended because, unlike wool, it will not

> ## >>Camping Tip<<
> An extra pair of socks will not warm your feet if they make your boots tighter. Toes need to be able to wiggle in order for the blood to circulate most efficiently.

keep you warm when wet.

Some socks are made with extra padding at the toe and heel as well as extra arch support. These socks are usually a nylon-orlon-polypropylene blend; liners are not necessary with them. Try several brands and find out what's right for you. I discovered that socks of mostly wool retain too much foot odor for my taste. Frank has absolutely no complaints with his wool-polypropylene blend.

Sports Sandals

Colorado river rats became fed up with tennis shoes rotting from repeated soakings. Necessity proved once again to be the mother of invention, and in the early 80s, sports sandals were born. Once the footwear of choice for river guides, Tevas and other brands of sports sandals have taken the footwear market by storm and changed the way we look at sandals. They are now as popular in the brick and concrete canyons of Chicago and New York (where they are worn with socks in cool weather) as they are in the Grand Canyon. Prices range from $10 from a cheap pair at a discount store to $100 for a name brand pair with all the extras. The more expensive styles offer added arch support, padding and soles designed to grip in slippery terrain.

Aqua Socks

These popular shoes are usually found in the vicinity of water. Like sports sandals, aqua socks were designed to meet the needs of folks participating in water-related activities. They are made with a mesh fabric that easily sheds water and a wrap-around outsole constructed of plastic for the protection of the soles of your feet. This outsole is also textured for gripping power in the water and out of it.

As with sports sandals, aqua socks can be purchased through discount stores for around $10. Brand name, high-quality models may be bought from outdoor retailers in excess of $30.

Tennis Shoes

If you are planning to spend most of your time hanging out around your campsite, tennis shoes are a good choice for camp footwear. However, they do not offer the firm soles needed for hiking on roots and rocks or the water resiliency offered by sports sandals and aquasocks. If your camping trip calls for special activities, you may want to opt for specialized shoes instead of the all-purpose tennis shoe. Prices for tennis shoes range from $15 to well over $100.

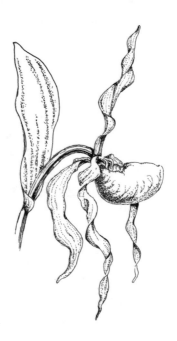

· 6 ·
Sleeping Gear

I will lie down and sleep in peace.

—*Psalm 4:8a*

The cry of seagulls and the gentle roar of the waves slowly and peacefully carried me from the depths of sleep to contented wakefulness. Slipping out of my sleeping bag and quietly unzipping the tent's door, I peered outside into the magnificent brilliance of a Hawaiian morning. The spring sun had already warmed the air, and the sea beckoned. My brother and sister soon joined me at the door. Without a word (for our parents were still asleep in the other tent), we donned our swimsuits and stepped out on the beach. Not a single footprint marred the sand, and the Pacific pounded against the Waimanalo's windward shore. As we waited for our parents to awaken, we combed the beach, searching for the sea's latest offering of shells.

I was only ten years old, but that morning is permanently engraved in my memory as one of the most peaceful moments of my life. It is not my first memory of camping nor is it my last. I intend to let my daughter experience many mornings of waking up in a tent; to let her fill her own treasure chest with memories of the outdoors.

Because about a third of your day is spent sleeping and because most people usually have an uneasy night's sleep in a strange place, choosing a sleeping bag that you'll be comfortable in is very important. It's probably wise not to go for an extreme unless you plan to buy several bags. Sleeping in a 0-degree bag (see Comfort Ratings in this chapter) on a muggy summer night in Pennsylvania can be as much torture as spending a night in a 45-degree bag when you're snowed in in the Sierras.

Important Features of Sleeping Bags

Choosing a bag really isn't as daunting as it may seem. The first consideration is how much you wish to spend (sleeping bags can be bought for less than $100 and in excess of $500 and everywhere in between); then decide on temperature rating, fill and weight. From there, you can narrow down your options by taking into consideration bag shape and shell material. The trick is finding a balance point between comfort and practicality. Care, cleaning, and the bag's construction should also be kept in mind. I won't even begin to recommend a bag because they (as with any piece of equipment you will

---

>>Camping Tip<<

Keep yourself warm in your sleeping bag by wearing a hat, drinking plenty of fluids, and warming yourself up before climbing in. A hat retains heat lost from the head, dehydration inhibits your body's ability to warm itself, and a quick stroll or a few jumping jacks will provide your sleeping bag with some heat to retain.

purchase for camping) really are a matter of preference, and there are so many options available. However, what follows are some characteristics to look for:

Comfort Ratings

A comfort or temperature rating is assigned to most sleeping bags by the manufacturer or retailer. The rating, basically, is the lowest temperature at which the bag remains comfortable.

Unfortunately, most comfort ratings are overly optimistic and vary widely among manufacturers. They assume you are an average person under normal conditions. The problem lies in trying to define who is "average," what conditions are "normal," and what is considered "comfortable." What it really means is that you are neither fat nor thin and you are not overly fatigued. It is also assumed that you are using a sleeping pad and are not sleeping out in the open. What it does not account for is whether or not you are using a bag liner or overbag, what type of sleeping pad you are using, and what you might be wearing. For example, you'll be a lot cooler sleeping in the nude and a lot warmer wearing long johns. Keeping all this in mind, comfort ratings are helpful when compared to one another: a 10-degree bag will keep you warmer than a 20-degree bag.

Before deciding on a comfort rating, try to determine the range of temperatures in which you will most often be camping. If you intend to do a lot of cold-weather camping, you'll probably want a bag rated between zero and twenty degrees. What if you intend to camp in both cold and hot weather? You may want to buy a 20-degree bag and a bag liner, which can raise your bag's temperature by as much as fifteen degrees. Of course, if money is no object, you may prefer to buy several bags with ratings ranging from zero to forty-five degrees or so.

A 20-degree bag is adequate for three-season camping except at high altitudes. But if you get cold easily, a 20-degree bag may be a bit chilly when the temperature dips below freezing. It is better to buy a warmer bag (or at least, a bag liner or overbag) than to face the new day after a cold and sleepless night. If it's too warm to slip into your bag, you can always sleep on top of it!

On hypothermic days (when it is wet and cold), a sleeping bag may save your life. Some people prefer to carry blankets and sheets rolled up (a bed roll) instead of a sleeping bag. Whether camping on the West Coast, the East Coast or anywhere in between, it is unwise to forfeit your sleeping bag for a bed roll when tent camping. Any meteorologist will admit that weather is unpredictable, seemingly changing at whim from hot and muggy to cold and stormy within twenty-four hours. If you are camping in a tent in the backcountry (even if you only intend to make overnight trips), a sleeping bag could be the difference between life and death. Why? Because most sleeping bags contain fillings that keep you warm even when you and/or the bag is wet.

Fillings
There are really only six fillings to consider when purchasing a bag for backpacking. They are the lightest and warmest to be found currently on the market: Quallofil, Hollofil, PolarGuard, Lite Loft, Micro-loft, Primaloft and down.

In general, bags made with Quallofil and Hollofil are cheaper and bulkier than those made with other synthetics. They are the fillings of choice for car campers who confine themselves to low altitude trips in the summer. PolarGuard, Lite Loft, Micro-loft and Primaloft are all used in bags made for three and four season camping. Down offers superior insulation for the weight to all of the synthetics, but loses its loft (or the thickness of its filling) and consequently, its warmth when wet, which the synthetics do not.

>>**Camping Tip**<<

Doing isometric exercises in your sleeping bag will help pre-warm your body before you leave the comfort of your sleeping bag.

Quallofil: The fibers of this polyester filling are hollow, each with four microscopic tubes that allow for good insulating ability and more surface area. Quallofil, which is as soft as down, is non-allergenic, and retains most of its loft when wet. So when Quallofil gets wet, it doesn't become thin and hard or lose its warmth.

Hollofil: Also polyester, Hollofil fibers are about two inches long and must be sewn to a backing to prevent clumping; this leads to cold spots in a sleeping bag. Similar to Quallofil, Hollofil has a single hole in the fiber, but it allows for more "air" per ounce and thus provides more insulation. The added insulation is gained at a price because the backing materials used for filling mean added weight. Like other polyester fills, Hollofil loses only about a tenth of its warmth when wet. The new Hollofil II has silicone added to make the fibers easier to compress and the bag, therefore, easier to fit into a stuff sack.

PolarGuard: PolarGuard is a continuous filament. The fibers, which are long and interwoven, don't become matted, which eliminates the need for a backing to prevent cold spots. PolarGuard also retains it loft—thus its warmth when wet. The new PolarGuard HV is twenty percent warmer than the old PolarGuard, weighs about twenty-five percent less and is more compressible. Its only drawback is that it is not quite as durable as the first PolarGuard.

Lite Loft: Thinsulate Lite Loft by 3M is the warmest synthetic insulation available for its weight. Its microfine polyester/olefin fibers make it lightweight, even when wet, and easily compressible.

This high loft fill features fibers with an inner polyester core. The fibers are arranged for the greatest loft possible and then are "frozen" in place, which helps the bag to retain its loft when wet.

Micro-loft: This is the latest fill from Du Pont. Micro-loft boasts the smallest of the micro fibers. These tiny fibers enable Micro-loft to trap more heat and remain soft and supple.

Primaloft: It mimics the structure of goose down with tiny fibers interspersed with stiffer fibers. Unlike down, Primaloft is water repellent and retains its warmth when wet. Manufactured by Albany International, this loft was engineered to feature an excellent warmth-to-weight ratio, superior compression, and water repellancy.

Proprietary Fillings: Several companies use a filling material that goes only into their own bags. Lamilite is the continuous filament polyester fiber used by Wiggys in bags for the military and in a line made for sale to the public. It is warm when wet and has been "lubricated" to improve its stuffing and draping. Lamilite reacts to washing and drying better than most synthetics. Feathered Friends and Gold-Eck of Austria also make their own synthetic fibers to fill their bags. These fibers are all similar in merit to the synthetics listed above.

Down: Down has long been lauded and is still number one when it comes to providing maximum warmth and comfort for minimum weight and bulk. Down sleeping bags breathe better and are less stifling in warmer temperatures than their synthetic counterparts. But when a down bag gets wet, it loses almost all of its warmth and gains much more in weight than synthetic bags. Down bags also mat and clump worse than synthetic bags. For hay-fever-sufferers, down bags are notoriously bad; and if you're allergic to feather pillows, you'll be allergic to down bags.

Both goose down and duck down are used as fillings with the difference discernible only under a microscope. But, goose down is generally considered structurally superior. The fill power or loft of down is measured in cubic inches and simply represents the number of cubic inches one ounce of down will expand to in a twenty-four hour period. For example, 600 cubic inches is considered to be a superior loft, 500 to 550 is very good, and so on. That infamous tag (Do not remove . . .) called the bedding or law tag will inform you of the bag's loft. By the way, the consumer is allowed to remove the law tag once the product has been purchased.

According to test conducted by Recreational Equipment Incorporated (REI), "a synthetic bag will lose about 10 percent of its warmth while gaining about 60 percent in weight" when the sleeping bag gets wet. Conversely, they said a water-soaked, down-filled bag "will lose over 90 percent of its warmth, gain 128 percent in weight and take more than a day to dry."

What this all means is that your ability to keep a down bag dry is a major factor when deciding to purchase a bag. All six fillings have strong proponents. When purchasing a bag, decide how much trouble you want to go through to keep your bag dry. Stuffing your sleeping bag into a plastic garbage bag before putting it in a stuff sack will keep it dryer. If you're expecting hard rains, put the stuff sack into another bag for extra protection. You and your tent may get wet but at least you'll have the warmth of your sleeping bag.

Down bags are clearly a favorite with cold weather

campers, but they may lose ground to the new synthetics—
Lite Loft and Primaloft—that are designed in the image of
down without its failings.

Shape
Sleeping bags come in three basic shapes—rectangular,
semi-rectangular and mummy. Most campers choose the
mummy-shaped bag because it offers the most warmth.
Many bags offer what is called a draft tube over the zipper to
prevent air from leaking into the bag. If you intend to use your
bag in windy or even cool weather, be sure that the bag you
choose has a draft tube.

Rectangular: These are the roomiest and the heaviest of
sleeping bags. Two sides of the bag are zippered, allowing you
to ventilate to the point of making the bag a blanket. However, room and ventilation become the bag's drawbacks on
cold nights because there is more air to heat up and no hood
to prevent heat from escaping through your head.

Comfort ratings for rectangular bags are usually 30
degrees or more, making these bulky bags for summer use
only in many parts of the country. Even in the South, you
don't want to spend a fall or winter night in these hard-to-
warm-up bags. Still, these bags can make a convenient
bedroll for cabins, RVs and tent camping in mild weather.

Semi-rectangular: The taper of a mummy bag without the
hood, this design saves some on weight, provides good ventilation because it, too, is zippered on two sides, and has a bit
less air to heat up because of the taper. Like the rectangular
bag, this style has no hood for cold nights. This bag shape is
a compromise between the roominess of a rectangular bag
and the excellent warmth-to-weight ratio of a mummy bag.

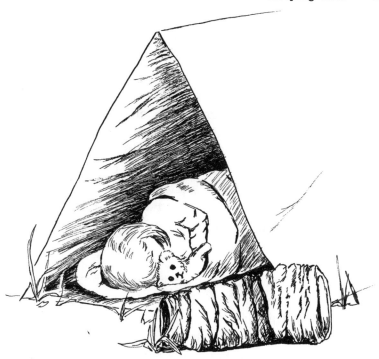

Mummy: The name describes the shape. Formed to the contours of your body, the mummy has the least amount of air to warm and takes less material to make (and, therefore, to stuff). This saves on weight as well making it the bag of choice for bike campers and backpackers. The mummy's "head" is designed to be drawn down over and around your own on cold nights, limiting your body's heat loss. Most mummy bags also feature a "boxed" foot section, which keeps the insulation in place over your feet so that they stay warmer. Comfort ratings for mummy bags start at around 30 degrees and drop to well below freezing. These bags are the best choice for camping from Labor Day through Memorial Day anywhere around the country. But like everything, the mummy has its drawbacks. There is absolutely no room to turn around in it.

You either toss and turn the entire bag or sleep in one position through the night. Also, the short zippers hamper ventilation.

When purchasing a sleeping bag, make sure it fits. A bag that is too narrow or too short will affect the quality of your sleep. Because a mummy bag follows the contours of your body, make sure that it is not too tight in the shoulders and around your head. If you are planning on a lot of cold weather camping, you may want to buy a bag with extra room at the feet. The extra room will accommodate water bottles, boots, socks or anything else you might want to keep from freezing.

Shells
Another important consideration when buying a bag is the shell or outer covering. Although there are numerous materials to choose from, you will only want to consider shells made from ripstop nylon, nylon taffeta, waterproof/breathable fabrics and polyester taffeta. Polyester and cotton shells are a possibility only when the bag will be used in a cabin or RV.

Ripstop nylon: This material features heavier threads interwoven in the fabric every quarter inch or so to prevent rips from running down the bag. The heavier threads also form a web of reinforcement to reduce stress. Strong for its weight, ripstop nylon is also wind resistant. On the other hand, it does not repel water and therefore gets wet easily—although it does dry quickly.

Nylon taffeta: This flat-weave fabric is softer than ripstop nylon but isn't as strong or as resistant to the wind. It, too, gets wet easily although it dries quickly. Nylon taffeta is often used as an inner lining.

Waterproof/breathable fabrics: These are being used more and more as shells because they ventilate better than other fabrics and repel water. Brand names such as Gore-Tex and VersaTech are the more popular waterproof/water resistant products. Microfiber fabrics, which feature a super tight weave that repels water, are also gaining in popularity. No bag is truly waterproof, but these fabrics will keep fillings dry in a tent and are often wind-resistant enough to improve a bag's temperature rating by ten degrees.

Polyester taffeta: A more durable, abrasion-resistant version of ripstop nylon. It is also more water resistant.

Polyester/cotton: Anything with cotton in it is never a good choice if you intend to use it in the outdoors, ie., anywhere it can get wet. When cotton gets wet, it is slow to dry. If your camping is confined to a temperature-controlled RV or cabin, you may prefer to use a cotton- or polyester-shelled sleeping bag.

Weight
Weight is not as much of an issue when you are car camping in parks, etc. However, for backcountry camping, the lighter your bag, the better. Unfortunately, the lighter the bag, the more its going to cost. If you are concerned about weight and bulk, try not to buy a bag that weighs more than 5 pounds.
Weight is related to the comfort rating and the filling. Usually the lower the comfort rating, the more the bag weighs.

>>Camping Tip<<

Glow-in-the-dark shoelaces are great for zipper pulls, flashlight handles and other items you might need to grab hold of in the darkness of your tent.

Fillings other than those mentioned above weigh a lot more than most people will want to carry, even on overnight trips. Save the weight for extra food and other luxuries.

Caring For Your Bag
Synthetic sleeping bags can be washed by hand or in a commercial washer with warm or cold water. They should be cleaned with a mild soap such as Ivory. If not air dried, they should be dried at a low setting in your dryer. When air drying any bag, make sure it is well supported. Never hang it by one end, because the weight of the wet filling may tear out the inner construction and ruin the bag. Supporting the bag on a slanted board is a good option.

Down sleeping bags should be hand washed in a bathtub with as little water as possible. And, if you must use a cleanser, use something extra mild like Woolite. If washed in a machine, your bag could lose its loft because the detergent breaks down the natural oils of the goose down. Down bags should not be dried in a household dryer; rather, they should be drip dried for several days and supported well so that the loft isn't broken up. The bag can then be placed in a commercial dryer on air dry to fluff it. Throwing in a clean pair of tennis shoes will break up the matted down.

Never wash a sleeping bag until it is so dirty you can no longer stand it. The more a bag is washed, the more quickly the loft is broken down.

Sleeping bags should not be stored in the tiny stuff sacks they are normally carried in when heading off on a camping trip. A big, loose bag is the best container for keeping your bag in good condition when you're not camping. Stuffing your bag into a small sack every day while camping (unless you leave your tent set up) is all right because you are taking your bag out every night. But if you store it that way at home, the filling becomes packed together and it is hard to restore its loft. Never roll your bag up neatly because this compresses the insulation. Stuffing the bag into its sack assures you of a different pattern of compression each day, which is better on the loft.

Another way to increase the life of your bag is to wash up each night before you crawl into it. Otherwise, the dirt and oil on your clothes and body will find their way into your bag's fill and inhibit its ability to insulate. If you can't wash up, change into clean clothes.

Mated Bags

For couples interested in camping, sleeping bags using the same size zipper can be zipped together, even if they are made by different manufacturers. Two right-hand zipper bags can be zipped together, but mated mummy bags will feature one hood on top and one on the bottom. To solve this problem and make mating bags more comfortable, many sleeping bag manufacturers offer bags with right and left zippers. Mated bags have more empty space to warm up than two separate bags. That is fine in mild weather, but if you get too cold in the night, you will want to each zip up in your own bag.

If you intend to buy mated bags, you may want to consider one lightweight (approximately 40-degree) and one heavier (about 20-degree) bag. That way, if it's warm, you can use the cooler bag on top—and vice versa.

While on the subject, some sleeping pads are also made to be joined together. These couple pads are more comfortable than trying to deal with two pads sliding around independent of each other.

Bag Liners

Purchasing a bag liner is a good way to warm up your bag without adding much cost or weight. There are three types of bag liners—overbags, vapor barriers, and plain inner liners.

Overbags: The overbags slide on over the sleeping bag and have a filling that increases the warmth of your bag by as much as twenty degrees. They cost approximately $50 to $100 and weigh about 2 to 3 pounds—kind of bulky and on the expensive side as well.

Vapor barriers: These liners are inserted inside your sleeping bag and can raise its temperature by as much as fifteen degrees. Basically, with the vapor barrier, you're sticking yourself inside a plastic bag. They are constructed out of fabric which weighs only ounces. Also, they cost much less than the overbags—approximately $20 to $30 a bag. The drawback to the vapor barrier is comfort; they are designed to trap your body heat. Using your own warmth to keep you warm can work wonders, but it can also result in your sweating uncomfortably. Vapor barriers are recommended for temperatures well below freezing.

Plain inner liners: You can also purchase simple bag liners made of flannel, cotton, breathable nylon, silk, synthetics, and down costing anywhere from $5 to $100 and weighing three ounces to two pounds. The degree to which they warm your bag varies and should be clarified by the salesperson before you decide to purchase such a liner.

Bed Rolls
Sleeping bags are the best choice for many campers, but they are not the only option. When we go camping at the beach in the summer, we find our 20-degree bags far too hot to sleep in. We pack a bedroll with a blanket to lie on and a sheet to cover us. Adding a wool blanket on top of this arrangement will keep you warm much of the year at low altitudes in the southern half of the country. This is a warm weather option that will not keep you warm when the temperature drops

below forty degrees. You must also be pretty sure that the blankets will stay dry because they could be difficult to dry.

Sleeping Pads and Mattresses

Sleeping pads or mattresses are a necessity for warmth as well as comfort. If you don't have something beneath your sleeping bag, you lose all your heat to the ground. Although the padding can be minimal, it will still make a big difference, especially when the alternative is sleeping on the hard earth.

If you're a minimalist, you'll probably want to try a Therm-a-Rest or a Ridgerest. The Therm-a-rest is a self-inflating pad that can be purchased in three-quarters or full length and in thicknesses varying from 1-inch to 2.5-inches. The pads range in weight from just over a pound to close to 4.5 pounds. Prices range from $40 to $100. The Therm-a-rest is an open-cell foam pad with a nylon cover and is available with a repair kit.

A "couples kit" also can be purchased for the Therm-a-Rest that allows two pads to be joined together. It is simply two nylon tarps that hold the pads so that they do not move around during the night.

The Ridgerest was given *Backpacker* magazine's product design award. It, too, can be purchased in three-quarters and full lengths, both of which weigh under a pound and cost less than $20. The "ridges" in the Ridgerest were designed to trap air to keep you warmer. It is a closed cell foam pad.

Dozens of other pads are also available as more and more companies take advantage of the popularity of backpacking and camping and create their own versions of a good night's sleep.

Other options include the blue foam or closed cell pads available at most camping stores and other foam pads. These pads weigh anywhere from 8 ounces to 1 pound and can be purchased in the $10 to $15 range.

For those who prefer more luxurious accommodations, you might want to try an air mattress. Air mattresses come in a variety of styles and weights, but in the end they all boil down to: you must pump them up yourself.

The lightest air mattresses weigh in at about 6 pounds; the heaviest, more than 12 pounds. Air mattresses also vary in size from single to double to queen. They cost anywhere from $15 to $50. Most air mattresses are purchased packed down to a relatively small size. Unfortunately, after they have been inflated once, they are harder to pack down again. Because of their size, they are strictly for car camping.

Cots

To some people, even an air mattress is too close to Mother Earth for peace of mind. For those who like a little air between their bed and the ground, there are always cots. Cots are definitely for the sort of camping where you will pull everything out of the car and stick it in your tent.You're not going to want to carry them even a tenth of a mile.

Coleman, Sierra, Byer of Maine and many others offer cots. They can be found at discount stores as well as outdoors stores. Basically, a cot is made of a metal (usually aluminum) or wood frame and a canvas-type material stretched across the frame. Cots usually fold up for easier storing, packing and carrying. As for weight, they range from 5 to 20 pounds, basically the same range as air mattresses. They cost any where from $20 to $60.

Pillows

For some people, a pillow is the adult version of a security blanket. If you feel strongly about your pillow, by all means bring it along on your camping trip. For most camping trips there is absolutely no reason not to bring one, even your old, familiar pillow from home. But if you have to walk any distance at all, you might prefer to carry a smaller camping or backpacking pillow.

We always bring pillows along in our RV but usually rely on rolled up jackets or sweaters on tent-camping trips. The weight of a pillow is nearly negligible, but for those who are weight or bulk conscious, there are a variety of camping pillows out there that range from inflatable pillows to a choice of small (10 to 12" by 16 to 20" inch) synthetic-stuffed ones. Basically a smaller version of home pillows, they are usually filled with a synthetic such as Hollofil or Quallofil or down and are covered with a combination of fabrics, often flannel and nylon. They are both light and inexpensive, weighing less than a pound and costing $5 to $15. Relatively inexpensive, these pillows are (like everything else) a matter of preference.

Backpacking pillows are nearly always self-inflating so that they can pack down to a reasonable size to carry. Oddly enough, they weigh as much or more than camping pillows, and cost more, too—$5 to $20, with the average price around $15.

· 7 ·
Tents

Camping can be the greatest expression of free will, personal independence, innate ability, and resourcefulness possible today in our industrialized, urbanized existence.

—*Anne LaBastile*
Woodswoman

We had promised our daughter Griffin wild horses, but we didn't realize how close they would get. All the way up from Georgia we told her about the ponies at Grayson Highlands State Park in southwest Virginia. The more we talked, the higher the stakes became. By the time we got to the park, Frank and I were a little nervous that the ponies wouldn't follow through on our promises.

But within minutes of setting up our tent, a curious pony had ventured close enough to poke his head into our dome tent for a closer look. Griffin, then two years old, was enchanted by the nose to nose encounter in our camp "home."

That night, we could hear the ponies grazing near the

>>Camping Tip<<

Before heading out on your first camping trip with a child, let them take naps or spend the night in your tent at home. The claustrophobic environment takes some getting used to, and its best for both you and the child to accustom yourselves to a tent at home rather than the outdoors where it is darker and you might bother other campers.

---

tent. Occasionally, one would venture over to snuffle the tent fly before plodding off. The sounds weren't all that much of a distraction, but we wouldn't have been able to get Griffin to sleep through the night if we hadn't had our refuge from equine curiousty.

Almost any tent camper can tell you of a time they were glad they had the refuge of their tent. They can also tell you of a time they cursed it. While tents have their advantages over tarps and over sleeping under the stars, many have drawbacks, and as always, it comes down to personal preference—how much discomfort you're willing to withstand on a camping trip.

Strictly speaking, a large piece of plastic and some rope is all it takes. When asked what type of shelter he prefers, the camper will give you a range of answers. From tarps to roomy dome tents (obviously recreational vehicles do not come into play here!), campers will tell you that their tarp or tent has proven adequate.

Tents, which can range anywhere from $10 to $1,000 in price, are the most practical alternative for staying dry on a rainy night. Tents keep out the rain and bugs; they are warm on cold nights because your body temperature helps warm the tent (sometimes by as much as ten degrees), and the tent itself dulls the force of the wind. When it is cold, wet or buggy, tents are invaluable.

Features to Look For

What shape tent you purchase is just one of the many factors involved in finding the tent that is just right for you. The shape of the tent, of course, determines a lot, but you will also find that even if you are in a car, the weight, size, ventilation, tent materials, tent poles, workmanship, waterproofing, set up and color will also matter. For example, if you drive a Geo Metro, it is doubtful you'll want to fill your car with a full-sized cabin tent.

Size

The most important thing to look for in a camping tent is roominess. Are you tall? Is there enough room to stretch out to your full length when you are in your sleeping bag? What about headroom? Do you have enough room to sit up comfortably? Do you intend to spend a lot of time in your tent? Decide how much room is important to you before purchasing a tent. Also will you be cooking in your tent? Some tents offer cook holes for cold weather camping. On cold mornings, it is not unusual to see steam rising from beneath the vestibules of tents as campers heat water for coffee or oatmeal. If you think this is a possibility (something that never occurred to me but that I have done many a time), make sure the vestibule has enough space beneath it so that it will not ignite when you light your camp stove. Whenever possible, I have placed a flat rock beneath my stove for further fire insurance.

Tent manufacturers tend to overestimate the number of people their tents can accomodate. If a tent claims it holds one to two people, it usually means exactly that and with little room for much else. Two people will be a tight fit without their gear, and one person will fit with plenty of room for clothes, food, etc. Keep that in mind when considering how much you want your tent to hold.

Weight

When you are making your tent wish list, remember that you will be responsible for how the tent reaches the campground, be it a primitive site in a state forest or a fully-equipped site at the nearest KOA. For backpackers, the most important feature of a tent is its weight. Car campers, on the other hand, are more interested in roominess and comfort. Even so, carrying more tent than the camping trip calls for can be almost as much of a mistake as not having an adequate tent. Some of the larger family tents weigh in excess of 30 pounds.

Don't purchase a huge, bulky, heavy tent if your time in the tent is limited to the eight hours you will be sleeping in it. If your tent will be used only for the "rest" half of R&R, you might want to look into one of the less expensive small family camping tents.

However, if you head out on a camping trip in a heavy duty vehicle intending to set up a base camp for several days or more, the larger tents may be worth the bulk as well as the price. Many campers set up in state parks, particularly those on lakes or the ocean, and live in the campground for a week or more.

Ventilation

This is another important feature to look for when shopping for a tent. On hot, buggy nights there is nothing worse than being stifled in a poorly ventilated tent. Many tents these days offer plenty of no-see-um netting for cross ventilation as well as protection from bugs. Well ventilated tents also have less problems with condensation build-up inside the tent than tents sealed up tight. If you are planning only cold weather camping, this feature won't be necessary.

Most tents can be classified as three-season. In other words, their construction makes them comfortable from spring through fall. There are also tents that are almost entirely no-see-um netting for ultimate ventilation and which are perfect for camping in the summer, particularly in the South and Southwest. On the other hand, if you intend to hike in every season, a good rain fly will compensate in cold weather for the extra ventilation needed in hot weather.

Tents built for four-season use usually have very little ventilation and often feature a cook hole in the floor so that you can cook inside your tent. Four-season tents theoretically keep you warm or cool, whichever the case may be, year-round.

Tent Fabric

Most tents are made of strong but lightweight nylon taffeta or ripstop nylon, which weighs approximately 2 ounces per square yard. Some of the bigger tents use coated polyester or cotton poplin canvas, which weighs a good deal more.

The floors and flys are usually coated with polyurethane or another moisture-repellent substance to prevent moisture from passing from the ground into the tent. Although the body of a tent is often left untreated to increase the transfer of respiration and perspiration through the tent's walls, it is not unusual to wake up in a damp tent. Moisture can gather beneath sleeping pads or air mattresses (but not cots since they are raised above the floor). Large and airy tents have less of a problem this way because of the greater circulation of air throughout the tent. Some tents offer a double-roof construction, which further decreases unwanted condensation. I have spent a number of sleepless nights in tents that dripped continually from the ceiling.

Tent Poles

In the past few years, tent poles have evolved from unyielding aluminum to shock-corded poles of fiberglass or aluminum (except in the case of some of the larger, family tents, which

>>Camping Tip<<

Never shake out your shock-corded poles to snap them together.
The violent action causes nicks to form at the joints that will tear
your tent pole sleeves.

still use rigid aluminum poles). These new poles are threaded
in segments over elastic (shock) cord that allows the user
merely to snap the poles into shape rather than piece them
together. When dismantling the tent, the segments are
pulled apart and folded compactly.

There is still some controversy as to whether fiberglass is
superior to aluminum when it comes to designing tent poles.
Fiberglass is less expensive and more flexible than aluminum. It does not require pre-bending or any special attach-
ments. It also provides a better packing size when folded. Its
major drawbacks are that it is affected by weather and can
break into splinters and must be replaced. Aluminum is more
likely to bend and can be splinted when it breaks. Durability
is one of aluminum's main advantages along with the fact
that it is easily replaced.

Workmanship
Although any tent may be adequate for your needs, you may
want to consider how long you would like your tent to last.
Good workmanship means you can have a long-lasting rela-
tionship with your tent. A well-made tent should have lap-
felled seams around the floor seam. Lap-felled seams (like the
seams on the sides of your Levis) provide extra strength,
because they are actually four layers of interlocking fabric
joined by a double row of stitching. On uncoated nylon tents,
check for taped seams. Because nylon tends to unravel,
taping or hiding the end of the fabric behind the seam with
another piece of fabric will stop or stall this process. Finally,

make sure that all stress points are reinforced either with extra stitching or bar tacking. Tug at the material to make sure the load is equally distributed across the reinforcement. Unequal distribution can cause premature wear on your tent.

Waterproofing
Campers agree that waterproofing is an important feature to consider. There is nothing more miserable than sleeping in a wet tent. The better the material, the more water-resistant, the more likely you are to sleep dry. But there are some days that it rains so hard that no matter how good your tent, you're going to get wet (if for no other reason that you bring the rain in yourself going in and out of the tent). It may rain for days on end while you cower inside your tent waiting for the deluge to subside. During this time, your tent does not even have time to dry out, but as long as your sleeping bag is fairly dry, you can sleep warmly, if not entirely comfortably, in your damp tent.

There are occasions like these that have taught some campers to keep a spare tarpaulin on hand. The tarp can then be erected over your tent to provide an extra roof and a little extra protection from the rain. Just remember to give the tarp a little slant so that water doesn't pool up in the middle of it.

To keep your tent as dry as possible, it is important to seal its seams. Although parts of the tent are coated, the needle holes in the seams will allow water to enter your tent. Buy some sealer (available at most outdoors stores) and follow the directions. Then seal them again. Depending on how much

>>Camping Tip<<

When camping in the cold or snow, try to position your tent so that the early morning sun warms you and evaporates the dew or frost on your tent.

you use the tent, the sealer can last up to two years. If you use your tent a lot or have subjected it to a lot of rain or snow, seal the seams more often.

Set-up

You will also want to consider how easily a tent can be set up and taken down—important when it comes to pitching a tent in the dark or wind or rain. Practice setting up your tent before you camp in it for the first time. There may be occasions when knowing the set-up of your tent can save you fumbling in the dark, and it could mean the difference between wet and dry clothes.

There are several different methods of tent set up—clip systems, sleeve systems and grommet systems. In the clip system, the ends of the poles are held by grommets and the tent clipped to the poles; in the sleeve system, the poles are pushed through sleeves in the tent and the ends are held by grommets; and the simple grommet system, in which the poles, usually rigid aluminum poles, are held by grommets or loops with little or no bending of the poles. Some tents employ combinations of the two systems, the clip and sleeve combination being the most common.

Color

While color is a matter of personal preference, there are reasons why you may choose one color over another. Bright, neon-like colors are good only in a search-and-rescue situations because the blinding material will stand out against the snow or the green and brown of the woods or the sand in the desert. Since most camping involves designated sites, this situation rarely arises. It is more common among mountain climbers or others who find themselves in this situation having traveled in remote areas. For the very reason bright colors are effective in emergency situations as described above, these colors can be annoying to other campers, causing a visual disturbance in what is supposed to be a natural, outdoors experience.

The fabric color affects the quality of light inside your tent. If your tent is pale green or blue, the bright sunlight filtered through your tent will form a soft light inside. On rainy or overcast days, the light inside your tent could be slightly depressing. These colors are also a bit more inconspicuous in the backcountry. In contrast, orange and yellow fabrics are great in foul weather because they produce a brighter light inside your tent but few manufacturers use these colors anymore just because they are so bright.

As a matter of fact, there is a definite trend toward using more inconspicuous and environmentally pleasing colors such as grey, light grey, white and tan. These please the eye both inside and outside the tent. Blue and gold combinations are also used in many tents as are lodengreen or spruce, charcoal, burgundy, teal and aqua. Blue-grey and green are by far the most common tent colors.

Family Tents

Car camping allows you a lot more freedom when it comes to choosing a tent. You can use everything from a bivy sack (but why?) to the large two-room cabin and umbrella tents.

Most campers choose the larger umbrella and cabin tents for car camping because comfort is the ultimate goal. Not only does weight not matter, but car campers often spend more time in their tents, making headroom and legroom more important than weight.

Family tents can be purchased in both the dome and A-frame styles, although the A-frame tents are more often than not available only at discount stores. Umbrella tents are hexagonal tents, usually free-standing, that offer nearly vertical walls and sometimes more than six feet of standing

room. You will pay the price for the larger tent, though. Even the small umbrellas (those that sleep 2 to 3 people) start at $180. The lodges, which consist of two rooms, can cost more than $650.

Cabin tents are eponymous. With a peaked roof, four walls, screened windows and doors, they look like fabric cabins. With one or two rooms and sleeping as many as ten, cabins are rarely free-standing. Walls usually reach a height of about five feet with a roof peak of more than six feet or more. Cabin tents start out at about $350, and for the really large, double room models, can exceed $1,000.

Large dome tents often weigh much less than umbrella and cabin tents, making them a compromise in weight and bulk between the roominess of big family tents and the cramped quarters of a lightweight backpacking tent. A big dome tent might weigh 8 to 10 pounds, making it possible to use on a canoe camping trip or short backpacking or bike camping trips. It will still be too heavy and bulky for a long hike or bike trip, but it is a workable compromise. Big dome tents start at $100 in discount stores.

Backpacking Tents

Because backpacking involves carrying everything you will need on your back, your tent must be lightweight and not bulky. Therefore, backpacking tents are designed less for comfort than for size and weight. They are also usually designed to be set up quickly, since, in the backcountry, a tent is your only refuge in bad weather.

Because of the lack of head room and cramped quarters in backpacking tents, many campers will probably not want to consider purchasing a lightweight tent. If, on the other hand, most of your tenting will involve carrying your tent any distance, your best choice is a backpacking tent. Backpacking tents, by definition, rarely sleep more than two people comfortably. If the tent sleeps more than three, it is doubtful that it is a true backpacking tent.

Backpacking tents are designed in a variety of shapes: A-frame, dome, tunnel and ultralights or bivies. The A-frame is the classic shape that is also known as a pup tent. Both roomy (as far as backpacking tents go) and easy to set-up, A-frames are stable except in the wind. Drawbacks include the fact that they are rarely self-supporting, and many models have a support pole in the middle of the entrance. They are inexpensive, which can be a plus.

Dome tents were once the most popular backpacking tents because they were designed to solve the limitations of the A-frames. They are free-standing—that is, they do not have to be staked—and they are roomy as well as stable and taut in the wind. Dome tents also offer more head and elbow room than the A-frames; maximum space for the weight. Because of all these improvements, dome tents usually costs more than A-frames. Depending on the size of the dome, it can be on the heavy side, and some are too bulky for backpacks. Many family camping tents are just enlarged dome tents.

A note from experience—free-standing dome tents are stable in the wind only if there is something inside weighing them down (or if they are staked to the ground in windy weather). They make great kites if left empty on a windy day, especially if the door is open.

Tunnel tents have gained popularity over domes because of the relation of floor space to the overall size and weight of the tent. They are much lighter and more compact than other tents because of the covered wagon, two-hoop design. Tunnels are rarely free-standing and must be pitched in the right position to provide optimum stability in the wind. Sleeping in an unstaked tunnel tent is similar to bedding down in a bivy sack—it keeps you out of the elements.

Finally, there is the ultralight or bivy sack. This is really for hardcore backpackers as it is basically a sleeping bag for your sleeping bag. A scaled-down version of a tent in the tunnel design, this is lightest and most compact of tents and is definitely not for the claustrophobic.

Ground Cloths

A ground cloth or ground sheet is a piece of plastic (or canvas) cut slightly smaller than the size of your tent. Lying usually between the tent and the ground, it will keep your tent drier and cleaner. Don't be led to believe that you will not need a ground cloth. The one time I neglected to bring one, I woke up to a very moist tent floor. Condensation is bad enough without this added aggravation. A plastic ground cloth, cut to fit under the bottom of your tent, may not completely protect the tent from the damp wet, but it helps. Ground cloths come in handy especially when you find you must set up your tent on ground that has been waterlogged by days of rain.

If the ground cloth is larger than your tent, you are likely to wake up in the middle of a rainy night sitting in the puddle that has formed beneath your tent. By cutting the plastic to within an inch of your tent's width and length, you will wake up much drier. A ground cloth also helps the fabric of your tent's floor, protecting it from abrasion by rocks and keeping it clean from the mud or dirt, pinestraw, etc. that you set the tent upon.

If you are really opposed to the thought of getting wet on the floor of your tent, try putting the ground cloth inside. You won't protect the tent's bottom and the tent still gets wet, but you and your equipment will be drier. Some campers even put one cloth on the ground and another in the tent for more complete protection.

Digging a trench around your tent can help keep the rain from running under it, but this outdated practice is hard on the environment and in most camping areas prohibited, anyway; I recommend that you do not follow this outdated practice. Who wants to waste the time digging a ditch on the off chance there will be rainfall? And if it is raining, wouldn't you rather be snug and dry in your tent rather than fighting the elements (and the possibly rocky and rooty earth) to dig a trench?

Taking Care of Your Tent
Never store your tent when it is damp. Make sure it is thoroughly dry if you are going to put it up for more than a day. Otherwise, the next time you pull it out of its stuff sack, you're bound to find it spotted with mold and mildew. It is important to make sure that even the seams are dry and that all the dirt has been cleaned from the stakes, poles, and bottom of the tent.

When packing your tent, stuff it rather than rolling or folding it. If the fabric is stressed at the same points every time, it will eventually crack and peel. Never store your tent in a car, including the trunk. Cars can become as hot as a furnace, and those high temperatures can damage the coating on the tent's fabric.

Never leave your tent set up in the sun for long periods of

> ## >>Camping Tip<<
> Never use your foot or any other hard object to clear the area where you will set up your tent. Get down on hands and knees to pick up sticks, stones, pinecones, etc. Leave the pine needles, grass and leaves. This will lessen your environmental impact.

time. If you are camping in one spot for several days, cover your tent with its fly during the day to protect it from the sun's ultraviolet rays, which can damage the nylon material. Because of its coating, a rainfly is less susceptible to the sun's damage and can be replaced at less expense than the tent.

To clean your tent, use a damp sponge and mild soap. Set it up before wiping it down and then let it air dry. If your tent is smeared with pitch or grease, use a bit of kerosene to remove it. Never machine wash your tent.

Keep your tent poles clean to avoid corrosion of the metal or to keep the fiberglass from weakening. A silicone lubricant applied occasionally will help protect your poles and keep them in good working order. Apply the silicone to your tent's zippers to keep them working smoothly when it is freezing outside. Also, avoid damaging your tent by carrying your poles and stakes in a separate stuff sack.

Repair kits for your tent are very helpful and are available from most outdoors stores. There are several kits available, but the best in my opinion is made by Outdoor Research. This inexpensive kit contains adhesive-backed ripstop and adhesive-backed taffeta fabric to repair holes in the tent and fly fabrics; mosquito netting, needle and thread to repair holes in no-see-um fabric; an aluminum splint and duct tape to repair broken tent poles (fiberglass cannot be splinted); and braided Dacron utility cord in case you need to jerry-rig a guyline, tent-peg loop, etc. A small tent repair kit should take care of most of the mishaps that can occur to a tent on a camping trip, unless you set the tent ablaze with your cooking stove or campfire.

Tarps and Sleep Screens
A simple, inexpensive alternative to a tent is a tarpaulin. One of the problems with a tarp is that it doesn't keep the bugs out. When the mosquitoes or black flies start to swarm, you probably won't want to be sleeping under the stars or under a tarp. But, some people are not bothered by bugs, and a tarp is a good way to be close to nature when the sun drops below the horizon. Some people use tarps only to protect themselves from rain or wind and carry along a sleep screen for especially buggy nights.

Escaping from bugs is no joke, and most campers agree that a tent or sleep screen is indispensable when the no-see-ums, mosquitoes, deerflies and blackflies arrive to torture innocent campers. When camping out West (because of snow, grizzly bear, etc.), you are probably better off in a tent. On the other hand, should you be camping along the beach in the summer, a sleep screen and a tarp to protect you from bugs and rain is likely more than adequate if you like the bare essentials.

If you decide on a tarp, you have a number of options. Tarps are generally both inexpensive and lightweight, although some can end up weighing and (in the case of the Moss Parawing) costing as much as a tent.

One option tarpers have is to purchase a polyethylene sheet (one brand is Visqueen) that is translucent white and comes in both 9' by 12' and 12' by 12' sizes. Unfortunately, these tarps do not come with grommets for you to attach your ropes, so you will need to find some sort of clamp—be it a stone wrapped in the tarp fabric and secured with a rope or the popular Visklamp that uses a rubber ball and a device to secure the ball and rope.

A number of tarps are available with metal grommets, including ripstop woven polyethylene and coated nylon. While the reinforced polyethylene is cheaper, it will decay faster in the sun than nylon. The best tarp size is the 10' by 12', to keep two campers dry without carrying around more tarp than you need.

Once you have chosen your tarp, you will need the following to set it up: approximately fifty feet of one-quarter inch braided nylon rope for the tarp's ridgeline; a hundred feet of one-eighth inch braided nylon rope for guylines; six to eight tent pegs to secure the tarp should there be a lack of other objects (trees, roots, rocks, bushes); and of course, cloth tape or a tent repair kit. Braided rope is stronger than nylon cord and will not unravel like other ropes.

Setting up a tarp
There are many ways to set up a tarp, but the most common is the shed roof. This is the easiest method of rigging a tarp and requires only two trees reasonably close together. The high side of the tarp is suspended six to eight feet off the ground (facing away from the wind) with one corner attached by rope to each tree. The low side faces into the wind with two to four tent stakes pegging it to the ground.

The A-frame is another common tarp configuration, with the tarp set up between two trees at least ten feet apart. Your fifty feet of rope is used as a ridgeline for the tarp and attaches to each tree six to eight feet off the ground. Make sure the ridgeline is pulled tight so that the tarp does not sag in the middle. Depending on the weather, guylines are then tied to grommets or clamps on both sides of the tarp and then nailed to the ground with tent pegs in bad weather or set several inches off the ground in good weather for more room and ventilation.

Should the area where you are hiking be devoid or scarce of trees or boulders large enough to support your tarp,

Shed Roof Tarp

another possibility is rigging the A-frame with four make-shift poles—sound branches, driftwood, whatever is handy—at least a few feet long. One end of the ridgeline is pegged into the ground. Making a tepee shape with the first set of poles, wrap the ridgeline rope twice vertically and twice horizontally around the top of the A-frame where the poles cross. With enough space left to lay your tarp over it, lash the other end of the ridgeline rope in the same way to the second set of poles. Make sure the ridgeline is tight then lash the end of the line to a peg and then stamp it into the ground. Throw your tarp over the ridgeline and lash the edges to the ground as needed.

Sleeping Under the Stars
If you have a wonderfully comfortable sleeping bag (or if you can sleep on a bed of nails), sleeping out under the stars is a viable option as long as you have a tent or tarp as a backup.

A variation on the A-frame tarp

Keep in mind that if you are hiking in the mountains, weather can change in an instant, and you will need a backup plan.

Advantages to sleeping outdoors (other than not having to set up a tent or a tarp) are falling asleep beneath a canopy of stars, or, as Shakespeare called it, "that brave, overhanging firmament, that majestical roof fretted with golden fire." Dawn's first rays of light will awake you and you are nearly one with your environment.

As long as you're in a relatively safe area, the weather is good and your sleeping bag warm or cool enough for the conditions, there is no reason not to sleep outdoors. Only insects will bother humans as they sleep. Since you are not threatening to the predators of night, if they should happen to find you, it is more than likely all you'll receive is a curious sniff or two. When they discover you are human, they'll want to get out of your way as quickly as possible.

The only place to use a little extra caution is in grizzly country, because these bears can be very unpredictable. If you find yourself nose-to-nose with a grizz, follow the suggestions mentioned in Chapter 9. As long as you use a little common sense, you should be able to reap the benefits of fresh-air camping.

Pitching Tents in the Wind, Rain and Snow

Before going on any camping trip, you should know your tent (and all your other equipment for that matter) backwards and forwards. Set it up in your yard (or if that is impossible, your living room) over and over again until you can do it in your sleep. This practice will be invaluable once you're at a campsite and setting up your tent in a downpour or in a raging wind. When it comes time to set up your tent (it should be about the first thing you do when car camping), you'll appreciate the practice, particularly if there is a knock-you-off-your-feet wind blowing. First, go over in your head the

> # >>Camping Tip<<
>
> Once you have chosen your tent site, you might want to spread out your ground cloth and lie down on it to determine where you'll want to place your head, etc. This will also give you some clue as to how rocky and bumpy the site is.

steps for setting up your tent. If you get panicky, the process will take twice as long.

Before rolling out your tent, get the poles, pegs, or whatever you need to set up, ready. Stretch out your ground cloth and lay the rolled up tent on top of it. As you slowly roll out your tent, stake it to the ground if it is not a freestanding tent. If it is free-standing, place heavy objects on the tent to keep it from blowing away if it's windy.

Once pegged or weighted to the ground, insert poles windward side first. This sounds easier than it is, but with a little determination and imagination, your tent will soon be up. If it is a free-standing tent, throw your sleeping bags or other gear inside the tent to keep it pinned down until you can get in. If it is a pegged tent, make sure none of the stakes threaten to pull loose.

Pitching your tent in the rain is merely a matter of speed. It all comes down to how quickly you wish to get out of the rain. The faster you set up your tent, the quicker you can get dry. Getting the rain-proof fly on as quickly as possible is very important as the tent itself can get soaked if you take too long. If possible, wait for a break in the rain before pitching your tent. When taking down your tent in the rain, you may be able to do most of the work beneath the fly, keeping the tent a bit more dry.

If you plan a camping trip in the snow, making sure your tent is securely pegged is especially important. Make sure that you have pegs that will hold in both soft and hard snow.

Most outdoors stores offer special anchors and pegs for snow camping. You may want to purchase a full-time replacement for the spindly pegs that come with your tent. Some of the heavy-duty options available are T-stakes, I-beams, half-moons and corkscrews. The staff at your outdoors store will be able to tell you which stake best suits your purpose.

Before you can set up your tent, you must first stamp down the snow, including an area for you to walk around while pitching your tent, a broad area for the entrance, and troughs for the guylines, if you need them.

To keep your tent as dry as possible, make sure that you rid yourself of as much snow as possible before climbing in. You are not stepping into a ski lodge that is used to standing puddles of water. A large garbage bag outside the entrance to your tent can work as a waterproof doormat.

If you intend to camp in extreme snow conditions, you will need either a snow shovel or something that can be used as a shovel, like a snowshoe. If your tent is buried in the snow, death by asphixiation is a possible result. If snow keeps falling for more than a day, take down your tent and rebuild your platform by shoveling snow onto the stamped down area and re-stamping. Finally, re-pitch your tent.

Dining Canopies

There is a variety of canopies available for those who prefer a little protection over their heads when eating but don't want to eat in their tent. Dining canopies or flys offer protection against rain, droppings (bird, sap and insect), and the sun. The simplest, basically a tarp, can also be pitched to protect you against wind. Occasionally, you can find tarps that are constructed specifically for pitching over a picnic table (almost all campgrounds feature picnic tables at the site). Tarps range in price from $3 to $100, depending on how big they are, what they are made of, and whether or not they have grommets. Poles are extra and usually cost less than $25 for each set.

Canopies, which are sturdier than tarps, are basically freestanding, sideless tents that use rigid aluminum poles in the frame. They cost around $75 or more. The most popular dining canopy today seems to be the screen house. These houses are essentially tents with walls that are constructed nearly entirely of screen. They are popular, no doubt, because they protect hungry campers from bugs as well as from the sun, rain, etc. Most of these screen houses offer optional wind/rain curtains. Two curtains will cover the entire house, but since rain and wind rarely blow four directions at once (except perhaps in a hurricane or tornado) it is doubtful you will need two. If you do suspect a hurricane or tornado, dismantle camp and get the heck out of Dodge.

Because they are so large and versatile, screen houses are not cheap. The tent, itself, costs in excess of $200, and the curtains are approximately $50 to $100 each. Some family tents these days are built with two rooms—a sleeping area and a screened dining area. Others offer net enclosures that can be attached with clips.

· 8 ·
Recreational Vehicles and Campers

Make voyages. Attempt them. That's all there is.
—*Tennessee Williams*
Camino Real

The campground host dropped another pine log onto the waning fire, sending sparks dancing up into the night like a thousand fireflies in frightened flight. A dozen campers sat in an assortment of chairs and talked about their lives on the road by the light of the fire in Georgia's Crooked River State Park. The park is just off I-95 and close to Georgia beaches and the Florida state line. Like many other winter nights in the park, there were no tents in sight. The campground was about a third full, with twenty travel trailers and motor homes scattered among the pines along the salt marsh.

"Now I know what it's like to live in an elevator," one man

remarked on his first three months of living out of a twenty-two-foot travel trailer with his wife.

Several RVers returned surprised glances. "You don't like it?" a woman asked.

"No, I love it," the man replied. "I can't wait until we make our trip to Alaska in it. But, we're just having to get accustomed to bumping in to each other."

Everyone laughed in agreement and soon advice was flowing around the campfire on how best to get to Alaska and back. To many people, RV is a two-letter word for freedom. Life on the road with all the necessary comforts and few commitments. Though most noticeably popular with campers fifty-five and older, recreational vehicles of all types are popular with young families as well.

Within the broad label of RV, there is one fundamental choice—to tow or not to tow. Towable options include pop-up camping trailers, travel trailers and fifth wheel trailers. The non-towable RVs are self-powered. They range from a camper on the back of a pick up through mini-motorhomes and the big bus-like Class A motorhomes. As with all vehicles, the basic models cost less but offer very little in the way of luxury.

Towable RVs
There are two main advantages to these units over self-contained models. They depreciate more slowly than a motorhome, which depreciates with the mileage on the engine, and they allow you to drop off the trailer and travel around in your towing vehicle. Passenger space may be limited in the towing vehicle, and most state laws prohibit passengers from riding in towable RVs.

Pop-up Camping Trailers
Also known as folding camping trailers or pop-ups, these RVs are built around a collapsible tent, which makes the trailer

smaller and easy to tow. In fact, some are made to be towed by motorcycles. They are also simple to set up and because of their compact size, the most economical of RV options. Like most RVs, pop-ups range from the basic, with a table and seats that become beds, to the fancy, with a bathroom, electric range and refrigerator and wiring for a stereo system. They usually sleep from four to eight people and the basic models run about $2,500. You can purchase a fancier model for anywhere from $2,900 to $10,000.

Travel Trailers
These trailers come in a range of lengths and can vary greatly in the amount of luxury afforded. Many trailers have a kitchen/living room area and a separate bath and bedroom. The living area has a pull-out bed to convert the area into a second bedroom at night.

Although they cannot be pulled by small cars, the larger family cars, station wagons, vans and pickups, can tow them. However, with a large travel trailer, you may have to modify your car with special shocks to support the weight on the hitch.

Travel trailers average about $7,000 for a basic model. The more popular models range from $10,000 to $35,000. An added option is the power-driven slide room, which enables a portion of the trailer to expand outward with the push of a button (when the RV is parked, of course). The slide room adds extra space without increasing the length of the trailer and costs range upward from $2,500.

Fifth Wheel Trailers
These RVs are so named because of the hitch which connects the front of the trailer to the bed of a pickup truck. These large trailers have four wheels (two on each side in the rear) and it is the hitch that is considered the fifth wheel. The hitch, a

fixed pivot point in the bed of the truck, makes this trailer very maneuverable, particularly when backing into campsites. Unlike some trailers, many states allow passengers to ride in the fifth wheel trailer because of their stability and maneuverability. The section of the trailer that hangs over the hitch is usually a bedroom with space large enough for twin beds or a queen-size bed complete with bedside tables.

The trailer can be hitched and unhitched easily, and once again, you have a vehicle for use in sightseeing or errands.

You can pick up a basic model fifth wheel for about $10,000, although the more luxurious models cost up to $75,000. The fifth wheel RVs can also be purchased with the slide room mentioned above.

Self-Contained RVs
Pick-up campers and motorhomes usually make driving easier than towing a trailer. They are still susceptible to being blown by tractor trailers on the highway (this is less of a problem for fifth wheel trailers and the big Class A motorhomes), but backing into a campsite is easier. In a motorhome, passengers can ride in the back. This is a bonus for families, as it gives children room to color in a coloring book or play games while riding.

The downside for motorhomes is that you must take the camper with you wherever you travel. This is unlike towable trailers, which can be left in a campground while you take a sidetrip in the towing vehicle. Self-contained RVs also depreciate more quickly as you put mileage on the engine. This does

---

>>Camping Tip<<

When parking in a shopping center, make sure the doors to your RV face the entrance to the store. When the doors cannot easily be seen, you leave yourself open to burglary. The doors to an RV can quickly and easily be popped by a crow bar.

not hold true for pick-up campers, which can be dropped in the back of a new truck.

Pick-up Camper

These RVs involve a camper unit that is installed on the bed of a pick-up truck. They range in size from the bed of a pickup truck covered with a shell to a large camper unit installed on the bed or chassis of the truck. Some of these units, which are accesible only by a rear door, are large enough to support a refrigerator, a water tank, sink and toilet. They might also have twin beds or a queen-size bed.

These are the smallest self-contained RVs. A truck camper with very basic living accommodations costs about $4,500. The more popular models range from $5,500 to $22,000.

Mini-Motorhome

These are also called Class C or cab-over models because they are built onto a truck chassis and contain a sleeping area over the cab of the truck in what is called a cab-over. They also tend to be smaller than Class A motorhomes. Prices usually start around $26,000 for the basic model. Larger models, or motorhomes equipped with microwave ovens and other luxury options, range from $30,000 to $55,000.

Class A Motorhome

These motorhomes vary in their construction and size, but they have one thing in common—the engine and driving compartment are all part of the unit. They are built on a metal bed that extends behind the engine, thus resembling a bus.

Class A motorhomes have numerous interior options and passengers can ride in back with accessibility to the cab. Self-powered, many are sturdy enough to tow a small car. The basic models cost about $28,000; the more luxurious models range from $37,000 to $250,000.

What to Look For
How will the RV be used? How many people will use it? Which features would be nice to have and which will be necessary? These are all factors that must be considered when matching an RV to your camping needs.

Sleeping
Of paramount importance is how many people will be sleeping in the RV. Keep in mind that RV manufacturers tend to overrate their vehicle's capacity for sleeping people comfortably (just as tent manufacturers do). Two adults cannot sleep comfortably in a space of less than forty-eight inches wide, and even two small children need a width of at least thirty-six inches.

Bench-style dinettes, which convert into beds, can easily handle two small children but are a bit on the crowded side for two adults. Couches that convert into beds can sleep two adults, but the flip-lounges will really only sleep one adult comfortably. Overhead cabinet bunks will sleep one small child (under 100 pounds), and the over-cab bunks found in most mini-motorhomes will sleep two adults pretty comfortably. The swing-down bunks in Class A motorhomes will sleep one adult or two small children.

If you purchase an RV with a bedroom, make sure that there is storage space beneath the bed. An innerspring mattress is preferable to several inches of foam, and lighting should be optimum for before-bed reading.

Eating
Where to sleep is not the only concern. Can you also seat your family easily at the dinner table? Keep in mind these guidelines when looking at RVs: a sofa facing a table will seat three to five people only if there are chairs available to move close to the table; bench-style dinettes seat two adults and two

children easily, but are a tight fit for four adults; and U-shape dinettes seat four to six people.

Also keep in mind how you intend to use your RV. Entertaining, weekend camping, short vacations, touring, wilderness camping, extended cross-country trips, one-day outings, and parking in one campsite all season are among the possibilities. Long-term wilderness camping and cold-weather camping are impractical though not impossible for RVs. Because your use of fuel determines your use of the vehicle, fuel accessibility is particularly important in the wilderness and in cold weather.

Living Space

Another thing to consider is how much living area your family (or you, alone) will need. Do you need plenty of seating/lounging space for entertaining, watching TV, playing games or hiding away on rainy days? Do you need quiet sections to segregate the younger or older folks from those who are loud or stay awake longer? Depending on your RV lifestyle, you may need movable chairs, a television, stereo system, bar, game table, etc. You will also have to think about lighting, cross-ventilation and space for storing refreshments.

The Bathroom

Another room you may or may not need is a bathroom. This may be an unnecessary luxury if you intend to use only campground showerhouses. But if you have a young child or two aboard, their ability to have use of an on-board bathroom may be a lifesaver on long-distance trips. You may wish to have a small bathroom available for those few times it might be necessary, while some people want a fully-equipped and large bathroom instead of using those at campgrounds.

The Kitchen

The kitchen is an area of great importance. RVs, except for the smallest, offer a variety of choices from L-shaped to split to in-line. But no matter the size or style, you will want overhead cabinets, refrigerator, and overhead lighting. An overcounter window is a big plus as are twin-bowl stainless sinks and a range with four burners, an exhaust hood and fan.

The refrigerator should be in easy reaching distance, with the top of the freezer no more than six feet off the floor. Also, make sure the refrigerator has at least two or three main shelves, shelves on the door, and a small freezer compartment. Vegetable crispers and meat keepers are a nice bonus. Also consider the refrigerator's power source. Some RV's offer dual power sources—electric and propane. You can also find three-ways that accept AC/DC power. If you will camp only in established campgrounds with electrical hook-ups, then you will not need an alternate power source. But you are always covered as long as you have at least a two-way source, particularly if it is propane-electric.

Judge your needs in a refrigerator similarly to your use of a refrigerator at home. Do you eat a lot of meat? You'll need a large freezer compartment. Drink a lot of milk? Your refrigerator door should be capable of holding a half-gallon carton (or jug) or two. Two door refrigerators cool more efficiently than one-door models but are not as common. Also, make sure that you can light or start your refrigerator without opening it. The controls (if you have dual-power) should be outside the refrigerator so that you can switch from gas to electric or turn the appliance off without opening the door and losing precious cooled air.

Luxury RVs offer a wide variety of appliances, everything from microwaves to coffeemakers to icemakers and blenders. Sometimes you can add these options, but if you want a lot, step up to the next model. You'll usually be better off than paying extra for these add-ons.

Storage

Storage space in an RV is very important. Because things can't travel out in the open without becoming an unusual sort of missile, you have to make sure everything has a place. There should be cabinets for keeping food, cooking utensils, plates, glasses, bowls, pans, clothing, bed linens and pillows. There should be a closet for hanging clothes, a medicine cabinet or under-sink storage for toiletries, towels and cloths, and room to store lawn chairs, toys and games, leveling blocks, tools, water hose, sewer hose, electrical cords and anything else you might want to carry along. Most importantly, make sure the cabinets stay latched when items lurch against them, or you'll experience a rain of stored items upon your head.

Other Things to Consider

Look, too, for upholstery that is easy to clean and doesn't show dirt. Curtains should be a color that does not fade quickly in the sun. Cushions should be at least four inches thick. Windows should open easily, be screened, and situated for good cross ventilation. Make sure there is adequate lighting throughout the RV.

An RV's furnace should be a forced-air, ducted model that is electronically ignited. RVs in excess of twenty-four feet should have an input rating of at least 20,000 btu; 30,000 btus for those over thirty feet. A wall-mounted thermostat should be conveniently located but not in front of a door or elsewhere where outside temperatures can change its reading. Make sure that ducts are located all over the RV so that air is distributed everywhere.

Think of what you want or need in your RV. Make a list.

Other items that can be purchased for an RV include a water heater, water purifier, generator, washer/dryer, clothes hamper, food processor, awning, reclining seats, swivel chair, pedestal tables, roof air conditioner/heat pump, systems monitor panel, CB radio, portable TV, TV antenna, cable hook-up, leveling jacks, floor-level courtesy lights, roof storage pod, vacuum cleaner, room divider, shoe storage rack, entertainment center, self-storing table. The list goes on.

Don't forget to inspect the outside of the RV. Does it have an electric patio outlet if you want one? Are the sewage and waste tanks conveniently located and large enough for your needs? What about the water, propane and gas tanks? If there are twin LP-gas bottles, are they equipped with an automatic changeover regulator?

Don't buy accessories that are appealing but that you probably will never use. On the other hand, don't sacrifice something to spare expense, only to find yourself sorry later on. Accessories will make your trip more comfortable and will add to the resale value later on.

Packing your RV

When loading your RV, make sure you pack the heaviest items close to the floor and in front of the rear axle or between the front and rear axles in motorhomes. In pickup campers, make sure the load is as far forward as possible.

Closets, cabinets and drawers are for use in storing items while the RV is in motion. Use them but make sure everything is secured. Use other items such as clothing, towels and linens to make sure everything is snug. Instead of carrying along china and glass, use plastic and melamine. Latch drawers, cabinet doors and the refrigerator. Any heavy items that cannot be packed into a closet or cabinet should be secured with rope or bungee cords so that they cannot shift and upset the balance of the RV, particularly if it is a trailer.

And keep in mind, the more you bring, the more clutter you have to deal with.

Most importantly, keep the weight down. Don't travel with a lot of water in your tanks, if possible. Tank up when you reach your campsite.

If you are carrying a lot, you will probably want to weigh your RV once it is fully packed, including passengers. Moving and trucking companies have scales you can use for a small fee, and there are a number of conveniently located state weighing stations. Don't just weigh the vehicle, though. Weigh each axle to make sure the weight is distributed evenly. If you are overloaded (the owner's manual will tell you what the limits for your vehicle are), you could tax the safety capacity of the suspension system. You are not required to stop for weigh stations when traveling; using their scales is for your own assurance only.

Driving an RV

Depending upon the type of RV you own or are renting, there are a few things you should learn about driving an RV. Most RVs are very maneuverable once you have become accustomed to the extra height and length. If you are pulling a trailer or driving a mini-motorhome, your point-of-view will be about the same as in any vehicle. It is the Class A motorhomes that sit higher off the road, allowing the driver greater visibility, adding to enjoyment of the trip as well as ease of driving.

On the other hand, all RVs take longer to accelerate and decelerate, an important point to keep in mind when merging onto a highway or other busy road. It will also take you longer to make a turn through an intersection and to pass other vehicles. It follows that you need to slow down sooner than you would were you driving a regular automobile. If you downshift when going downhill rather than riding the brakes, your brakes will not overheat and you don't risk losing complete control of your brakes. If you have trailer brakes, pump them intermittently and only for a second or two.

If you keep a safe distance between yourself and the vehicle in front of you, there should be no problem when sudden stops are involved. The key to maintaining a safe stopping distance is by allowing a second for every ten feet of your vehicle's length (and a minimum of four seconds) when you are stopping. If the road is wet and slippery, you will probably want to add a few seconds to this figure.

You can maintain a safe distance between vehicles by taking the length of your RV from front to back (if you are pulling a trailer, include the vehicle that is pulling) and multiplying the number by each ten miles per hour you are traveling. For example, if your RV is total of 25 feet long, and you are traveling 60 miles per hour, a safe distance between vehicles would be 25 x 6, or 150 feet.

Large Trucks

RVs often suffer from the turbulence caused by passing semis, trucks and buses. Keep an eye on your mirror so that you can be prepared for passing vehicles. Your hands should be at the ten o'clock and two o'clock positions on your steering wheel so that you can keep the wheel steady. If you are driving a motorhome, take your foot off the gas and edge as far as possible to the right of the pavement, slowing down five to ten miles per hour. If you are driving a trailer, move as far as possible to the right and (rather than slow down), accelerate slightly to keep tension on the trailer hitch. When passed while going downhill, step only on the trailer brakes (if you have separate brakes for the trailer). The longer your trailer, the more problems you will have with truck suction, where the trailer is pulled forward by the suction of the passing semi. If the suction caused by trucks continues to be a problem, your trailer may be hitched up incorrectly.

Wind

Strong winds are also hard on RVs because they can sway, particularly if you are hauling a trailer (though even the mini-motorhomes can be buffeted pretty badly). Decreasing your speed will help because it gives your wheels a better grip on the pavement. If the wind is really bad, however, don't just slow down; pull to the side of the road, stop and set your emergency brake.

Turning

It is also important to turn carefully, as height and weight of some RVs make them susceptible to tipping over if you turn suddenly. When turning at an intersection, you will have to pull further into the intersection before beginning your turn. If you are towing a trailer, try turning from the center of the intersection, pulling into the right side of the lane before aligning the vehicle that is towing and the trailer, itself, into the center of the lane. If you use the hand-over-hand method of steering as you turn, you will have greater control over your RV. When driving on curvy roads, drive a bit slower than the posted speed limit.

Clearance

The height of an RV can also be a problem. Know the clearance of your RV, taking into account for anything that sticks up from the top of your RV such as luggage pods or air conditioners. Most RVs can drive easily beneath a highway underpass, but you could have problems at gas stations, drive-thrus, shopping centers, motels and under tree branches on the side of the road. Learn to tell whether or not your RV will fit beneath an overhang, but if you have the slightest doubt, don't take any chances. Also check your ground clearance. RVs usually have a higher ground clearance than automobiles, but when passing over bumps or holes, a trailer, particularly, reacts to a downward thrust that could break a hitch or bust an axle or spring.

Backing an RV can be difficult, particularly if you are towing a trailer. You can have a TV monitor installed at the rear of the vehicle, or you can, with help, develop a backing routine. Motorhomes, since they are one with the engine, are easier to back and only take a little practice, but trailers must be backed a lot more slowly, with as little movement as possible of the steering wheel. Too much movement, and your trailer can turn at a right angle to the hitch. No big deal. It just means you have to pull forward and start again.

Because a trailer turns opposite to the way the towing vehicle's wheels are turned, you get a delayed reaction with the trailer, which is why it is important to move slowly. Once the trailer begins to turn, it will not continue to back up straight, for example. Instead it will continue in the direction it was turning. You will have to continually adjust the rate of turn until the trailer is maneuvered into place. Just remember to take your time and to stop frequently. Get out and look to see how the procedure is going. Pull forward as often as necessary. It won't be long before you learn exactly how your trailer reacts and what it takes to get it in place.

A final point to consider is that nearly all RVs have trouble getting up hills. The best advice is to reduce your speed and learn to get used to it. If you push your vehicle too hard, it could overheat. Finally, if you are slowing down

traffic (that long line of cars behind you), pull over and let them pass. They will appreciate it, and you won't end up frustrated and embarrassed.

RV Clubs

If you intend to do a lot of traveling in your RV or even if just want to get away for an occasional weekend, you might consider joining one or more of the numerous national RV clubs, which offer their members wonderful benefits, including RV-related magazines, camping fee discounts, emergency road service, discounts on parts, special financing, insurance, directories, trip routing services, mail forwarding services and more.

A good travel club should do two things: serve your needs while you are on the road and keep you informed when you aren't. But, before you join a club, look to see who is trying to get you to join. An oil company? An insurance company? Is there an ulterior motive? Discover what the club knows about camping and traveling first. It is your time, your money and your trip that are on the line.

Two of the more popular clubs are The Family Motor Coach Association and The Good Sam Club. The former has 325 chapters and 90,000 members. The Good Sam Club, run by TL Enterprises, has more than 900,000 members worldwide. Woodall's, who publishes a popular campground directory, also operates the Travel America Club.

RV Rentals

One way to try out RVs before making a purchase is to rent a unit from an RV dealer, most of whom will take the rental price off the sale price if you buy an RV from them. Rentals also make sense if you want an RV for an annual trip, but don't really need it the other fifty-one weeks of the year.

RVs of all styles and sizes can be rented. Make sure that

you are fully oriented to all of the units features before you leave the RV dealer. You will want to rent from a company that offers roadside assistance once you leave the dealer. Renting from an individual will not offer you the protection in an emergency that dealing with an RV dealer or rental agency does.

· 9 ·
Where to Camp

Of what avail are forty freedoms without a blank spot on the map.

—*Aldo Leopold*
A Sand County Almanac

There wasn't a "no trespassing" sign (or the Swedish equivalent) in sight when Frank and a group of ten other Scouts and their leader passed through the gate onto private property. After a three-mile hike, the group stopped in view of a vast lake with an unpronounceable name and made camp for the night. The next morning the group looped back around to their starting point and crossed back onto public property.

When arrangements were made for this foray into the Swedish countryside, the Scouts had told the landowner they were coming, but they didn't ask for permission; because of the early 1800s Swedish law "Allemanstratten," or "everyman's right," the group didn't need permission for the overnight stay on private property.

The Swedish law gives hikers, campers, birdwatchers and other outdoor enthusiasts the legal right to cross onto private property, even when it is fenced. You can even camp for the night without permission. The law protects landowners from damage by constraining interlopers from damaging property, camping too close to a house or in planted crops. The law has worked well in Sweden for more than 150 years, and there is no change planned for the foreseeable future.

In America, where ideas of property rights hit at the core of most Americans' concepts of freedom, every person's right is to enjoy our public lands. Fortunately there are millions of acres of national and state lands to choose from. Tens of thousands of established campgrounds and backcountry campsites await. Amenities range from fully developed campsites with full hook-ups, bathhouses, laundromats, swimming pools, and more, to a flat place on the side of a trail or stream.

National Forests

More than 10,000 recreation sites and 4,500 campgrounds are scattered among the 156 National Forests throughout the country. Administered by the Department of Agriculture, the U.S. Forest Service has multi-use management goals for the nation's working woodlands. The Forest Service routinely balances concerns about logging production and recreational uses for its 191 million acres of Forests (roughly the size of California, Oregon and Washington) including more than 370 wilderness areas. The Forest Service also administers nineteen National Grasslands, which are primarily located in North Dakota, though some are dotted down through the middle of the country to Texas.

Camping, backpacking, hunting, fishing, hiking, skiing and whitewater rafting are among the recreational activities in the National Forests. For more information on National Forests in your area, write to National Forest Service, Department of Agriculture, 14th St. and Independence Ave., SW, Washington, DC 20250, or call (202) 205-1760 and ask for the free brochure, "A Guide to Your National Forests."

National Parks

There are 49 National Parks in the United States. There are also numerous National Recreation Areas, Seashores, Monuments and other specially designated national sites that offer campgrounds or primitive camping. While backcountry camping is usually free, permits are often required. Before heading off on a trip, check with the park you intend to visit to see if you need a permit to head off into the backcountry.

Keep in mind when planning a trip to a National Park that although backcountry sites are still available, free-of-charge, on a first-come, first-served basis, many sites require reservations. All developed campgrounds charge a fee and most require reservations. Ticketron offers a computerized reservation system for the National Park Service. If you are planning a trip to Acadia, Maine; Assateague, Maryland; Cape Hatteras, North Carolina; Grand Canyon, Arizona; Great Smoky Mountains, Tennessee-North Carolina; Joshua Tree, California; Ozark Riverways, Missouri; Rocky Mountain, Colorado; Sequoia-Kings Canyon, California; Shenandoah, Virginia; Whiskeytown-Shasta-Trinity, California; Yellowstone, Idaho-Montana-Wyoming; and Yosemite, California, you will need to make reservations.

Ticketron can be reached by calling (800) 452-1111, and fees range from $8 to $16 a night. Ticketron also charges a $5 fee for making the reservation.

Some National Parks also charge an entrance fee, and if you intend to visit one park regularly or a number of parks in one year, you would be wise to get a Golden Eagle Pass, Golden Age Passport or Golden Access Passport from a National Park or Forest area. The Golden Eagle Pass, which costs about $25 annually, allows your private vehicle to enter all federal recreation areas—parks, monuments, battlefields, etc. Camping fees are separate and are not included in the pass price. The Golden Age Passport is for those sixty-two years of age or older; the Golden Access Passport for the permanently disabled. These two are free and have the added benefit of providing the holder with a fifty percent discount on camping fees. You must apply for The Golden Age and Golden Access passports in person at any National Park or Corps of Engineers reservoir.

The public library is a good source of information about national public areas. You can also contact the National Park Service and ask for the "Guide and Map: National Parks of the United States." This free publication can be obtained by calling (202) 208-4747 or writing National Park Service, Department of the Interior, 1849 C St, NW, Room 1013, Washington, DC 20240.

Bureau of Land Management Lands
The BLM, like the Forest Service, manages its 272 million acres guided by a multiple-use ethic. As a part of the Department of Interior's Land and Mineral Management Office, the BLM looks out for the competing interests of livestock grazing, mineral production, timber harvesting and recreational uses. The BLM has 3,700 miles of hiking trails and a roughly equal system of trails for all-terrain vehicles. Most of the BLM's vast holdings are concentrated in eleven western states. For more information, contact the Bureau of Land Management, Department of Interior, 1849 C St, NW, Washington, DC 20240, or call (202) 208-4200.

Corps of Engineers Reservoirs
The 460 Corps of Engineers lakes boast thousands of campsites close to some prime fishing, boating and swimming

> ### ❦ *Camping Secret* ❦
>
> Looking for solitude on America's public lands? Alaska is the place to go. That state's Kenai and Arctic National Wildlife Refuges alone offer more than 20 million acres of wilderness.
>
> If that's just too far from home, try these lesser visited areas: Great Basin National Park, Nevada; Isle Royale National Park, Michigan; Bob Marshall Wilderness, Montana; Guadalupe Mountains National Park, Texas; and if you stay away from the large tourist draws, Adirondack State Park, New York.

spots. The lakes, impounded to control flooding, produce hydroelectric power, protect the shore and provide a reliable supply of water, are a great place for recreation. More than 500 million visitors each year fish, boat, camp, swim, hike, bike and enjoy other forms of recreation on Corps-impounded lakes.

A small use-fee is charged for camping at the Corps' 93,000 campsites. Golden Age and Golden Access passports, mentioned in the section on National Parks, are good for discounts on fees on Corps lakes. However, Golden Eagle passports, sold for entrance to National Parks, are not accepted at all lakes; ask at the time you get your passport about specific lakes in your area. The passports are available at Corps district offices and lake headquarters.

For more information on Corps of Engineers facilities, write to U.S. Army Corps of Engineers, CECW-ON, 20 Massachusetts Ave., NW, Washington, DC 20314, or call (202) 272-0660.

State Parks and Forests

National Parks and Forests offer many well-known opportunities for campers and outdoor enthusiasts, but don't overlook opportunities that may be closer to home. From the

600,000-acre Anza Borrego Desert State Park in California to the 3,000-acre Cape Henlopen on the Delaware coast, state parks and forests offer a diverse array of places to camp.

Appendix B lists addresses and phone numbers to contact for information on state or provincial parks in all fifty states and the Canadian provinces.

Private Campgrounds

There are so many campgrounds across the nation that each year Woodall's updates *The Campground Directory*, a guide to U.S. and Canadian campgrounds, both public and private. There are also regional editions of the directory, which are smaller and cheaper, listing only campgrounds in one section of the country. A similar guide is offered by the Good Sam Club through many bookstores and the club itself.

Each entry begins with a town and map coordinate and continues with the campground's name and a descriptive phrase about the campground and directions. Information on rentals, facilities, recreation, rate information, phone number, reservations, discounts, group camping, tenting and other special features are included in the listing.

Purchasing a huge directory isn't the only way to discover where to camp. If you have a particular itinerary or destination in mind, you can write the local Chamber of Commerce for the information. Many libraries also subscribe to Woodall's and other guides, and you can get your information there as well.

Campground chains, such as KOA and Jellystone, offer directories to their campgrounds for free.

Solitude

Looking for a campsite away from the maddening crowds can be a challenge, but following a few guiding principles will help you find some peace and quiet.

At popular campgrounds, camp in the off-season. The weather and bugs are not usually at their best, but you will have less company.

Seek out less publicized areas. The Great Smokies and Yellowstone may be crowded, while a nearby state park has sites to choose from. Talk with other campers about places they have camped to learn about little-used areas.

Camp in primitive sites. The Forest Service, BLM and Corps of Engineers have thousands of sites without hook-ups, restrooms and other facilities. These campsites are used less than more developed areas.

Take a walk. Crowds in parks are almost always confined to within a mile of a parking lot or on well worn trails to prominent landmarks. By taking a day hike away from these popular attractions, you can share a park or forest with just a few other visitors.

· 10 ·
In Camp

There is a pleasure in the pathless woods; there is a rapture on the lonely shore; there is society, where none intrudes, by the deep sea, and music in its roar.

—*Lord Byron*

After a better night's sleep than I generally expect on my first night in camp, I crawl out of my sleeping bag. Being careful not to disturb my husband Frank or our four-year old daughter Griffin, I dress, pull on boots and climb out of the tent into the cool morning air. By noon it will be a little on the warm side, but we're camped in sight of a clear pool beneath a small cascade on a mountain stream to take advantage of the natural air conditioning.

I fire up our camp stove and put some water on to boil. We are within a mile of at least a dozen other campers, but I can see or hear nobody else. By the time I hear my "big girl" telling her papa the dream she just had, I've enjoyed my first cup of coffee in peace.

There are only so many days any of us can spend in the wood, which makes choosing the right site and setting it up properly very important.

Getting There

Packing up your car or truck properly will make your camp set-up go easier. Exactly how you pack your equipment varies greatly by the type of vehicle you own. A small sedan may have no more room in the trunk than a backpack, while two campers traveling in a truck with a camper top may have more storage space than most apartments. What matters is that you can find the gear you need when you need it. That means that you must pack the things you will need first (such as a tent and ground cloth) last. With your essential gear on top, you can set up camp and then unload the rest of your gear.

If you travel by car and are pressed for room, a luggage rack can give you added space. It will likely be required to get bikes or a canoe to your destination, and with a luggage box, you can take other gear as well. Yakima is one well-established brand of car racks; their basic roof rack starts at about $150, with accessories including locks ($60 for eight locks using one key) and luggage racks ($400 to $500) adding to that. Another option is the Kanga Roof Pouch, a lightweight, water-resistant nylon packcloth bag that straps to the top of your car with or without an existing roof rack. It costs about $150 for 15 cubic feet of storage space.

>>Camping Tip<<

Instead of starting a fire, try using a hot water bottle to keep you warm on chilly nights. Heat the water up on your stove, fill the bottle, and cuddle up against it in your sleeping bag. It is a good alternative to sparks and smoke.

Put your lightest gear, such as clothes, in the rooftop luggage box. Saving the heavier gear for the car itself will keep your center of gravity lower and reduce risk of accidents. Your car should also have weight distributed evenly from side to side to similarly balance the load.

Selecting a Campsite

Whether you are camping at a campsite next to your car or canoeing to a site on the river bank, selecting a good campsite will make your overnight stay more enjoyable. So what makes a good campsite?

A good campsite will have a good source of water nearby. In a campground, that water source will be a faucet. On the trail, the water source may be a spring or stream. Unless you are planning to carry all of your water along with you, you will need a good water source and a means to purify. There is more on water and water purifying in Chapter 1.

The second most important criteria for a good campsite is enough open area to pitch your tent or tents without being too exposed. This can pose a challenge for large groups, which is one of the reasons that groups should confine themselves to camping in designated areas.

There are many factors to consider. If you are in a mountain meadow in a thunderstorm, a lightning strike will find your tent an attractive target. Trees around your campsite will protect you from the wind but will drip water on your site long after the rain has stopped. Also check overhead for rotten limbs that can blow down in wind or rain.

So, an ideal site would be a fairly level area in a small clearing in the woods. Another good site is a meadow with high trees nearby. An attractive site that may be a bad idea is on the banks of a stream. Flash floods can wash through a camp even though its several feet higher than the stream bed (even more in a narrow gorge or canyon). Minimum impact camping guidelines call for setting up camp at least 200 feet from water. Finally, remember it is usually several degrees colder beside a stream, so keep some distance away from a stream (except on hot nights) to avoid the natural air conditioning of the cold water.

You will want to pick a site that is flat or on a very slight slope, but don't pick a low spot, because rain will puddle up around your tent. Make sure the slope is very slight. If not, you will spend the night slowly sliding down the tent and then waking to crawl back into position again. If there is a slight angle, put your head at the high end for the best night's sleep.

If you are camping at a developed site, your "kitchen" will be set up on the picnic table. Covering the table with a rain fly will give you shade from the sun and protection from rain; however, the fly should be high enough above the table to not catch fire or trap fumes from the stove. Putting the stove near the edge of a picnic table will make it easier to stand and cook. Whether a picnic table is available or not, your tent should be ten to twenty feet away from the kitchen area. This will keep food smells from the kitchen from attracting animals to your tent. It will also keep a stove flare up from damaging your tent.

In many campgrounds, you will not have a choice, but will be assigned a site when you check in. These designated campsites are almost always just right. If the site you are assigned has too little or even too much room, you may want to suggest to the person who assigned the site that another would be better for your group. If you want a quiet campsite, get one away from the bathhouse and main road into the campground.

Making Camp
Once the site has been selected, you will want to pitch your tent and roll out your sleeping pad and sleeping bag first thing. This way you won't have to fumble around in the dark

later on to get settled for the night. Before you lay out the ground cloth for the tent, get down on your hands and knees and remove all of the sticks and rocks under the tent site. Preparing a relatively smooth spot now will make for a much better night's sleep later. If there are roots sticking up above the ground, look for another spot. Like the fairy tale princess who could feel a pea through dozens of mattresses, you will find that a small rock or root will feel like a boulder under the sleeping pad at night.

Depending on where you are camping, another important part of setting up camp for the night is selecting a site for your "bathroom." If you're staying in a developed campground, there may be toilets already there; if not, you will have to improvise. Now is the time to agree on an area that will be your outdoor bathroom. It needs to be a couple of hundred feet from any streams, springs, or other water sources and well out of sight of the camp and trail. You will bury your solid wastes there in a "cat hole" as described in Chapter 3.

If you are camping in an area with bears or an area that has problems with raccoons or other animals breaking into packs and tents for food, now is the time to protect your food and smellable toiletries that attract animals. If you are car camping, locking these smellable items away in the trunk will prevent problems. If not, you need to hang a smellables bag. Hang it about ten feet off the ground and at least four feet from the tree. As you are making camp, you should select the tree and get a rope over a branch so that you can get the bag up easily in the dark. Weight a rope with a stick and toss it over the branch you selected. Pull hard on both ends to make sure the bag will hold. Make sure that when you are testing the branch you step to one side in case the branch breaks. Tie one end to the tree and leave the other free to attach the bag to later. When it's time to hang the bag, fold the end of the bag over a stout stick (about two inches thick and a foot long). Tie a knot around the bag below the stick, pull the bag up to about

---

>>Camping Tip<<

Washing your pots and pans isn't enough if there are hungry animals in the vicinity of your campsite. Hang up or otherwise put away everything from the pot you boiled water in to the sponge you scrubbed it with. You may think they are spotless but the animals can scent otherwise and may carry things off or chew them up.

---

ten feet off the ground and tie off, on a second tree if possible.

When going to sleep, change into sleepwear or other clothes before climbing into your sleeping bag. The clothes you wear during the day collect moisture that will keep you colder at night. Changing into fresh clothes will help your sleeping bag keep you as warm as the manufacturer's promised comfort rating.

If you are car camping and have to arrive at the campground at night, you will need to pack your vehicle accordingly. A lantern, your tent, sleeping bags and pads should be packed at the top and easy to find. Determining a good site will be difficult in the dark, so you may have to move things around the next day if you are staying for more than one night. It will be best to have already eaten if you are going to arrive at night. If this isn't possible, have the food for your first meal easily accesible along with the stove, fuel and utensils you will need. By having all the things you need for the first night readily available, you can delay completely unpacking until the light of morning.

Campfires

If you want to have a campfire, you may want to bring wood from home. That may sound a little extreme, with your car trunk bulging at the seams already, but faced with a constant onslaught of campers, most developed campgrounds are groomed of their downed wood soon after it hits the ground.

You will want only downed, dead wood. Not only is it irresponsible to cut up a live tree for your fire, but the green wood won't burn well anyway. Be sure to get plenty of twigs (about as big around as a matchstick) to use to get the fire going. You will need to put on progressively bigger pieces of wood as the fire begins burning in earnest, so go ahead and have some on hand before lighting the fire.

Select a previously-built fire pit or ring, or create one in a safe area. Build a tepee-shaped cone of small branches by leaning the wood together. Leave the side away from the wind open so that you can add fuel and light the fire. Break up your small twigs for kindling and place them inside the tepee. If you have brought a fire-starter, place it inside the tepee with the twigs around and over it. If not, you will want to use a few dried leaves or some crumpled paper in with the small twigs. Light the firestarter, leaves or paper, and the fire should get going easily. As it burns, continue to feed it, always making sure that you don't pile on too much fuel at once, which can smother the fire.

Once the tepee fire gets going, you can let it burn down to a low flame with coals and add the big pieces of wood, log-cabin style. Start by adding a log on either side of the fire, pushing the edge of it up against the coals from the tepee fire. Place two more logs on the opposite sides of the fire, laying them on top of the first two as if building a log cabin. Continue adding to your cabin to build up a supply of fuel. Five or six layers of logs are usually enough to bring the sides up to the top of the tepee fire. At the top level, lay logs across the middle, like a roof, but leave several inchs between them to allow air to circulate.

Keep water and a trowel handy when the fire is burning so that you'll be ready to put out the flames if your fire spreads outside of the ring. If your fire is popping sparks into the air, the risk of spreading a fire is greatest. Using only dead, dry wood will lessen sparks.

When going to bed at night or breaking camp for good, make sure the fire is completely out and douse the fire pit with water. Wind can cause coals to come back to life if they are not thoroughly drowned.

Day Hikes

Your campsite can be used as a base to hike away from during the day and come back to each night. This way you will get many of the rewards of backpacking without having to lug a quarter to a third of your body weight on your back all day. Do not leave valuables behind in camp; lock them away in your car or carry them with you.

Although, you will be relatively unburdened with equipment, there are a few essentials every well-prepared day hiker must have. Comfortable clothes that don't constrict your movement are essential. For many hikes, a sturdy pair of shorts, a T-shirt and hiking boots are adequate. You will also need a daypack or fanny pack (covered in detail in Chapter 3) to carry the gear you need. For all but the shortest hikes (a mile or less), you should carry a liter or more of water. You will also need rain gear, such as a rainsuit, poncho or umbrella.

Items you may want to consider include a small first aid kit, a lighter or matches, a pocketknife, a snack or lunch, toilet paper and trowel, a camera and film, binoculars, wildlife and plant guides, a map or guidebook, and a compass. Also if you are going to be hiking at high altitudes, carry some warm clothing; the temperature on the mountain tops can be much lower than in the valleys.

>>Camping Tip<<

Glue gun sticks make great emergency repairs. Just melt the end of the stick and press against tears in your tent, rain gear, stuffsacks, etc.

Hunting

Many outdoor enthusiasts camp in order to be at a favorite hunting spot early in the morning, and sitting around a campfire telling stories (or swapping lies) is an unmatched way to end a day of hunting. A hunting camp is also a great place to introduce youngsters to the sport.

When it comes to getting that first buck of the season, you will be sure to have other like-minded sportsmen around, as campgrounds near game lands can fill up near opening day. But you will most often find that after Labor Day, you can have your pick of sites as many family campers will stay at home until the next Memorial Day.

If you are not in a developed campsite, be sure that your camping area looks like a hunting camp to other hunters. Bright colors in camp should keep other hunters from shooting in close proximity to your camp. I will not go into specifics on how to hunt here, as I am no expert, and there are many good books on hunting available. But here are a few camp oriented tips to consider.

For safety reasons, it is good to have someone in camp at all times during the day. Campground thefts are not uncommon, and you should always be a little wary of abandoning camp entirely.

A few extra pieces of gear you may want to pack for a big game hunt are a game cart and a block and tackle to ease hauling and cleaning your game. A box to lock up ammunition will also be needed if children are in camp. If you are setting up a long term hunting camp, you may want to bring an outdoor cooker or grill, fueled by a bulk propane tank. It will feed a crew of hunters quicker and easier than a smaller camping stove.

Fishing

Whether you are an avid fisherman or only occasionally dip a line in the water, you will sooner or later want to combine camping and fishing trips. The 93,000 campsites the Corps of Engineers maintain alongside their reservoirs are reason enough to consider a combined camping-fishing trip. Some of these lakes, such as Lake Seminole on the Florida, Alabama and Georgia state lines, are renowned for their fishing potential.

If fishing is the main purpose of your camping trip, then the equipment you carry will be determined by how and where you are fishing. If, however, your main interest is a camping trip, you can get by with these few essentials: a rod and reel with appropriate line, a net, stringer and small tackle box with a few lures or hooks and bobbers for live bait.

To get your gear to camp, you can make a fishing rod holder to strap on the roof of your car. A four-inch wide piece of PVC pipe of appropriate length, capped at each end, will keep the rods safe and out of your way in the car.

Because evening hours are prime time for fishing, you may want to adjust your eating schedule to allow fishing from an hour ahead of sundown into dark. But, do not leave fish caught at night on a stringer until morning. Not only will most be dead, but they will likely have been nibbled on or stolen by turtles, otter and other animals. Clean these fish soon after they are caught and pack them away in a cooler for breakfast.

Identifying Flora and Fauna

Honk, hink. Honk, hink. Honk, hink. The call and response come so close together, that it is often hard to tell that it's the male Canada goose supplying the honk and the female replying hink. None of that matters, as the goose music is building to a crescendo. The geese you were hearing turn in a final arc and line up on the pond in front of you. With their feet spread wide to greet the water, the geese stretch their wings and cup them to put on air brakes as they glide down

> ## >>Camping Tip<<
>
> Try blending environmental self-education into a camping trip. Carry along a couple of field guides or make "special" trips. Take a flower camping trip one spring weekend, bring your guide along and take a couple of day hikes to explore, using your guide. Take a bird trip or tree trip another weekend. Look up species you are likely to encounter ahead of time and refer to the book as you hike to broaden your enjoyment of the outdoors.

to the water. The fourteen geese slide to a halt and begin to honk and hink again as mates pair up on the pond.

The joy of watching wildlife or identifying plants in the wild is hard to describe in a carpeted, dry-walled and comfort-controlled room. It is a slightly untamed thrill as you learn where and when to be to find different species. From wildflowers under the sun of the California desert or alongside a cool Smoky Mountains creek to Brown Bear catching salmon on an Alaskan creek, the search for plants and animals can be an exciting way to pick your camping destinations.

In addition to the usual camping equipment, you will need guidebooks such as the Peterson Field Guide Series or those created by the Audubon Society, a pair of binoculars, a notebook for either a journal or field notes on the species seen, and a camera with macro or telephoto lens and tripod (if you want to bring your find home).

Remember that removing plants or animals (other than game animals in season) from public lands is illegal. The exception to this general rule is that seashells may be collected in state parks and National Seashores without special permission.

Many parks have ranger-led talks and nature walks to help you get started, and the ranger-naturalists are great sources of information about a specific area or ecosystem.

Evening programs in a park, such as an outdoor slideshow
and talk, are another good opportunity for learning while
camping. Check at the park office for a schedule of events.

What Else?
The above activities are, of course, only a partial listing of
things you can do while camping. Other popular activities
range from reading books to boating, swimming, biking and
collecting seashells or rocks (where permitted). Check your
local bookstore and library for books on these and other
specific activities.

· 11 ·
Camping Green

To waste, to destroy, our natural resources, to skin and
exhaust the land instead of using it so as to increase its
usefulness, will result in undermining in the days of our
children the very prosperity which we ought by right to hand
down to them amplified and developed.
                                    —*Theodore Roosevelt*

The morning sunlight filters through the trees and
haze to cast a soft glow on the tents in Yosemite Village.
Hundreds of tents are clustered in a campsite where the haze
isn't all from morning fog, but is caused in part by the
thousands of cars vying for parking space in the "wilderness"
of this city in a park. The golf courses, gas stations, hospital
and motel are all thankfully blocked from view at the moment.

Nearby lies the pristine beauty of Yosemite Valley with
Half Dome and El Capitan rising majestically above the
meadows, but squeezed in among the other campers, it is

hard to see this beauty. It is also hard to see this camping trip as earth friendly.

Minimum Impact Camping

In recent years, "minimum impact camping" and "Leave No Trace" have become the catchphrases for responsible outdoors behavior. This philosophy, once summed up by the National Park Service as "Take nothing but pictures, leave nothing but footprints," is now widespread. Groups such as the Boy Scouts, who once espoused techniques like trenching your tent to prevent water from running under it, have adopted low-impact techniques. The following are measures you can take to eliminate any trace of your presence wherever you camp.

Maintaining a Clean Camp

If you camp at established sites with a clear-cut means of disposing of your waste—trash cans or dumpsters for trash, dump stations for RV sewage and grey water—make sure you take advantage of it. Do not leave paper, matches, foil or any other item at the site, including organic trash.

Orange peels, apple cores and egg shells may strike you as natural trash, easily biodegradable, so why not leave it in the brush to rot? Because it takes five months for an orange peel to decompose. Toss it in the nearest trash can or carry it home with you. Never burn trash. You cannot guarantee that your campfire or grill fire will totally eradicate it.

If you are camping in the wilderness, with no means of disposing of your trash, pack it out! Established camp-grounds have either latrines or flush toilets, but if you are camping somewhere where the woods are your privy, pack out the toilet paper you use to wipe yourself. Imagine heading back into the woods to relieve yourself only to discover a trail of paper proving you weren't the first one to have this idea at

>>Camping Tip<<

Always camp at least 200 feet from water sources. This prevents contamination and lessens your impact on the banks of the stream or lake.

this spot. Soggy, used toilet paper is probably one of the uglier reminders of human presence.

I have seen campsites littered with candy bar wrappers and cigarette butts. If you smoke, carry along a plastic bag just for your butts. If you want to smoke, that's your prerogative but you shouldn't think of the outdoors as one big ashtray. Not only is the litter of cigarettes ugly, but it only takes one stray spark to start a forest fire that will turn the woods into a huge ashtray. If you're a snacker, carry a plastic bag for your candy wrapper, orange peels or apple cores. Pack it in, pack it out, and you're already one giant step toward improving the environment you've supposedly escaped to.

Clean Up Trash Left by Others

If you arrive at your campsite to find that it has already been trashed by the folks before you, don't despair and add to the filth. Always carry along an extra garbage bag and fill it up with others' trash. When I camped as a child, we were each required to fill a bag with trash (if possible) before we could settle in to play or swim (since we mostly camped at lakes). Sadly, the three of us kids usually had no trouble filling our garbage bags. Unfortunately, the enviro-conscious among us do not outnumber the abusers of America's great outdoors, and we have to make up for their ignorance and sloth by picking up after them.

In fact, camping areas abound with trash. For some reason, people who wouldn't dare throw trash on the ground at home (or even out the window of their moving vehicle) do so freely in the outdoors. You can make the outdoors an even better place to be by occasionally stopping to pick up other people's trash. You do not have to be ridiculous and carry out nasty toilet paper or rotting organic material, but you can take a minute to cover it with leaves, moss, dirt and twigs. Pick up trash, you'll find you'll feel a whole lot better about yourself.

Keep Campfires to a Minimum
It is now illegal in many places to build fires, particularly in state and national forests. And for good reason. If not cared for properly, a campfire can start a forest fire. Campfires are also damaging to the environment. Scars from fire rings last a long time, and blackened earth and rocks are messy and far from aesthetically pleasing. Using a cook stove puts less wear and tear on the environment.

If you build a fire, resist the temptation to burn trash or leave it in the fire pit. This is as ugly as finding trash scattered about your campsite. Once you've started something burning, you'll have the tendency to leave it in the pit whether it is fully burned or not. Do not put tinfoil-lined packages in fire pits, because they will not entirely burn up. The easiest thing to do is to avoid this problem altogether by packing out all your trash.

If you do decide to build a fire, use only downed wood. Breaking branches from trees or chopping dead or live trees for wood should not even be considered a possibility. Killing plant life for the sake of atmosphere is inexcusable. Obvi-

---

>>Camping Tip<<
If you find more than one fire ring at your camp site, use one and disassemble the others. Scatter the rocks and burned logs and pack out any trash you find.

ously, rules change for just about anything if a life or death situation is involved. Once again, if you do intend to build a fire, do so only in designated fire pits or grills. Many camp-sites offer permanent grills in which you can build a small campfire.

Limit Your Group Size to Ten or Less
Any time you have ten or more people camping in one spot, you're going to have a major impact on the environment. If latrines aren't provided, you've got ten people using the surrounding area as a toilet, and you have ten people beating down the ground to set up tents. The environmental impact a group of ten or more can have on a backcountry campsite is shocking. If you are interested in camping with a larger group, find a state park or other site that offers group campsites. Many do have sites set up just for use by large groups.

Obviously, some large groups are environmentally con-scious. If you become involved with a group that is interested in camping or backpacking trips, make sure you find a group camp or divide yourselves into groups of ten or fewer before setting out.

Camp in Designated Sites or Off-Trail
If possible, camp in designated sites only. These places have been chosen because they are more resistant to constant use. If you should feel it is too dangerous (in grizzly country, for example) to camp in a designated area, or if one is not available, camp well off the trail or road you have been following. Trails and roads obviously already receive a lot of impact, and camping away from the trail will cut down on wear and tear.

When you leave a campsite, take a long, hard look at it. It should look better than when you found it. If you camp off the trail, it should look as if you had never been there. This can be done. I go so far as to rescatter leaves and fluff up grass (though given time it will spring back, itself) so that other travellers could not tell where the tent had been pitched. It only takes a few minutes and your efforts are more than compensated for with peace of mind.

Stay on the Designated Trail
Don't cut switchbacks, which are there for a reason. They slow down the erosion of the trail when it must climb steeply up a hill or mountain. Although it might be shorter and seem easier to scramble up the hillside ten yards or so to the next section of trail, if too many people do so, the rain will begin using the newly exposed earth as a watercourse—washing away both trail and mountain. Stay on designated trails. You may curse the person who blazed it and those who attempt to keep it passable for you, but remember that a lot of time and effort (and volunteer hours) go into keeping a trail hiker-ready.

Don't Use Soap In or Near Bodies of Water
There are a number of reasons to avoid using of soap in or near a body of water. Unless you are using a biodegradable soap, you could poison the water for any animal that drinks from it, including yourself. Even if you do have biodegradable soap, do you really want to drink water that has any type of soap in it? If you need to wash your body or hair or your dishes and there is no established means provided, such as a spigot or dishwashing station, use lake or stream water, but carry it well away from the water source.

One green method for washing your hair is to get it wet while at the water source, then with a pot-full or waterbag of water, walk about 150 feet away from the water source. You can then wash your hair and rinse it with the water in your pot or bag. If you have a waterbag with a shower attachment, you can hang the bag from an appropriate tree and rinse your hair out that way.

The same goes for washing clothes and dishes. Carry the water away from the source. You can wash both dishes and clothes out of your largest cooking pot. For more information on cleaning up after meals, see Chapter 2.

Solid Waste Management
In other words, how to dispose of your excrement. For most campers, this is not a problem and involves nothing more than a quick trip to the bathhouse with its modern flush toilets. In some cases, the toilets may be a bit on the primitive side, little more than a seat over a pit. And some RVs provide toilets than can later be emptied at the camp's dump station (if a dump isn't provided at the site). But what about those folks who like to head off into the woods and set up camp in the most primitive of styles? Kathleen Meyer has written a book, which she calls "an environmentally sound approach to a lost art." To learn about the fine details of relieving yourself in the woods, Meyer provides plenty of advice in *How to Shit in the Woods*, which is available from Ten Speed Press.

There's more to being green than just packing out trash. Disposing properly of your solid waste will keep the wilderness much more appealing. Always, always, always (I can't say it too many times) dig a hole. Even more importantly, make sure that you're at least 150 feet away from the nearest water source. If you are camping in a canyon through which water runs, climb up. If it is winter, and you cannot dig through the snow and ice (if you can, make sure you dig into the earth as well), pack your waste out. Yes, it sounds horrifying but if it's cold enough, it can be done. Just line the hole in the snow with a plastic bag, do your thing and then tie-twist or zip lock the bag shut, and carry it out. Otherwise,

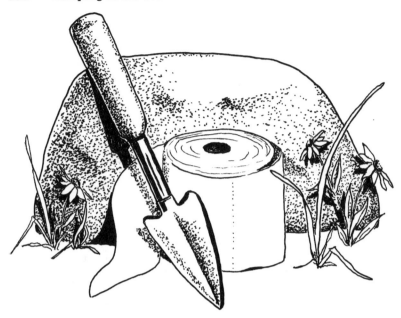

when the snow melts, your feces will end up on the ground surface and make an unwelcome sight (not to mention odor) for any springtime campers.

What Else Can You Do?

There are a number of little things you can do to decrease your environmental impact. Here are a few examples:

- Reuse your zipper-lock bags. Not only can they be reused during a camping trip, but once you're at home, you can wash and dry them to use on your next trip. However, don't reuse bags that carried raw meat or human and animal waste.
- Buy camping equipment in environmentally eye-pleasing colors such as forest green, grey, light blue, tan and brown.
- Purchase environmentally-sound toiletries by manufacturers such as Aubrey Organics, St. Ives and Tom's of

Maine. Catalogs from The Body Shop, The Compassion-
ate Consumer, Ecco Bella, Seventh Generation and others offer environmentally safe products. The Green Consumer supplies lists of both catalogs and manufacturers.
Wear a pair of soft-soled shoes around camp to lessen your
impact on the site.

This chapter is not a list of rules; it is a way of living that
is becoming increasingly important to adopt. If these techniques are not used by everyone (and currently they're not),
the outdoors will lose its natural beauty. Although nature is
resilient, its ability to fight back is limited. It takes a campsite
a long time to recover from a single overnight stay by an
inconsiderate group of campers.

A little bit of help goes a long way toward improving the
world we're escaping to. If everyone pitches in—even just a
bit—we'll be able to enjoy our outdoor experiences even more.

Buying Green
Like Kermit the Frog says, "it's not easy being green."
Camping is not really the greenest form of recreation. It often
means piling into your car for a long drive, and arriving in
camp to eat overly packaged and processed foods beforing
retiring for the night to the synthetic womb of a sleeping bag
and tent. Although we revel in the environment, do we trade
price, nutrition, safety and convenience for environmental
quality?

Some questions to ask about anything we buy include:
Are the products we buy and use dangerous to the health of
people and animals? Do they cause damage to the environment during manufacture, use or disposal? Do they consume
a disproportionate amount of energy and other resources
during manufacture, use or disposal? Do they cause unnecessary waste due to either excessive packaging or a short useful

life? Do they involve the unnecessary use of or cruelty to animals? And, finally, do they use materials derived from threatened species or environments?

John Elkington, Julia Hailes and Joel Makower use these questions to determine whether or not a product is "green." In their book, *The Green Consumer*, they agree that it is difficult to find a perfectly green product. But when purchasing camping equipment, you may want to take some of these factors into account. Fortunately, camping gear already has one major factor in its favor—minimal packaging! Most camping gear comes as is: sleeping bags and tents are packed in stuff sacks and stoves in environmentally sound cardboard cartons.

In the book, *Shopping for a Better World*, by the Council on Economic Priorities, manufacturers are rated on how green they are. Criteria used to determine the rating include: how environmentally clean the company is, if animals are tested, and if the company is associated with nuclear weapons. The book focuses on manufacturers of food, personal care products and other items typically found in a grocery store. To find out about the manufacturers of boots, tents, stoves and other camping equipment, contact the company and question them about your concerns.

There are a number of companies involved in environmental protection these days and many outdoor businesses are members of the Outdoor Industry Conservation Alliance, which helps out the environment by providing grants to grassroots conservation organizations. Other businesses are helping to purchase land for the Nature Conservancy and similar groups. Chevrolet, Coleman (one of the largest manufacturers of camping equipment), ACG (Nike), AT&T, Canon, Duofold, Kodak, Merrell, Mountainsmith, Nalgene, Nature Valley Granola Bars, Nike Hiking, REI, Spenco, Trek, Wild Country USA and Yakima are all sponsors of the new American Discovery Trail, which travels from the East Coast to the West Coast.

Recycled Gear

One of the biggest changes taking place in the 90s is that manufacturers of camping equipment are making gear using recycled products. One example is Patagonia's line of Synchilla fleece jackets made from recycled plastic soft drink bottles. They contain eighty percent recycled polyester (including post consumer plastic) and twenty percent virgin fibers.

Other companies using recycled materials include Nike, which uses reground rubber in the soles of its boots, and Reebok, which includes pigment-free leather and recycled plastic soft drink bottles in their lightweight Telos hiking boot's uppers. The Telos also have outsoles made of seventy-five percent recycled car tires. REI and other clothes manufacturers are producing their own recycled clothing and camping gear.

Other manufacturers are joining the green bandwagon with decreased packaging and increased use of recycled materials in both their packaging and in the products themselves. Most of the earth-friendly products are competitively priced with gear made from virgin materials. As consumers buy more green gear, manufacturers will continue to offer more environmentally sound options for campers to choose from.

· 12 ·
First Aid

"Did you get lost?" he asked mildly.
"Yes, yes we did! We never got to Terror Lake at all."
"Good!" exclaimed my enigmatic boss. "Now you're no
longer a novice. You're on your way to becoming a real
woodswoman. From now on you'll respect the woods, you'll
take fewer chances, and calculate your risks. And you know
what? You'll enjoy camping more than ever."

—*Anne LaBastille*
Woodswoman

The report tacked to the bulletin board caught my eye. It was the National Park Service's daily incident report, and once I started to read, I couldn't stop. I had been waiting for a meeting to begin in the Park Service's Mather Training Center in Harpers Ferry, West Virginia, but the report carried me away as I read. The clipped, bureaucratic language took me to an accident in the fog on the Blue Ridge Parkway where a car and a deer had collided, to a fatal heart

attack in Arches National Park, to a rescue attempt under-
way in Glacier National Park, on through several pages more
of incidents, big and small. Millions of people visit our
National Parks each year and problems are inevitable. It
does not seem to matter how careful you are. Accidents
happen.

Murphy's Law stands correct whether you are in a primitive camping area of a state park or at a luxurious park for
motor homes: If something can go wrong, it will. You could
trip and wrench your ankle as you walk to the bathhouse,
burn yourself lighting a stove or lantern, cut yourself whittling some wood or discover that your child has collected a
beautiful bouquet of poison sumac and a horrible rash to go
with it.

A general knowledge of first aid will help you in any
situation. Whether you are at home or in the woods. Knowing
what to do when that flaming marshmallow falls off the stick
and burns your companion will relieve some of the stress of
the situation.

The most important way to prepare for emergencies that
may come up on a camping trip is to get trained in first aid.
The overview of first aid procedures in this book cannot

replace an approved and appropriate course by the Red Cross or other qualified organization. Preparation also means planning. *Emergency Medical Procedures for the Outdoors* by Patient Medical Associates outlines what to do before you go:

- If you are camping with one or more people, it is to your benefit to discuss beforehand any existing medical problems and knowledge of first aid.
- If any of your party suffer from chronic illnesses, such as diabetes and epilepsy, or from serious allergies, make a list of names and illnesses. Also note types of medication, dosages, when the medication is given, and where it is kept.
- If there is no one in your camping group that knows CPR, the Heimlich Maneuver, artificial respiration, or basic first aid, it would be wise to have one of the group take a course that covers these important techniques. If one of your party is trained, he should review the procedures before heading out.
- If you don't have a first aid kit, prepare one. A kit containing the basics is described in Chapter 3. Put the list of names, illnesses, and medications in your kit.
- If children are camping with you, explain to them how to get help in an emergency.
- Before you leave, inform a close friend or relative of your whereabouts and when you intend to arrive at the camping area and depart for the return trip home.

This all sounds a little scary, but chances are you will face nothing more than a scraped knee or a stubbed toe. Just remember that even the best prepared person cannot anticipate every overturned cooking pot, hidden patch of poison ivy or lightning strike. But, being prepared for emergencies can lessen their impact. I will never forget the time my foot was slashed by a sharp object beneath the shallow but cloudy

waters of the Gulf of Mexico. We were wading in the tepid
water when the accident occurred, and I insisted at the time
that I must have stepped on a dead gar because of the pattern
of the incisions. We never discovered what was responsible
for the wound, but my father was prepared for emergencies,
and the bleeding was soon stanched and my aching foot
wrapped in bandages.

Preparing yourself for camping emergencies is simple—
know the environment around the campsite and know what
to do when you or someone else is injured. Many state parks
are built on lakes, ponds, rivers and other bodies of water, so
drowning is a possibility. Parks with bears have occasional
problems with people being nipped as they try to feed these
wild animals; parks with waterfalls and cliffs have to deal
with serious falls from time to time. And, in areas such as the
White Mountains in New Hampshire, rangers must deal with
campers and day hikers unprepared for rapid changes in
weather. Knowing what the recurring problems are will help
you avoid getting in to trouble in the first place. Rangers in
parks and forests go to great lengths to educate visitors about
potential problems, making bulletin boards in campgrounds
and at trailheads required reading.

It is next to impossible to pack everything you might need
should an accident occur. In their book, *Medicine for the
Backcountry* (by ICS Books), Frank Hubbell and Buck Tilton
state that the first commandment of first aid kits is, "Thou
shalt find it impossible to put together the perfect first aid
kit."

"Go ahead and try," they write, "but eventually, if you
spend enough time in the backcountry, you will one day wish
for something that is not there."

This holds true not only for camping but also for your
medicine cabinet at home. How many times have you peered
into your medicine cabinet only to find the antihistamine

expired a year ago or the calamine lotion turned to dry clay rattling in its bottle? Because it is impossible to carry everything you might need for a camping emergency, you have to rely heavily on knowledge. Or in other words, learn what to do in an emergency. If you are worried that you might forget what to do, carry along a first aid instruction manual on your camping trip. But, taking a first aid course (wilderness first aid—a course and book offered by Outward Bound—is best) is highly recommended to those who spend a lot of time in the outdoors. Learning how to perform CPR should be a requirement for every capable person on this planet. My husband has already put his knowledge of CPR to good use, saving the life of a young woman with heart problems who nearly died from cardiac arrest.

Other than carrying along a first aid kit and a knowledge of outdoor medicine, it is important to know your limits. Decide first which style of camping is for you. Camping ranges from the most basic, backpacking, to the most luxurious, RVing in a motor home. You can also "camp" from a houseboat, a canoe, a bicycle, a horse, a motorcycle. . . . Am I forgetting anything? Each form of camping has differing risks and benefits.

While camping, I have been burned, stung by insects, become swollen and rashy from poison ivy, and suffered from a wealth of bruises, scrapes and scratches. All of these injuries were easily treated with a basic first aid kit. However, I am not an expert, and I am not going to try to be. What follows is a list of the major categories of some of the medical emergencies that can occur on a camping trip. Each category gives you some idea of how to treat the emergency. For the most part, I have listed them in alphabetical order in order not to imply that one medical emergency is more significant than another. While that is generally not true—one medical problem in the outdoors is just as great as another—two medical emergencies are so important that they need to be mentioned first. If a person is not breathing they will die. If a person is bleeding profusely they may well die. If a person is breathing and they are not bleeding to death, however, you usually have time to react. A by-product of many medical emergencies is shock, which is a life-threatening situation only if not treated. But, because it is a threat to life, it is covered after breathing and bleeding. And so follows the list:

Stopped Breathing
As I said above, if a person is not breathing they will die. Breathing can be stopped by a lightning strike, choking, drowning or a heart attack. If you do not know how to establish an airway and perform artificial respiration, you should take a CPR course before you head out into the woods. Even at a campground, who knows how quickly you can find a ranger or other responsible person. Artificial respiration is part of cardio-pulmonary resuscitation and will be taught in a CPR course. There are many instances, particularly in drownings, lightning strikes and heart attacks, where CPR has saved lives. The popularity of shows such as Emergency 911 attest to peoples' fascination with accidents, and if you watch one of these shows you're bound to see CPR used several times in every episode.

Bleeding
Unless you have a severe aversion to blood (that is, you get sick or faint at the sight of it), you should be able to handle minor injuries while camping. (See the section on wounds in this chapter.) But what if you or a camping partner slice an arm or a leg while whittling? Knife wounds often demand an emergency trip to the hospital where a professional can stitch their knife wound back together.

How do you stop the bleeding until you or the victim can

reach help? Direct pressure on the wound, accompanied by elevating the wound higher than the patient's heart, will stop even moderately severe bleeding and should be all that is required for almost all wounds you will encounter. If bleeding persists, applying pressure to the major arteries supplying the area can help. Risk of contracting HIV and other blood-borne diseases has made surgical gloves required wear for all emergency medical personnel. A first aid course will help you learn how to help others without putting yourself at risk.

If the cut is serious, get the injured person to a doctor/ emergency room as quickly as possible. In established camp-grounds, a campground host or ranger will no how to get to the closest hospital.

Shock

To some degree, shock occurs after every injury. It can range from something so minor it is not even noticeable to some-thing so extreme that it results in death even when the injuries received wouldn't normally have resulted in the loss of life.

The signs and symptoms of shock range from the physical to emotional and include a dazed look, pale or ashen skin, nausea and vomiting, thirst, weak and rapid pulse, cold and clammy skin, shallow and irregular or labored breathing, dilated pupils, dull or lackluster eyes, and cyanois (the skin appears blue). Among the emotional signs are feelings of weakness or helplessness, anxiety, disorientation or confu-sion, and finally unconsciousness.

The two most important things to do when a person is in shock have to do with the two previous sections—maintain an airway so that the victim may breathe and control any bleeding. Once you are sure the victim will not bleed to death or suffocate, you can treat the shock by lying the victim down and elevating the lower extremities (if the elevation doesn't aggravate any injuries, including abdominal and head injuries).

If the person is suffering from a head injury, sunstroke, a heart attack, stroke, or shortness of breath due to a throat or chest injury, you may need to raise his head. If a spinal injury is possible, keep the victim flat.

Once positioned, make sure the victim has plenty of fresh air and loosen any tight clothing that might inhibit breathing and circulation. Keep movement of the victim to a minimum and handle him as gently as possible.

Also important is keeping the victim warm and dry. Reduce the loss of body heat by keeping the victim covered both on top and underneath, but don't overdo it. Making the victim sweat is not desirable. The idea is to keep the body as close to normal body temperature as possible.

Finally, don't give the victim anything by mouth. Remember, also, that his emotional well-being is just as important as his physical. Keep the victim calm, continually reassure him and try to keep talk of his injuries to a minimum. Don't let people crowd around as their discussion and interest will only upset the victim more.

Anaphylactic Shock

Bees, wasps, yellow jackets, hornets, ants and black flies can cause in some people an extreme allergic reaction referred to as anaphylactic shock. If you know that you are susceptible to anaphylaxis, then it would be wise to carry an Anakit whenever you go camping. The kit contains a couple of injections of epinephrine and several antihistamine tablets. Your doctor should be able to prescribe one for you. If you must use the injection, always get to a hospital as soon as possible in case the anaphylactic state returns.

Anaphylactic shock occurs when the body produces too much histamine in reaction to a bite or sting. The reaction turns skin red and itchy hives appear; and airways begin to close down and will eventually shut completely, causing asphyxiation.

If you are presented with a first-time case of anaphylaxis, give the victim antihistamine tablets if he can swallow. You should be carrying Benadryl or some similar antihistamine in your first aid kit. Seek help immediately.

For those not allergic to bites and stings, Sting-eze is supposed to be a superior product when it comes to relieving the pain and itching caused by most insects. It is said to combat infection from poison oak, cuts, burns and abrasions as well.

Blisters

Blisters are not usually a problem unless you do a lot of day hiking from base camps. If you like to amble along a nature trail or intend to embark on a serious hike of more than a mile or so, you need to be aware of the possibility of blisters.

Blisters heal slowly if you continue to hike, and they will be aggravated by the extra friction caused by walking. The best way to avoid blisters is to treat them before they occur. When a part of your foot feels hot or tender, stop hiking immediately. Take your shoes and socks off (hopefully you are wearing a decent pair of boots if you intend to hike several miles) and inspect the tender area. If you are carrying moleskin (a good idea on long day hikes), cut out a piece that is larger than the "hot spot." Apply it to the hot spot and put your socks and shoes back on. If you can do this right away, you may prevent blisters from developing.

When hiking on a nature trail or if you are hiking without moleskin, your best bet would be to return to the campground by the shortest route possible. But, stay on the trail! Don't add to your misery by taking a shortcut through the woods. Getting lost is not the only possibility. You can hurt yourself

further by slipping or tripping on leaf-covered roots, rocks or
fallen limbs.

If you do get a blister, try to leave the blister unbroken. If
it is still small and relatively flat, cover the blister with
moleskin and resume hiking. But if the blister gets worse, you
should return to your campsite, wash the area with soap and
water, and make a small hole in the bottom of the blister with
a sterilized needle so that the fluid drains. To sterilize the
needle, hold it over a flame until the tip turns red, then wait
for it to cool before you apply it to the blister. Once the blister
is drained, apply a sterile bandage to prevent further irritation and infection.

If the blister is already broken, treat it like an open wound
(cleanse and bandage) and watch for signs of infection. If
necessary, limit your walking for a few days so the blisters
may heal.

Bruises

When camping, bruises occur much as they would around
your home. For example, you might bump into the picnic
table on your way to the bath house or trip or fall while on a
day hike. If the bruise is severe, it is not helped by elevation
and cold compresses, and also increases in both pain and size,
it could indicate internal injuries or a fracture. Help should be
sought quickly.

Burns

Most burns are easy to prevent because you need use only a
modicum of caution. Sitting too close to a campfire, carelessly
lighting your campstove, ignoring the sun and refusing to
wear sunscreen, and improperly stabilizing your cookpot (on
the stove or over a fire) are all sure ways to get burned. With
a little extra care and caution you should be able to avoid
burning yourself. But, accidents do happen.

First-degree burns, including sunburn, appear bright

red. Treat these minor burns by pouring cold water over the burned area and applying cold compresses for five to ten minutes. The skin should be allowed to air dry if possible. Sunburn can be prevented by the use of a sunscreen with a sun protection factor of fifteen or more. Continued exposure to sun can cause severe burning and, eventually, skin cancer. Antiseptic burn sprays may be used with first-degree burns but should not be used with second- or third-degree burns.

Second-degree burns are characterized by bright red skin, blisters and swelling. Do not break the blisters. Rather, immerse the burn in cold water or pour cold water over the burned area. Quick action will help reduce the burning effect of heat in the deeper layers of skin. Cover the burn with a sterile bandage.

Third-degree burns are highly unlikely on a camping trip, but clothes, and even tents and RVs, can catch fire. These burns are distinguished by charred flesh and must be treated in a hospital. If third-degree burns occur, do not remove clothing that may adhere to the burns. If you cannot get to a hospital within an hour, give the victim a weak solution of salt water to sip on. The solution will help replace essential fluids that have been lost because of the burns. Unlike the treatment of first- and second-degree burns, do not immerse the burn in cold water. Cover the burned area with a clean cloth and get the victim to a doctor immediately.

Stop, Drop and Roll

A church youth group was camping in the mountains of Georgia when they were awakened by the screams of a fellow camper. It was a cold November morning, and Ed Stewart decided he'd rather remain in the warmth of his sleeping bag and tent rather than venture out into the frosty morning air.

Dreaming of a cup of hot chocolate, Ed pulled his camp stove just inside the tent and lit the small burner. As he reached behind him for the stuff sack that held his drink mix, he inadvertently brushed against the stove, which tipped, igniting Ed's sleeping bag and clothing. Screaming for help, Ed leapt out of the tent and quickly dropped to the ground, smothering the flame against the earth. His fellow campers reacted quickly, dousing Ed with cold water from their Nalgene bottles. While his injuries were being assessed, several campers scurried down to the spring where they refilled their bottles with cold water. Ed's friends and leaders continued to douse him with water for the next ten minutes until they were sure that his skin and the tissue beneath it were no longer hot.

Due to his quick reaction and the nearly instantaneous response of his fellow campers, Ed escaped with only second-degree burns. If you ever find yourself on fire, it is important to remember—Stop, Drop and Roll.

The natural tendency is to run, but running only fuels the flames. By dropping immediately, flames to the ground, you can smother the fire. By rolling back and forth or in complete circles (depending on the extent of the flames), you will completely smother the flames by denying them oxygen.

Fortunately, this type of situation is rare. But keep in mind that many of today's synthetic fibers are prone to melting rather than igniting. This can make burns more dangerous because the material melts into your skin instead of ashing and flaking away.

Cold Weather Medical Emergencies

You are unlikely to face hypothermia or frostbite when car camping, but there is always the possibility that the weather could become nasty while on a day hike or while you are out fishing or boating. Any number of activities can lead to hypothermia when the weather is cold, humid and windy, especially if your clothes are wet. Fatigue, smoking, drinking alcoholic beverages and emotional stress further reduce your body's ability to fight off the cold and wet. You can prevent hurting yourself in cold weather by keeping these things in mind. If it is really cold, wet, and windy, your best bet would be to remain in your tent or camper. Crawl into a sleeping bag if your tent is too cold. A little warmth and rest may be all you need to combat the cold.

Hypothermia

The scariest aspect of hypothermia is that it is most likely to occur when the weather is only moderately cold (40 degrees), but wet and windy. Your body has the ability to keep you relatively warm as long as you are moving. But, as soon as you stop, it is harder for the body to fight off the cold, wet and wind.

The first signs of hypothermia—shivering, numbness, drowsiness, and marked muscular weakness—are followed by mental confusion and impairment of judgment, slurred speech, failing eyesight, and eventually, unconsciousness. Death, if it occurs, is usually due to heart failure. Be aware that the most serious warning sign that a hypothermia victim is going down fast is when the shivering stops. It means the victim is close to death.

As I said above, you are most likely to become hypothermic once you have stopped moving, especially if you are tired. Because it is the movement that keeps you warm, your body's core temperature can drop once you stop.

Fortunately, hypothermia is easy to combat if caught early. If you arrive at your campsite on a cold, wet day and are experiencing any of the symptoms mentioned above, drop everything and make yourself warm. Strip yourself of your wet clothes and put on dry clothes if possible. Crawl into your sleeping bag, and if you're able, heat up something hot to drink—tea, soup, hot chocolate. Anything hot will help raise your internal temperature. Drinks with a high sugar content are best. You may want to carry along a pack of fruit gelatin whenever you go camping—stick it in your first aid kit. It tastes great when heated and contains a lot of sugar. But get your body warm first! Don't take the time to heat yourself something to drink until you've rid yourself of the wet clothes.

If you're with someone else or happen upon someone showing signs of hypothermia, try sharing body heat. If you are not too shy or modest, strip down to your underwear or to nothing at all and crawl into a sleeping bag with the victim. Direct skin contact does wonders for transferring heat. Once the victim is in dry clothes, wrapped in a warm sleeping bag, and sipping something hot to drink, you can try building a fire for added warmth. If you are car camping and the vehicle is nearby, get inside and use the heater. The same goes for recreational vehicles. If you are really unsure of your ability to warm the victim, head for a hospital or home.

Remember to take hypothermia seriously and you can easily prevent you or someone else from dying.

Frostbite

It was winter in the Adirondacks, and a group of four men had met for their annual winter camping trip. From their base camp, the group traditionally trekked by snowshoe to a viewpoint where they could watch the sun set. They did not worry about the hike back to base camp even though it would be in the dark, because on this particular trip, they had a full moon. The moonlight, combined with the reflection of light off the snow, would illuminate their path. They wouldn't even have to use flashlights. Not only that, they could easily follow the tracks their snowshoes had formed earlier when they made their return trip back down the mountain.

They started out in the late afternoon and arrived at the viewpoint to watch the early winter sunset. It was on the trip back that they ran into trouble—the wind had picked up while they were admiring the setting sun, and their tracks had been covered by drifts of snow.

Because they were not prepared to spend the night outdoors, the men decided it was best to keep moving. They quickly lost their way and wandered through the woods for hours, battered by the frigid wind. Although one member of the party begged them to stop (all he wanted to do was sleep), the other three forced him to keep moving. It was 3:00 A.M. when the group finally stumbled into their base camp, exhausted and nearly frozen.

Upon checking themselves out, it was discovered that three of the four men had suffered frostbite on their toes, fingers and ears. Fortunately, they knew how to treat frostbite. Because there was a chance that the parts might refreeze before they reached a doctor, the men packed up quickly and headed toward their cars, and sought immediate medical attention. All three managed to escape without losing any of their skin.

Frostbite occurs when crystals begin to form either superficially or in the fluids and soft tissues of the skin. Keep in mind that the effects of frostbite will be more severe if the affected area is thawed and refrozen. Fortunately, the areas affected by frostbite are often small. The nose, cheeks, ears, fingers and toes are the most common areas.

Before frostbite occurs, the affected area will look flushed and then become white or grayish yellow. Pain is often felt early but usually subsides—if you feel any pain at all.

If you suspect frostbite, the first thing to do is to cover the frozen part, and provide the victim with extra clothing and blankets or double wrap the victim in sleeping bags. If possible, bring the victim indoors (a tent will do if nothing else is available) and provide him with a warm drink.

Rewarm the frozen part quickly by immersing it in lukewarm water. Continue to keep the water warm. If water is not practical or available, wrap the affected part gently in warm blankets, clothes, etc.

Handle the frostbitten area gently. Do not massage it. Once thawed, the area will swell severely and become flushed once more. At this point, discontinue warming it and have the victim exercise the part if possible.

Cleanse the frostbite with water and soap and rinse it thoroughly before blotting it dry with clean towels or whatever you have handy that is clean and dry. If blisters have formed, do not break them.

If fingers or toes are involved, place gauze between them to keep them separated. Do not apply any other dressings unless you intend to transport the victim to medical aid. Also, elevate the frostbitten parts and protect them from contact with bedclothes. If toes are involved, the victim should not walk and additional heat should not be applied once the part is thawed. If the victim must walk before the part has recovered, do not thaw the frostbitten parts. Also, if you intend to seek medical assistance, do not thaw any parts that may refreeze on the trip.

If you decide to transport the victim and have thawed the frostbitten parts, cover the affected areas with a clean cloth, apply temporary dressings, keep affected parts elevated, and continue to give the victim fluids, if possible.

A note on windchill: When the wind starts to blow, even temperatures in the fifties can be dangerous. The lower the temperature and the greater the wind, the more hazardous the conditions. Believe it or not, the relatively mild winter temperature of forty degrees can feel like twenty degrees when the wind is gusting at twenty miles per hour. The following chart will give you some idea of the temperature your body feels when the winds are blowing:

Wind	Actual temperature in degrees Fahrenheit						
(MPH)	40	30	20	10	0	-10	-20
	Wind chill equivalent temperatures						
Calm	40	30	20	10	0	-10	-20
5	35	25	15	5	-5	-15	-25
10	30	15	5	-10	-20	-35	-45
15	25	10	-5	-20	-30	-45	-60
20	20	5	-10	-25	-35	-50	-65
25	15	0	-15	-30	-45	-60	-75
30	10	0	-20	-30	-50	-65	-80
35	10	-5	-20	-35	-50	-65	-80
40	10	-5	-20	-35	-55	-70	-85

· Wind Chill Chart ·

Diseases

Insects and mammals carry diseases which can be contracted by outdoor enthusiasts. Campers should take appropriate precautions to avoid problems with the following diseases.

Hantavirus

Well-publicized cases of Hantvirus Pulmonary Syndrome in the Four Corners Area in the Southwest and a single case on the Appalachian Trail in the East have raised concerns about this rare disease. Campers can contract Hantavirus by sleeping in a confined area with the droppings of a mouse infected with the disease. The disease is very rare in mice, making it difficult to contract. But it is better to be safe than sorry. Clean out mouse droppings and sleep in ventilated areas.

Lyme Disease

More than 100,000 cases of Lyme disease have been reported in forty-five states since it was first identified in 1982. Among the symptoms of Lyme disease are fever, headache, and pain and stiffness in joints and muscles. If left untreated, Lyme disease can produce lifelong impairment of muscular and nervous systems, chronic arthritis, brain injury, and in ten percent, crippling arthritis.

Lyme disease proceeds in three stages (although all three do not necessarily occur):

The first stage may consist of flu-like symptoms (fatigue, headache, muscle and joint pain, swollen glands) and a skin rash with a bright red border. Antibiotic treatment wipes out infection at this stage.

The second stage may include paralysis of the facial muscles, heart palpitation, light-headedness and shortness of breath, severe headaches, encephalitis and meningitis. Other symptoms include irritability, stiff neck, and difficulty concentrating. Pain may move around from joint to joint.

The third stage may take several years to occur and consists of chronic arthritis with numbness, tingling and burning pain, and may include inflammation of the brain itself. The disease can also lead to serious heart complications and may attack the liver, eyes, kidney, spleen and lungs. Memory loss and lack of concentration are also present.

Although antibiotics are used for treatment in each stage, early detection and diagnosis are critical. If you suspect you have Lyme disease, see a doctor immediately.

Rabies

This disease has terrified me ever since Atticus shot the rabid hound in *To Kill a Mockingbird*. Then, of course, there was Cujo. My husband and I have had some frightening run-ins with dogs in Nepal and along the Appalachian Trail. Now, if an animal even looks at me cross-eyed, I avoid it. And, for those of us who enjoy camping, it is wise to keep in mind that ninety-six percent of the carriers of rabies in the U.S. are wild animals. Skunks are the chief carrier followed by raccoons and bats. Cattle, cats, dogs, wolves, bobcats, coyotes, groundhogs, muskrats, weasels, woodchucks, foxes, horses and humans also host the disease.

Transferred through saliva, death from rabies is very rare in the U.S. because treatment is available. Symptoms appear anywhere from three weeks to a year after being bit and include headache and fever, cough and sore throat, loss of appetite and fatigue, abdominal pain, nausea, vomiting and diarrhea.

If you have been bit by a mammal and are experiencing any of these symptoms, get to a doctor immediately. The rabies vaccine (a series of five shots in the arm—no longer the painful abdominal shots) may be recommended and has so far always been successful.

When bitten by any mammal, it is best to thoroughly cleanse the wound and see a doctor. You may need nothing more than a tetanus or antibiotic shot. Please don't take the risk and forego seeing a doctor. Rabies is an incredibly painful and unpleasant disease, and past a certain stage—fatal.

Rocky Mountain Spotted Fever
This tick-borne disease is misnamed today, as it is as common on the eastern seaboard (North Carolina routinely has the highest number of cases reported) as it is in the Rocky Mountains. The disease is caused by Rickettsia, a microorganism similar to bacteria, that is transmitted by tick bite. Ticks transmit the disease after being attached for four to six hours, making checking yourself for ticks frequently the best line of defense against spotted fever.

Rocky Mountain Spotted Fever is easily treated with Tetracycline or other antibiotics if diagnosed early, but, as it resembles other infections, it is hard to distinguish by symptoms. Headache and fevers are the most common symptoms.

Other symptoms include a rash on wrists, hands, ankles or feet; loss of appetite; and abdominal or chest pain. The rash can be a late sign and may not appear until the disease has progressed far enough to make it dificult to treat. Bleeding problems, including coagulation abnormalities, will result if you let the disease go untreated. About five percent of victims die from the disease.

Drowning

Bodies of water are the biggest draw when it comes to attracting visitors to parks, campgrounds, forests and other outdoor areas. Whether it be a beach, lake, pond, or even a waterfall, people love to watch water, swim in water, wade in water, and boat on water, fish in water, and camp next to water.

The troubling thing is that between six and eight thousand people die each year by drowning. Why? Carelessness mostly. Knowing how to swim is essential, particularly if your camping revolves around spending lots of time on or in the water. Lifeguards are on duty at some swimming areas, but very few, considering the amount of water on planet Earth.

I will never forget the time my brother, who was no more than six at the time, stepped off our houseboat. My parents were in the cabin with my sister, and I was the only one to see him drop overboard. He didn't thrash about or cry for help but rather waited patiently, calmly, to be rescued or to drown. Fortunately, my father had recently had a discussion with us on what to do should something just like this happen. Remain calm, he said. If you get hysterical, it will take us longer to understand you and longer to react.

So, I very calmly went to the door of the cabin and said, "Breck just fell off the boat." Within seconds my father was in the water, and shortly thereafter, Breck was safely aboard and seemingly none the worse for the experience. On a humorous note, he had been reprimanded earlier for swallowing his gum, and he was very proud to show us that even though he had almost drowned, he had not swallowed it this time!

Like our family, stay calm and be prepared. Missteps and carelessness cause many water accidents, and when they occur, you will want to respond quickly and effectively. Once again, I must stress the importance of CPR. Before taking a camping trip that will bring you near water, make sure that either you or someone you are camping with has recently taken a CPR course. Because, once the drowning victim has been removed from the water (and sometimes even before), you may have to perform artificial respiration. If there is no pulse, you will have to use CPR. When dealing with a drowning, always send for help, even if the victim appears to have recovered completely. Without proper care, lung infections and other problems can set in that might lead to death.

Hot Weather Medical Emergencies
Stupidity resulted in a mild case of heat exhaustion for me a number of years ago. My husband and I drove to Cloudland Canyon in Northwest Georgia for a day hike. At that time in our lives, we regularly skipped breakfast, so we arrived at the state park hungry. Although my husband has the regular habit of drinking a couple of glasses of water when he awakes, I neglected to drink anything that morning—not even my usual cup of coffee. By the time we arrived, I was ready for both lunch and something to drink.

We decided to take our picnic lunch down to the base of the falls, where the temperature was much cooler. Unfortunately, the only liquid in our cooler was beer. As thirsty as I was, I drank it, never considering the possibilities of alcohol on an empty stomach and in a dehydrated body.

It was during the return hike to the brim of the canyon

that I began to experience cramps in my legs and abdomen. At the time, my only thought was, "How am I going to hike the Appalachian Trail if I can't even make this short hike?" We were nearly to the top when I suddenly felt weak, dizzy and nauseous. I was lucky enough to find a bench to sit on and rested until I felt I could finish the last leg of the trail.

As soon as we reached the top, we headed for the car and quickly drove to a store where Frank bought me Gatorade. I sipped at it slowly, and soon the symptoms began to pass. But that one experience was enough to convince me to change my habits and make sure I always drink enough liquids.

If you drink enough water, you probably won't experience heat related problems while camping unless you're involved in vigorous activities such as hiking or volleyball. You can also suffer from heat-related problems if you spend too much time out in the sun (suntanning on the beach, for example).

Heat Cramps

Muscle cramps are an early sign of heat exhaustion, especially if the victim is dehydrated. Cramps occur first in the muscles of the legs and abdomen. If you're are experiencing heat cramps, sip salt water (one teaspoon of table salt per quart), drinking sixteen ounces over the period of an hour. Massaging will help relieve the cramped muscles, according to the American National Red Cross book on first aid. The book *Stretching and Massage for Hikers and Backpackers*, a Nuts 'n Bolts Guide from Menasha Ridge Press, will teach you how to massage a partner as well as yourself.

Heat Exhaustion

If the heat cramps are not treated and lead to heat exhaustion, you will find that the body temperature is nearly normal. The victim's skin, however, will feel pale and clammy. It is possible that the victim will faint, but lowering his head will help him regain consciousness. Weakness, nausea, heavy sweating, severe headache and dizziness are symptoms of heat exhaustion.

As with heat cramps, the victim needs to drink a diluted solution of salt water. Lay the victim down, loosen his clothing, and raise his feet eight to twelve inches. Applying cool wet cloths will also help relieve heat exhaustion. If you were struck with heat cramps while on a day hike, it would be wise to take the remainder of the day off, particularly if you plan to do more day hiking during your camping trip, or even cancel the remainder of your trip.

Heat Stroke

Treatment of heat stroke should be immediate. You will know when a hiker has heat stroke because his skin will be hot, red, and dry. His pulse will be rapid and strong, and he will probably lapse into unconsciousness.

Undress the hiker and bathe his skin with cool water or place him carefully in a stream or other cold body of water if possible. Once his temperature is lowered, dry him off. If cold water is not available, fan him with whatever you have on hand. If his temperature rises again, resume the cooling process. Never give someone with heat stroke stimulants such as tea, coffee or some colas.

In the case of heat stroke, the victim should receive medical attention as soon as possible. Heat stroke is a life threatening situation.

Lightning

Massive flooding in the early 90s dropped lightning to the number two position when it comes to the natural disaster that kills the most people. But it is highly likely that lightning will regain the top position.

Lightning kills between 100 to 300 people each year,

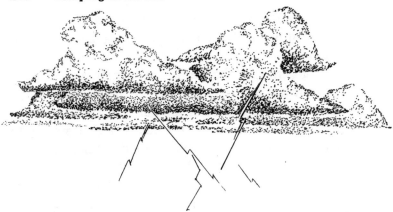

particularly between May and September. And, when you think about it, doesn't everyone know someone who was either killed by lightning or struck but survived? Both my great-grandmother and brother-in-law are lightning survivors. It is surprising that anyone survives considering that lightning strikes a hundred times a second worldwide with as much as 200 million volts, 300,000 amps, and 8,000 degrees Centigrade. Even worse, when you are outside during a lightning storm, it is only a matter of luck that you are not hit.

Lightning can strike three ways—within a cloud, cloud-to-cloud, and cloud-to-ground. It is the cloud-to-ground lightning that is most dangerous for humans and it can injure you in four different ways: by direct strike, when the bolt hits you dirfectly; by the splash or side flash, when the lightning hits something else but flashes through the air to hit you as well; by ground current (the most common injury for humans), when the lightning strikes a tree, for instance, and the current runs through the ground or water and into you; and by the blast effect, when you are thrown by the sudden expansion of air caused by a strike. Some people get lucky when the ground current charge passes over and around them without entering their body. This is called the flashover effect.

There are a number of types of injuries a lightning victim can receive—traumatic, respiratory, neurologic, and cardiac injuries, as well as burns and everything from loss of hearing to vomiting. Treatment is for the type of injury the victim has sustained. Knowing cardio-pulmonary resuscitation will be invaluable to you in the case of a lightning strike because most victims can be revived by this method. Never assume that a lightning victim is all right. Always go for help.

Lightning can strike from a mile away, so once you see your first flash, begin counting—one one-thousand, two one-thousand, etc. If you hear the thunder before you reach five one-thousand, you are within range (one mile) of the storm. That's when you need to find a safe spot. Storms move quickly, it's doubtful you can outrun it.

So what's safe? Not much, but if you are near a car, head for it. It is probably the safest place you can be outside of a building or motorhome and other enclosed vehicles. Do avoid bodies of water and low places that can collect water. Avoid high places, open places, tall objects, metal objects, wet caves and ditches. Your best bet is a small stand of trees. If you can sit on something that doesn't have metal in it—a sweater, plastic-zippered day pack, etc.—you put a little extra protection between yourself and the ground. Sit with your knees pulled up against your chest, head bowed, arms hugging knees. If you are in a group, spread out, but make sure you can all see at least one other person in case anyone gets hit.

Rashes

I react as violently to the presence of poison ivy as I do to the sight of most stinging insects. Both have caused me great pain, but only poison ivy has left me bedridden for a couple of days and my face fire-engine red for more than a week while I was on cortisone.

The best thing to do once you realize you've had one-on-

one contact with one of the poisonous plants—ivy, oak and sumac—is to take a cool or cold bath and completely cleanse yourself with soap. After that, use Calamine or other poison ivy-specific lotions. Cortisone creams help some, although if you have a really bad reaction, you may have to head to your doctor for a shot and a prescription. Antihistamines such as Benadryl also offer some relief. Prophylactics are available, although how well they prevent you from getting rashes from poison plants is debatable.

Your best defense against poison ivy, sumac and oak is to able to identify and steer clear of them. As the saying goes— "leaves of threes, let them be."

If you intend to do some day hiking while camping, you may run into another type of rash. Rashes caused by friction, heat and humidity are also common, especially in the crotch area. One way to deal with this problem is to apply petroleum jelly to the areas that rub against one another. If heat is the problem, try to keep the area as cool as possible. Shorts with built-in liners will keep you drier than shorts and underwear because liners are made to allow moisture to escape. Powder will also help keep the problem area dry. If the rash begins to look fungal, there are a number of over-the-counter products, such as Desenex, that will clear it up. If the heat rash gets to be a real problem, try sleeping nude at night to allow the area to dry as thoroughly as possible.

Snakebite—Nonpoisonous

By making a little extra noise in areas where snakes may be hidden from view, you should avoid any chance of snakebite. If a bite should occur, proper treatment is important.

Even the bite of a nonpoisonous snake can be dangerous. If not properly cleaned, the wound can become infected. Ideally, the victim should be treated with a tetanus shot to prevent serious infection. Although, if you intend to do some camping in wilderness areas, you might want to consider a booster shot before you go. Nonpoisonous snakebites will cause a moderate amount of swelling. If large amounts of swelling take place, the bite should be treated as if it were caused by a poisonous snake.

Snakebite—Poisonous

The body's reaction to the bite of a poisonous snake will be swift. Discoloration and swelling of the bite area are the most visible signs. Weakness and rapid pulse are other symptoms. Nausea, vomiting, fading vision, and shock also are possible signs of a poisonous bite and may develop in the first hour or so after being bitten.

It is important to know that tourniquets can cause more damage to the victim than a snakebite. If improperly applied, the tourniquet can cause the death of the infected limb and the need for amputation. The cutting and suction methods, the tools for which are a part of most snakebite kits, are also not recommended.

The best treatment is to reduce the amount of circulation in the area where the bite occurred and seek medical attention immediately. Circulation can be reduced by keeping the victim immobile (which won't be easy if you are any distance from a road or car); by applying a cold, wet cloth to the area; or by using a constricting band. A constricting band is not a tourniquet and should be tight enough only to stop surface flow of blood and decrease the flow of lymph from the wound. The constricting band should not stop blood flow to the limb (you'll know it is loose enough if you can slip two fingers between the limb and the band). Cold compresses and constricting bands are now said to localize tissue damage. If you are near medical help, you may just want to treat for shock and get the victim to a doctor as soon as possible. As with all medical emergencies, keep in mind that what you do is always a judgment call.

The Extractor, which I discussed briefly in Chapter 3, is

state-of-the-art, so to speak, in snakebite kits because it uses mechanical suction (rather than mouth suction), and it does not involve cutting the bite with a razor or knife. It is also said to remove approximately thirty percent of the venom if used within five minutes of being bitten.

Information on poisonous snakes is included in Chapter 13, including the fact that snake bites are rarely fatal to any but the very young and very old.

Wounds

It is not unusual to experience minor and sometimes major wounds—abrasions, incisions, lacerations and punctures—while camping. Avulsions, though rare, are also possible.

I've wounded myself any number of ways while camping. I've carved my finger with a knife while slicing salami, scraped arms and legs by falling, cut my feet while foolishly walking barefoot to a beach or bath house. Sometimes it doesn't matter how careful you are, you are just going to hurt yourself.

When someone is injured to such a degree that there is a flow of blood from the wound, you need to do three things: 1) stop the bleeding, 2) prevent infection, and 3) promote healing.

Here are two methods, described in order of preference, that should be used to stop bleeding:

1) With a dressing or a cloth, apply direct pressure over the wound. In most instances, this will stop the bleeding, and the thick pad of cloth will absorb blood and allow it to clot. Once the blood clots, leave the wound and dressing alone. If blood should soak the pad before clotting, do not remove the pad, but add another layer to the already soaked cloth and increase your pressure on the wound. If you need both your hands to help the victim, apply a pressure bandage with a strip of cloth. Place it over the pad on the wound,

wrap it around the body part, and then tie a knot directly over the pad.

2) Elevate the wounded part, unless there is evidence of a fracture, above the victim's heart. This will also help reduce blood flow. Wounds of the hand, neck, arm, or leg should be elevated and direct pressure should be continued.

These methods will stop most bleeding, but taking a course in first aid will teach you other options (too technical and risky for discussion here) to use if the bleeding doesn't stop with direct pressure and elevation.

Preventing infection goes hand-in-hand with proper cleansing of the wound. Your first step is to wash your hands to avoid contaminating the wound further. That is, don't breathe on it, cough or sneeze on it, drool on it, throw dirt on it, etc. Cleaning means cleansing around and sometimes in the wound, itself. You can make an antiseptic wash by using the povidone-iodine in your first aid kit. You may also use soap and water or just plain water if that is all you have.

Cleanse around the wound with a sterile gauze pad and in the wound only if there is foreign matter in it. Always rinse everything, even the antiseptic wash, from the wound before you dress it. You can irrigate the wound with water from a plastic bag that has a pin hole (to direct the stream of water).

If the foreign material remains in the wound after irrigation, you may try using sterilized tweezers (sterilize by holding them to a flame until red hot or by boiling them in hot water—make sure they cool down a bit before applying them to the wound). If you can remove all foreign objects and have stopped the bleeding, allow the wound to air dry a while before dressing it. If you can't remove the foreign objects or the wound is big, keep it moist until you can get to a doctor. If it is a gaping wound, apply a butterfly bandage after bringing the folds of skin together. Some first aid books do not advocate the use of butterfly bandages because it is felt that the bandages promote infection. Do as your conscience sees fit.

When dressing a wound, do not touch the sterile bandage except at the edges where it will not come in contact with the wound. If possible, the dressing should extend at least one inch past the edges of the wound.

The wound should be bandaged snugly but not too tight. Remember to check it often and never apply tape on the wound. Also, if you use tincture of benzoin on the healthy skin, the tape will stick better, but don't get the benzoin in the wound because it will hurt and encourage infection.

Abrasions
Most of the wounds you'll suffer when camping will be abrasions, which occur when the outerlayers of the skin are damaged, usually when the skin is scraped against a hard surface.

Although bleeding is usually limited, danger of contamination and infection still exists. Simply cleansing the wound, applying an antiseptic, and keeping it clean until healed will help you avoid serious problems.

Incisions
An incision occurs when body tissue is cut with a sharp object. When camping, most incisions are the product of poor knife handling. People (including myself) can never seem to remember that they are supposed to cut with the blade of the knife turned away from their body. It is not uncommon for a camper to be carried off to the nearest emergency facility because he sliced his hand while whittling.

An incised wound often bleeds heavily and rapidly, and if deep, can damage muscles, tendons, and nerves. Incisions need immediate attention, even if small, because they can easily become infected. Whether a deep or shallow cut, the bleeding should be stopped immediately and the wound cleaned. If the wound is large, you should also treat for shock.

Punctures

The most likely puncture wound you will receive when camping is a splinter. But if you walk around barefoot, you're asking for all manner of foot wounds. Keep shoes of some sort on at all times.

When several layers of skin are pierced by a sharp object, you have a puncture wound. Although bleeding is usually limited, internal damage can result if tissues and muscles are pierced. Infection is likelier because there is no flushing action from blood. Cleanse the wound; and if there is a foreign object (such as a splinter) that is easily removable, do so with a pair of sterilized tweezers or a needle. Objects imbedded deeply in the tissue should be removed only by a doctor.

Avulsion

If tissue is forcibly separated or torn from the victim's body, seek help as soon as possible. Bleeding will usually be quite heavy and should be stopped before transporting the victim, if possible. Send the avulsed body part along with the victim to the hospital. It can often be reattached.

To carry the separated part(s), collect them and label, if necessary. Place the part(s) in a plastic bag and set the bag in iced water but do not get the part(s) wet.

Getting Help

The above list highlights some of the more common emergencies you might face on a camping trip. There are a host of others—everything from abdominal pain to diabetic shock to spinal injuries. All of these take a knowledge of first aid that cannot be encompassed in this book. Taking a first aid course will introduce you to these problems and what to do about them.

While talking to a couple of rangers on a mountain trail in Washington, a friend of mine took a step backwards while saying farewell and stepped off a cliff. The rangers quickly sent for help, but it took a major evacuation effort before she could be reached and her injuries assessed. Even two rangers, knowledgeable in wilderness first aid, were forced to make a judgment call on how to handle this outdoor emergency.

I can't tell you how to evacuate a person who has just fallen off a cliff, but if I had to make that decision, there are a number of questions I would have to consider. How far is help? Is the person already dead? Is there someone around more qualified to deal with the situation? Can the victim be reached? Is the temperature detrimental (too hot or too cold) to the victim? Is the victim breathing? Bleeding? And so on.

In emergency situations that require evacuation, you will be faced with many choices. But unless you're trained in wilderness rescue, you would be best advised to go for help rather than try to evacuate the victim yourself. I cannot put it more simply than this: never evacuate the victim yourself. Let professionals handle it. If you try to evacuate the victim yourself, you may injure him further or perhaps, injure yourself as well. And unfortunately, that means you can be sued. The world is in a sad state when good samaritans are sued for trying to rescue someone, but it happens all the time.

If something has happened and someone(s) need to be evacuated, send for help as soon as possible. In the meantime, there are a number of things you can do to make the injured person(s) more comfortable. According to *Emergency Medical Procedures for the Outdoors*, you can:

- Set up a shelter and protect the victim from direct contact with the ground if possible.

- Cover the victim with a shirt, jacket, sweater, etc. to retain body heat.
- Leave or provide food and water.
- Make sure the victim is comfortable.

If it is an extreme emergency and time is of essence, you may want to use distress signals:

- Standard ground-to-air signals: one rectangular shape means "require doctor—serious injuries," two rectangular shapes, side by side, mean "require medical supplies." Build these symbols as large as possible by digging in sand, snow or earth. You can also use tree limbs, rocks, clothing or whatever else you might have on hand to represent the image. The most important thing is to make sure the image is clearly visible from above and that it contrasts with the ground color as much as possible.
- Universal distress signals: a series of three sights or sounds and can include shouts, whistle blasts, high-frequency beeps, gunshots and flashes of light.
- SOS or Morse Code distress signal: a series of three dots, three dashes, three dots (·······) means SOS or Help! They can be made by blows on a whistle, high-frequency beeps or flashes of light—three short blasts, beeps or flashes, then three long, and again three short.
- A large flag at the top of a tree, the brighter the better.
- A mirror or other shiny object can be flashed across the sky several times a day to attract planes.
- Flares.

If you must leave the victim, alone or with others, it is important to mark your trail, (unless it is already clearly blazed so that the victim can be found when help returns). You can do this with branches, cairns (rock mounds), arrows carved in dirt or snow, grass tied in bunches, sticks dug into the ground at the side of the trail, torn pieces of cloth tied to branches, or whatever you can think of to ensure help can find its way to the victim.

If you are in a public area—state park, recreation area, etc.—there will often be a ranger or some other person-in-charge around who can either provide you with help or make sure that help is sent to you.

It's a dangerous world out there and the Boy Scouts have the right idea when they chose as their creed the succinct, "Be prepared." Basically, if you plan on surviving on this planet that is predominantly water; in a world where every day you face the specter of death in automobiles and lunatics with guns; and within an environment where even fresh air and clear water carry potential hazards—you need to be prepared. It's easily done! Courses in CPR, first aid, and self-defense are offered in nearly every county, parish and township in the United States. So, before you head out into the woods, be prepared. Or camp with someone who is.

· 13 ·
Problem Animals

There were hordes and hordes of mosquitos, buzzing their high-pitched chainsaw whine, and equivilent armies of flies: the slow fat ones that merely annoy you by walking on your arms and legs, and the agile fast ones that bite, and bite hard.
—Karen Berger and Daniel Smith
Where the Waters Divide

It wasn't a question of whether the raccoon would get the food. It was question of how and when. The camp kitchen was set up in a screen tent with the bottom edge staked to the ground in eight places. The raccoon was fat from other campground feasts, and it was hard not to laugh watching him quickly waddling around the tent trying here and there to pull up the bottom. I happened upon the scene while heading back to my campsite from the beach. I didn't need to do anything as the campers whose kitchen was under attack were in camp. They sat by a fire ring and didn't move to chase the coon away. They were confident the staked-down screen would wear on the animal's persistence. But this was Hunting Island State Park in South Carolina, and the raccoon had the benefit of year-round practice at swiping food from confident campers.

It was less than a minute before the raccoon pulled up on the screen hard enough to coax a stake out of the sandy soil. Before the surprised campers could react, he was in the tent, turning everything inside out. A practiced thief, the raccoon was back out of the tent and headed toward the palmettos with a half-empty package of bread before the campers made it the fifteen feet to their camp kitchen.

Raccoons, bears and other animals are ingenious when it comes to parting campers from their food. When the recommended methods don't work, you're left with no other option than to cancel your camping trip or to head for the nearest town or trail store and restock.

Most people prefer the luxury of State and National Parks with their bath houses and easily accessible water, and

these well-visited parks have the largest population of camper-smart animals. Even mild-mannered deer have perfected their "Yogi" act and can scrounge food out of even the hard-hearted.

Bears

The Black Bear has a commanding presence and can summon an ominous "woof" to warn you away; but a face-to-face encounter will probably end with the bear ambling, if not scurrying, way. If you are camping in a National Forest, you will be lucky even to see a bear. Because they are hunted annually, they tend to be wary of humans. It is in the National Parks, particularly the Great Smokies, Yosemite and Yellowstone, that bears have become a problem. They have learned to be both conniving and aggressive in their search for food. Bears are also notoriously unpredictable and can be vicious.

The National Park Service offers some tips for how to handle bear encounters as well as how to prevent bears from getting into your food. The following list is based on those recommendations:

- If you are day hiking and stop to take a break, or if you are just sitting around camp, keep your food nearby. If a bear approaches, pick up whatever you have out, and leave the area. Bears have been known to bluff campers into leaving food behind. Don't fall for this ploy, but on the other hand, don't take your time leaving, either. If the bear persists, it's not a bluff. Drop your food or pack to distract the bear from following. Avoid trouble at all costs. Bears seldom attack, but when they do, they can cause plenty of damage.
- If the bear continues to approach, keep your face turned toward the bear and slowly back away from it, but never, ever look a bear (or any animal) in the eye. Direct eye contact is perceived as aggressive.

- If, while backing away, you lose sight of the bear, move downwind of the bear and continue on your way. Keep an eye out for the bear until you are positive the bear has not followed.
- If a bear charges, don't run. Like many animals, bears react to running as if it is food trying to escape. They can also outrun you. Don't bother trying to climb a tree, either; bears are adept at climbing trees, and can probably do so faster and better than you can.
- If the bear is a lone black bear, you can try and fight back by screaming, yelling and kicking at it. That is often enough to scare it away. If these ploys don't work, react as you would with a grizzly or mother with cubs.
- If you are charged by a grizzly or a mother with cubs, your best bet is to lie on the ground in the fetal position, arms drawn up to protect your face and neck. Most bears will leave you alone if you do this or content themselves with a scratch or two.
- Never, under any circumstances, try to feed a bear or leave food to attract one. Once a bear has tasted human food, he will continue to search for it, which means trouble for the bear as well as the humans.
- When making camp, stash your food in a bag (a heavy-duty garbage bag may mask the smell of your food) and tie it securely off the ground and between two trees. The bag should be approximately ten feet above the ground and ten feet from the nearest tree. In areas where there are a lot of bears, bearproof means of storage are often provided for campers. Bear poles are the most common defense against these not so amicable Yogis. These tall, metal poles have four prongs at the top from which you can suspend your food bags. A gaff is provided to lift the food to the top of the pole. Another option is to lock the food in your car, with your windows up and vents closed.

A special word about grizzlies: Edward Abby once wrote, "If people persist in trespassing upon grizzlies' territory, we must accept the fact that the grizzlies, from time to time, will harvest a few trespassers." But what if you're not willing to sacrifice your life to the Great Griz? Fortunately, when camping in griz country, there are some precautions you can take to avoid meeting up with one of these legendary creatures.

When day hiking, stop and listen every five minutes or so, especially if it is windy. Grizzly bears are loud, particularly when they are not yet aware that their territory has been invaded. Keep your head up, and ears alert. It is very likely that you can spot a grizzly before it spots you, and thus avoid a potentially dangerous situation. If you've got your headphones on and are just enjoying the exercise, you may not make it to your destination.

Whether or not you walk into or with the wind depends on whom you ask. Grizzly expert Doug Peacock says that he walks into the wind for the most part, confident in his ability to spot grizzlies before they spot him. Peacock does say he does this only when he's heading toward potential bedding sites that he cannot otherwise get around. The government says you ought to walk with the wind so that grizzlies smell you before you spot them and disappear before you arrive.

If you are day hiking in grizzly country, be on the look out for cached carcasses (if you're downwind of it, you'll smell it) because it probably means there is a grizzly nearby. If you see a carcass, freeze and look around to see if you spot any grizzlies. If not, retreat slowly without turning around.

While camping in grizzly territory, you do not have to be unusually loud to scare off the bears. A normal, conversational tone interspersed with some singing and a yell or two will suffice to alert bears of your impending presence. If you feel as if you must make lots of noise (bang pans, clang bells, etc.) just to feel safe, forget it and camp somewhere that is safe.

Always, always, always sleep in a tent (RV, cabin, you get the idea) in grizzly country and keep a knife (for cutting an escape hatch in the tent), flashlight and fire starter handy. Although often illegal, camp away from established areas and any area where a bear is likely to travel. If you bushwhack into the brush a hundred yards or so (check for bear beds, food and trails), you'll probably be safe.

Don't bother bringing a gun; a gunshot will only make the bear mad. Never drop your day pack or food. Grizzlies are intelligent animals and we don't need to teach them that they can find food in day packs or around humans. Bear repellents are iffy at best, and are better left at home. Never walk about in the dark and if possible, don't camp alone. Groups of four or more are the safest as grizzlies rarely attack a group of campers.

The first thing to do when you encounter any adult grizzly is to speak quietly, hold your arms out at your sides and turn your face away. Avoid direct eye contact, but keep an eye on the bear to continue to gauge its mood. Unless the bear flattens its ears back and looks directly at you, begin to retreat—slowly. If it does flatten its ears, freeze, wait and then slowly begin your retreat.

Never make sudden movements or loud noises. Don't try to climb a tree—it takes too long, and grizzlies can knock down some trees or possibly shake you out of your perch.

If you should be attacked, play possum but—in this case—don't expose your vitals. Draw up in a fetal position; use your arms, hands and day pack, if you have one, to protect your neck and skull. As painful as it might be, try to stay still. This might be your only chance to save your life.

Finally, when camping or hiking around grizzlies, don't worry too much about sex or menstruation; bears are not drawn irresistibly to these human odors. You should keep yourself as clean as possible. You don't have to avoid camping trips into grizzly country just because you might be menstruating, but if you can delay your trip by a day or two, it might make you feel safer. The same goes for sex. While a griz may not notice the sounds and scents of your coitus outdoorsus, do you really want to take that risk?

Snakes

In the wild, snakes lie in wait for the small rodents and other prey that make up their diet. Coiled along the edge of a trail or other likely area, waiting for food to pass by, the patient reptiles test the air with their flicking tongues for signs of game.

This image of the snake lying in wait just beyond our next footstep is a cause of concern among some campers; but what about the snake's view of things? The snake is aware of its place in the food chain; it must watch for predators as well as prey. A camper making a moderate amount of noise will usually be perceived as a predator, and the snake will back-off or lie still until the danger passes.

To avoid confrontations with snakes, remember to make a little extra noise when you are walking through the brush, deep grass or piles of dead leaves that block your view of the ground ahead. This will warn snakes of your approach. By kicking at the brush or leaves slightly, you will make enough noise to cause a snake to slither off or lie still. Be especially careful when stepping over logs, as a snake may be lying under them.

Many species of poisonous snakes prefer areas near rocky outcrops and are often found among the boulders that border rocky streams as well. In spring, they sun themselves on the rocks. Generally, rattlesnakes appear throughout the country, copperheads throughout the East, water moccasins in the wetlands of the South, and coral snakes in only the South. Poisonous snakes do not occur in the far North, where the temperatures remain cool or downright cold most of the year.

When in doubt, avoid all snakes. But keep in mind that more people die each year from insect stings and bites than from snake bites. Refer to Chapter 12 for information on treating snakebites.

Rattlesnakes

Rattlesnakes are heavy-bodied and can be from three to five feet long, although large rattlesnakes are increasingly rare. Rattlesnakes have large blotches and crossbands (though these are not hour-glass-shaped). There are two color phases of the background color—a yellowish and a dark, almost black phase. Sometimes their overall color is dark enough to obscure the tell-tale pattern.

The real giveaway is the prominent rattle or enlarged "button" at the end of the snake's tail. Rattlesnakes usually warn predators with a distinctive rattle; but this can't be relied on, because they may also lie still as hikers go by.

Rattlesnakes are frequently seen in camping and hiking areas both in the West and East, although their presence has been greatly reduced by development encroaching on their terrain. Although these snakes are found throughout the U.S., rattlesnake bites are almost unheard of; and when quick action is taken, they will almost never prove fatal, except among the very young or old. Even so, rattlesnake bites are extremely dangerous and more potent than those of the the copperhead and water moccasin because of the snake's size.

Copperheads

Copperheads are typically two to three feet long. They are moderately stout-bodied with brown or chestnut hourglass-shaped crossbands. The background color is lighter than the crossbands, anything from reddish-brown to chestnut to gray-brown. The margins of the crossbands have a darker outline. This pattern certainly helps the copperhead blend in among dead leaves. Other, non-poisonous snakes like the corn snake have similar patterns, but the hourglass shape is not so prominent.

Copperheads prefer companionship; if you see one copperhead, there are probably others in the area. In the spring and fall they can be seen in groups, particularly in rocky areas. Their nests have the strong and distinctive odor of cucumbers.

Copperheads avoid trouble by lying still or retreating, biting only as a last resort. The bite of the copperhead is almost never fatal. Rarely has someone weighing more than forty pounds died of a copperhead bite. While not necessarily fatal, the bite is dangerous, and medical attention should be sought immediately.

Copperheads can be found from Massachusetts south to North Florida and westward to Illinois, Oklahoma and Texas.

Water Moccasin or Cottonmouth
One of the largest poisonous snakes in America, the cottonmouth's head is diamond-shaped and very distinct from the neck. Water moccasins are dull olive to brownish in color and a bit paler on their sides. Their sides also sport indistinct, wide, blackish bands. The body is very stout in proportion to length—they can also be as long as five feet. With an abruptly tapering tail and eye shields, the cottonmouth is a very sinister-looking snake. It is also the most aggressive poisonous snake in U.S.

Water moccasins, as the name implies, can be found in swamps and along streams, ponds, lakes and rivers from Southern Virginia (sometimes) south to Florida and westward into Eastern Texas. They range northward up the Mississippi as far as Illinois and Indiana. They are not found in the mountains.

Coral Snake

Also called the Harlequin snake, the brightly banded coral snake reaches a yard long. When it comes to recognizing the coral snake, just remember, "red on yellow will kill a fellow." Broad bands of red and blue-black are separated by narrow yellow bands. Other snakes imitate the coral snake's colors but not its pattern.

Although small and rarely known to bite, the coral snake is the most venomous of the poisonous snakes inhabiting the U.S. An antivenin is needed to counteract the poison of a coral snake, which unlike the venom of the three pit vipers above, is a neurotoxin. Most coral snake bites occur when the snake is being handled because it has small fangs and needs prolonged contact.

The coral snake can be found from northern North Carolina to the Gulf of Mexico and westward through Texas. A smaller, less venomous species, occupies parts of Arizona.

Poisonous Lizards

There are only two poisonous lizards on God's Green Earth and both of them can be found in the United States, but not in the woods and forests. The Gila Monster and the Mexican Beaded Lizard occupy the deserts of the Southwest and will bite if picked up or stepped on. To be poisoned, you must come in direct contact with these critters because their jaws must clamp down on you for them to be able to drool venom into the wound they make with their primitive teeth. You may even have to heat the underside of their jaws with a flame before they'll let go. The bite should be treated as you would treat a snakebite.

Boars, Moose, Elk and Other Beasts

Boars, which are not indigenous to the United States (they were brought here from Europe for hunting purposes), can be found in the Southern Appalachians and throughout the South. They are rarely seen, and, like most animals, will disappear if they hear you coming. If you happen upon a boar, try to avoid direct confrontation; just continue about your business (unless, of course, it threatens the boar).

Male moose and elk should be avoided during rutting season because they may mistake you for a rival and attempt to chase you out of their territory.

Only the very lucky will catch glimpses of other wild animals—alligators, mountain lions, bobcats, wolf, coyote and big horn sheep. Chances of confrontation are slim.

Pests

Campgrounds and even primitive campsites often attract rodents and other small mammals. These creatures are searching for food and can do much damage, especially if you do not take care to protect your belongings. It is never wise to leave your food out on the ground for the night. Food, and even garbage, should be hung where these animals can't reach them. You will also want to protect yourself from insects.

Porcupines

These nocturnal creatures love to gnaw on anything salty. Hiking boots, picnic tables and outhouses are all fair game to the porcupine. That may sound strange, but they are after the salt from your sweat. So, if you have anything salty with you, make sure to hang it (boots and shoes, especially) when you're camping in porcupine country, and take particular care in areas known to be frequented by porcupines.

Direct contact is necessary to receive the brunt of the

porcupine's quills. Although it is unlikely for a camper to be lashed by a porcupine's tail, it is not unusual for a dog to provoke a porcupine into defending itself. Young children might unknowingly provoke a porcupine, as well. Porcupines quills become imbedded in the flesh of the attacker, causing extreme pain. If the quills are not removed immediately, they can cause death.

Skunks

Skunks can be found nationwide but are usually only a problem to people in high-use areas. Dogs, on the other hand, can provoke skunk attacks just about anywhere. Although we've only seen a few skunks, we've been aware of their presence (that telltale odor!) on many a camping trip.

The Great Smokies are notorious for their brazen skunks. I have listened to many a skunk tale and have experienced the agony of a skunk encounter myself. We sat, tensely, for a half-hour or more around a campfire waiting for the scrounging animal to startle and spray. It didn't, and it was with much relief that we watched it amble away from us. One of the skunk tales related to me concerned two British campers unfamiliar with the skunk. They attempted to chase the animal off by tossing a boot at it and were given a quick course in skunk etiquette! For those who don't know, skunks are about the same size as raccoons and are always black and white.

Mice

Mice are the most common pest to be found in the outdoors. If you leave your food sitting on the ground next to your tent, don't be surprised the next morning if mice have gnawed their way into your foodbag (if not a raccoon or other pest). If you don't hang your food, make sure it is locked in your car, or stored in a pest-proof container. Mice also like clothing. They are perfectly willing to chew away at your clothes to obtain fibers to use in their nests.

Raccoons

Raccoons are also a widespread nuisance. They, too, will invade your food and garbage and thus, you must hang or otherwise protect your food. On a camping trip to Cumberland Island off the Georgia-Florida coast, we very carefully suspended our food and garbage from the long and twisted branch of a live oak. It wasn't good enough. Around midnight, we heard the sound of ripping plastic, our garbage bag. The beam of our flashlight illuminated the fat raccoon that had shimmied down the rope and was currently tearing at the garbage bag. He was obviously attracted by the empty tuna can (even though we had rinsed it with hot water and bagged it in plastic). When hungry, raccoons are devious.

Dogs

Some dogs encountered when camping are companions, and others are strays or the property of people who live nearby. If they are strays, they can be very friendly as well as very hard to get rid of. They can also be aggressive, especially if they are hungry. Other dogs can be aggressive if they feel like they are defending their territory or their masters.

Fortunately, most of the dogs you will meet when camping are friendly, but many people have had bad experiences with dogs. I've been threatened any number of times but sometimes people have been attacked. My brother was bitten by a dog whose master was standing right next to him. So, even if the dog appears friendly and is with its owner, it doesn't mean it will be happy to see you.

How to Avoid Troublesome Dogs

As with bears and most other animals, don't run. Don't look

directly into a dog's eyes. If it is necessary to defend yourself, use a stick or small stones. Sometimes picking up a stone and holding it as if you're going to throw it is enough to dissuade a dog. Throw the rock only if it's absolutely necessary.

Insects

You can't escape them. They're everywhere. Even in the coldest reaches of the Arctic and Antarctic, it is not surprising to stumble upon a bug. No-see-ums, bees, hornets, wasps, blackflies, deerflies, horseflies, fire ants, scorpions, chiggers, mosquitos and ticks are among the millions of insects (and other small pests) out there that torment the human soul… and skin.

They invade our lives both indoors and out, and to be perfectly honest, I find insects much easier to deal with in the out-of-doors than inside my home or car. They may be demons outside, but they are Satan incarnate when trapped somewhere they do not want to be. So, because you can't live with them and you can't live without them, how do you handle insects, especially those that like nothing better than feasting on human blood?

No-see-ums

These are the smallest of our tormentors and perhaps those most likely to drive us insane; the tiny midges and gnats that tend to swarm otherwise happy campers. But there are ways to avoid that which you cannot see. First of all, camp away from running water and make sure the no-see-um netting on your tent is a very fine mesh; otherwise they will torment you all night long. If day hiking through a swarm, use DEET (more on this miracle repellent later) and wear a long-sleeved shirt buttoned up to your throat and closed at the cuffs. For those of you who are really irritated by no-see-ums, you can purchase headnets made out of no-see-um netting. The covering fits over your head and is secured by a cord around your neck. Be careful not to pull this cord too tight.

If you are bitten, grin and bear it, because there's not much you can do to stop the fortunately brief pain. On second thought, don't grin, because no-see-ums are not averse to flying in your mouth.

Bees, hornets, wasps
In years and years of camping, I have only been stung twice by yellow jackets. Mostly, stinging insects will try to avoid you, but they are attracted to food, beverages, perfume, scented soaps and lotions (including deodorant) and bright-colored clothing. Also, they nest anywhere that provides cover—in logs, trees, even underground (not to mention the wood siding of my house).

Yellow jackets are the most obnoxious of the bunch, often stinging more than once and without apparent provocation. By keeping your camp clean, and food and drink undercover, you should avoid these stinging insects. But keep in mind that, like animal pests, yellow jackets are more prevalent in high use areas. They know where to hang out for a free meal. I have been chased from countless picnic spots by this yellow and black-banded pest.

If stung by one of these insects, wash the area with soap and water to keep the sting from becoming infected. Apply a cool cloth for about twenty minutes to reduce swelling and carry an oral antihistamine to reduce swelling as well. Check your damp clothing and towels before using to make sure one of these stingers has not alighted on it.

Remember that bees, hornets and wasps kill more people each year than snakes. Numerous stings can induce anaphylactic shock, which can be fatal. Those who know they are allergic to bee stings should carry an Anakit (available by prescription) with them when camping. These kits carry an antidote for anaphylactic shock—epinephrine (adrenaline). You will find more information on anaphylactic shock in Chapter 12.

Blackflies, deerflies, horseflies
Most abundant during late spring and summer, these flies produce a painful bite as well as leave a nasty mark on your skin. They sponge up the blood produced by their bite, which is why the wound is often so big. Deer flies, in particular, seem to prefer to dine on your head. When swarmed by the monsters, I have covered my head, Arab-style, to avoid their nasty bites. If bitten, wash with soap and water and use an oral antihistamine to reduce swelling and itching.

Fire ants
So far these nasty little creatures are found only in the South. But nearly everyone in the South, as well as visitors, have experienced first hand their tenacity and painful bite. My husband found one little ant clinging stubbornly to his foot hours after he stepped in a fire ant bed. They usually build distinctive foot-high mounds, but you don't necessarily have to kick one to be the brunt of their anger. These ants are very aggressive, consider your passing a provocation, and will sting you repeatedly. Water-borne fire ants will attack you as viciously as those defending their territory, which often appears to be the entire universe. Treat a fire ant bite as you would a bee sting.

Scorpions
Scorpions hide under rocks, logs and other cover during the day; and although they pack a powerful wallop when they sting, only one species is potentially fatal. You'll rarely encounter scorpions, which are arthropods, not insects, in the woods unless you're picking up rocks for a fire ring or deadfall

for a fire. Lift the rocks carefully and you will avoid stings.

Keep a lookout for scorpions in the desert. Here, they will crawl into your shoes, clothing or sleeping bag during the night. Make sure you inspect your shoes and clothing before you put them on and shake out your sleeping bag before you climb into it.

If stung by a scorpion, treat the wound as you would a wasp sting. If the scorpion that stings you is about one-half to three inches long and yellow or greenish-yellow and you are in Texas, Arizona, New Mexico, southern California or northern Mexico, seek help immediately. It may be the one exception to the rule, the potentially deadly Ceturoides sculptuates. If unsure and if it's possible, kill the scorpion that stung you and show it to the doctor.

Chiggers or Red Bugs

Although reputed to burrow beneath your skin and to retreat only when full or suffocated, chiggers actually cause that red, itchy irritation on your skin when secretions are released during feeding. Treat chigger bites as you would bee stings.

Mosquitos

These blood-thirsty bugs have been the carrier of a number of diseases that have killed thousands of people. Until recently we had to deal with mosquitos only at night. But a new species has invaded the United States that is just as happy to feed during the day, even in the scorching heat of a Georgia summer. Now not only can we be driven insane by the buzz of mosquitos in our ears at night, but also we get to slap our selves silly during the day as well.

Only female mosquitos bite, but there always seem to be plenty of them around. Most of the time it is impossible to avoid mosquitos, but if you camp in breezy areas away from still water, there's a good chance your sleep will be mosquito-free. I say good chance because I have been bombarded by mosquitos while walking along a windy beach at night. Go for light-colored clothing that is too thick for mosquitos to penetrate. If that is impossible and those mosquitos are really bad, wear long-sleeved shirts and pants and use DEET.

Ticks

A relative of spiders (another pest that leaves nasty bites) and not actually insects, the tick has become a serious health threat. It is the carrier of both Rocky Mountain Spotted Fever and Lyme disease. Rocky Mountain Spotted Fever is carried by the wood ticks (West), lone star ticks (Southwest), and dog ticks (East and South). Lyme disease is carried by the deer tick, which is about the size of a pinhead.

Whenever you are camping in tick country—tall grass and underbrush—make sure you check yourself often for ticks. Wearing a hat, long-sleeved shirt, and pants with cuffs tucked into the socks will also discourage ticks. This can be very uncomfortable in hot weather. Using a repellent containing permethrin will also help, as will avoiding tall grass and underbrush.

Like mosquitos, ticks are attracted to heat, often hanging around for months at a time waiting for a hot body to pass by. Wearing light-colored clothing will help you to see ticks. Nearly any one who enjoys the outdoors can tell a tick story. If a tick attaches itself to your body, the best way to remove it is by grasping the skin directly below where the tick is attached and pulling, removing the tick along with a small piece of skin. Once removed, carefully wash the bite with soap and water.

It takes a while for a tick to become embedded. If you check yourself thoroughly each day spent in the outdoors—examining every mole and speck of dirt—you are likely to catch the tick before it catches you. Tick season lasts from

April through October, and peak season is from May through July. But in warmer climates, tick season may last year 'round if there has been a warmer than average winter.

Repellents

DEET is the hands-down winner when it comes to repelling insects. Short for N, N-diethyl-meta-toluamide, DEET is found in some percentage in most repellents—lotions, creams, sticks, pump sprays and aerosols.

This colorless, oily, slightly smelly ingredient is good against mosquitos, no-see-ums, fleas, ticks, gnats and flies. Although it can range in percentage from five to ninety-five percent, the longest lasting formula contains approximately thirty-five percent DEET.

Repellents containing DEET in the thirty-five percent range are (in ascending order): Deep Woods Off! lotion, Deep Woods Off! towelettes, Cutter's Stick, Cutter's Cream, Cutter's Cream Evergreen Scent, Cutter's Cream Single Use Packets (35%), Muskol Ultra Maximum Strength, Repel and Kampers Lotion (47.5% and includes suntan lotion).

Using a thirty-five percent solution on adult bodies is fine, but a number of children have died after being slathered with the stuff day after day. A seven to eight percent solution is perfect for children, and a good brand to try is Off! Skintastic.

Avon's Skin-So-Soft is a highly recommended deterrent against no-see-ums and some bigger bugs such as sand fleas and black flies. It does appear to work differently on each

>>Camping Tip<<

Marines on South Carolina's Parris Island, where sand flea abound, mix Skin-So-Soft with alcohol (roughly half and half) and put in an empty pump spray bottle to make their own DEET-free repellent.

person. I have better luck with it than my husband, for example.

During a trip to the low country of South Carolina, I was glad I packed the Skin-So-Soft. My daughter, Griffin, was bitten only on the head (where she was still greatly lacking in hair)—the only place I couldn't slather her with the stuff. I received only one bite, my husband quite a few more.

· 14 ·
Traveling by Boot, Boat or Bike

Never did we plan the morrow, for we had learned that in the wilderness some new and irresistible distraction is sure to turn up each day before breakfast. Like the river, we were free to wander.

—Aldo Leopold
A Sand County Almanac

You don't have to have travel by car to enjoy camping. The best way to see the world up close and personal is by foot, canoe or bike. These modes of transportation can take you to places an automobile has no chance of reaching. From overnight trips to treks of a week or more, backpacking, cycling and canoeing open up a whole new world of camping experiences.

Each of these forms of transportation comes with some of its own equipment and brings new possiblities and challenges to consider. This chapter considers each of these weight- and bulk-conscious forms of camping separately and covers some of the equipment and techniques needed to enjoy each.

Backpacking

A hiker's state of grace is something only avid backpackers can truly experience. Those are the days that the forty pounds on your back are weightless. Your booted feet skim over the trail, and all senses are acutely tuned in. The electronic trill of the vireo, acid sharp scent of pine and the leaf-filtered light increase your awareness of the outdoors. It is a total oneness with the earth and whatever supreme being you believe in.

At the end of one of these days, having hiked nearly twenty miles after a late breakfast, we set up camp at the top of a ridge. We watched as the sun set over the farmland below, tingeing the little white church and meandering stream orange. The sun was a blazing ball of fire slowly sinking below the far ridge, and, as my stepfather likes to say, everything was copacetic.

The thick layer of leaves beneath our tent was as soft as a mattress and we easily drifted off to sleep. A day unique to backpacking, something that can only be experienced away from developed campgrounds and roads.

Backpacking is essentially camping, and the two are so intertwined that they are nearly indistinguishable. The only difference from car camping, other than the fact the number of luxuries you carry is limited, is that you hike to your site. The joy of backpacking is that your choice of campsites is often unlimited. Your legs can carry you to mountain peaks and tarns, surf-tossed beaches, water-carved canyons. Backpacking brings you limitless possibilities. And with recent advances in backpack "technology," a backpacking trip no longer means blanket rolls and heavy, shapeless canvas rucksacks. Today, selecting a pack is almost as tough as finding a pair of boots. Dozens of manufacturers offer hundreds of options.

Backpacking in the 90s, published by Menasha Ridge Press, offers up-to-date information on the type of backpack that will best suit your needs, but basically there are two types of backpacks to choose from—internal frame and external frame.

Choosing a Pack

Both frame designs have their pros and cons. The basic differences are that the external frame is designed to distribute weight evenly and has a high center of gravity (perfect for established trails), the internal frame pack is designed to custom-fit each wearer and has a low center of gravity (popular for off-trail hiking and mountaineering). Also, the external frame is said to be cooler than the internal frame because it is designed to sit away from your back rather than on it like the internal frame. The external frame is also better built to carry heavier loads (more than fifty pounds), but it swings from side to side when you scramble over rocks and can catch on limbs hanging into the trail.

A 3,000-cubic-inch external frame pack is best for most trips. Externals come in top-loading, front-loading and combination models. Because the top-loading model works kind of like a duffel bag attached to a frame, it is not the preferred backpack. The best is a combination model with front and side pockets and a top-loaded section. A well-padded hip belt

>>Camping Tip<<

Develop your own system. Pack your backpack the same way each time you use it and try to keep from stuffing things randomly into pockets.

is one of the most important features of an external frame pack because most of the weight is supported by the hip belt and your hips. External frame packs cost from $50 to as much as $400.

Internal frame packs have rapidly gained popularity because they are a good compromise for all trails, as they alleviate most of the problems involved with external frames. Because they hug your body and have a lower center of gravity, they provide excellent balance and allow more upper-body mobility and flexibility. An average internal frame pack will need a minimum volume of 4,000 cubic inches to be comparable to a 3,000-cubic-inch external frame pack. This is because sleeping gear is attached to the frame of an external pack but is carried in a special compartment inside the internal frame pack. The drawback to internals is that they are mostly top-loading and rarely come with external pockets. Many manufacturers sell add-on pockets to strap on to internal frame packs. In general, internal frame packs are more expensive than externals, costing upwards from $100 to as much as $500.

How Much to Carry in Your Pack

Assuming you've purchased a pack, what should you bring and how much should you carry? An easy-to-use rule of thumb is to never carry more than one third of your body weight. That means the more you weigh, the easier it is to carry what you need. Since I weigh only one-hundred pounds, I often carry more than a third of my weight on week-long trips. I have carried in excess of forty pounds, with the only damage being a slower pace and minor welts on my hips. On shorter trips, it is wiser to carry even less—one-quarter of your body weight is about right.

Some hikers swear that you should carry only one-fifth of your body weight, but that can be extremely difficult to do, especially if you are winter hiking or carrying a week's worth of food. What if you pack your pack and it weighs sixty pounds, and you weigh only one-hundred twenty? Unpack and look at everything very carefully. Things like your stove, tent and sleeping bag are absolutely essential. But what about your clothes? You do not have to wear something different every day. Bring the bare essentials.

Another area where you might be overpacking is toiletries. If you must shave, deodorize, shampoo, etc., try to find sample sizes or transfer to travel-size bottles, if possible. Don't bring a radio unless it's the compact, "Walkman" type. The slender Mag Lites have become the popular flashlight for backpackers. And, a small flashlight that uses AA batteries will serve you just as well as one that uses C or D batteries.

Those are just a few examples. See Chapter 3 for more examples of what to bring along in your pack. The key is to study your pack's contents objectively. Are you sure you can't live without it?

What to carry
Most of this book is dedicated to the types of things you need to carry on a camping trip. In most cases, chapter by chapter, lightweight (backpacking-style) gear is discussed. For a complete list of what to carry and the options, see the Appendix on equipment lists at the back of the book. For the most part, a pack will contain a tent, sleeping bag and pad, cooking gear (including stove), pots and fuel, toiletries, lighting, food, clothes (including rain gear), and a small first aid kit.

Packing Your Pack
Once you've narrowed down what you intend to bring, you need to pack it. You are going to need certain items to be handy. Any system that you come up with will work as long as you know how to get at those necessary items quickly.

Rain gear, for example, will be something that you'll want to be able to lay your hands on immediately. It is not unusual to be caught in a sudden downpour, and if you have to drop your pack and dig through it to get to your rain gear, you and all your gear may be soaked by the time you find it.

You will also need a means to carry water so that you can reach it without taking off your pack. Some hikers use holsters for their water bottles, while others keep their canteens within easy reach in a side pocket on their packs.

It is also important to distribute the weight as equally as possible. A well-balanced pack will ride easier on your back. For example, don't put all your food on one side and all your clothes on the other. Believe it or not, food will be a good third of the weight you are carrying.

Packing the heavier stuff toward the top of your pack will keep the load centered over your hips, particularly in an external frame pack. On the other hand, don't follow this rule to its furthest conclusion, because an overly top-heavy pack is also unwieldy.

Sleeping bags are usually secured at the bottom of an external frame pack, strapped to the frame just below the pack sack. In the internal frame packs, the sleeping bag compartment is usually the bottom third of the pack.

Another suggestion: you will probably want your food more readily available than your clothes and cooking gear, particularly at lunch time. Nothing is more aggravating than having to dig through your clothes just so you can satisfy your craving for Gorp.

>>Camping Tip<<

Stand all fuel and water bottles upright in your pack to keep them from leaking and, with gas bottles particularly, from contaminating food.

Loading Tips:
* On gentle terrain, pack the heaviest items high and close to the back. Because the pack's center of gravity is about at shoulder level, it will take only a slight bend at the waist while hiking to align the weight over your hips.
* If balance is crucial (climbing, off-trail travel, rough terrain), pack heavy items in the center, close to your back. You may have to lean over more to offset the pack's weight, but your balance is better because the pack's top-heaviness is reduced.
* If you are carrying anything sharp in your pack, pad it well. The last thing you want is to be stabbed in the back.
* Women have a lower center of gravity and do well to pack dense items lower and closer to the back.
* Color-coded stuff sacks are a great backpacking tool.
* Make sure that all fitting points are properly adjusted to your torso.
* Long items should be lashed to the pack frame.

Pack Covers
Although all backpacks are made of water resistant material, moisture will seep through seams and zippers and saturate your gear if your pack is left unprotected. A pack cover can be anything from a heavy duty garbage bag, which will keep your pack dry when camping (and protect it from the dew at night), to a specially-designed cover made for the purpose. These coated nylon or Gore-Tex covers, when their own seams are properly sealed, fit over your pack but still allow you to hike. They are usually fitted to your pack by elastic or a drawstring.

No matter what kind of pack cover you purchase (and you do need to buy one), you will still want to carry a heavy duty (BIG) garbage bag to keep your pack covered at night, because pack covers are not designed to protect the straps

---

>>Camping Tip<<

Before turning in for the night, cover your pack. Even if the stars are shining overhead, clouds can still blow in before morning. The cover will also protect your pack from the dew and some pesky animals.

---

and back of your pack. A plastic garbage bag is indispensable when you are forced to camp in a downpour but don't have room for your pack in the tent.

The poncho-style pack covers work under ideal conditions only. The poncho is designed to be a one-piece rain gear, covering both you and your pack at the same time. Not only do ponchos tend to tear easily, but they work only when the wind is not blowing hard. If the wind whips up, so will your poncho, and both you and your pack will soon be soaked. For added insurance, anything you don't want to get wet can be slipped into a plastic bag before being stored in your pack.

Canoe Camping
Paddling the waters of North America (and elsewhere) brings you to places as remote as anything you can find on a backpacking trip. There are hundreds of lakes (in Maine, for example) that are accessible only by float plane. So you can imagine that there are many rarely-visited areas that are only miles from the nearest automobile. And many people consider anything off-road as uncivilized, primitive (which it can be) and terrifying (which it isn't). Some lakes and rivers offer oft-used campsites or even seldom-used primitive sites. For the adventurous, you can always make your own camp.

Assuming you already have a canoe or access to one, and before running out and purchasing gear for your canoe trip, you must first plan what type of trip you will be taking. Trips requiring a lot of portaging, will require different baggage than a trip on a river or lake.

The classic pack for canoe trips, particularly in the Boundary Waters, is the Duluth pack. Shaped like a canvas envelope, it features leather shoulder straps and nothing on the outside to get caught on the thwarts or sides of a canoe. The Duluth pack also sits well in the canoe and is pretty easy to carry. Refined over hundreds of years of use, this pack is now made of lighter weight but sturdier materials. The shoulder straps are padded and can be adjusted to fit and the sack has internal, flat pockets to hold maps.

Duluth packs are cheaper than internal frame packs and come in a variety of sizes depending on what you want to carry. For example, a #2 Duluth pack can carry up to thirty-five pounds of food. For larger Duluth packs you may want to invest in a tumpline, a leather strap that is worn like a headband and attaches to the pack to help support its weight.

Never purchase any hand-held packs or duffel bags for canoe trips. If you have ever carried a suitcase through a large airport, you'll know why. Always pick a bag with shoulder straps. A larger pack, an updated version of the Duluth pack, called the #3 Voyageur, is perfect for carrying sleeping bags, pads and extra clothes. There are also specially-made internal frame packs just for canoeing. External frame packs should be avoided because they are hard to get in and out of the canoe. If you will be doing a lot of portaging, one of these new internal frame packs (for canoeing, not backpacking) will make hauling your gear a lot easier.

While the Duluth packs cost less (around $50 and up), the internal frame packs cost substantially more ($100 and up). If you are just getting into canoe-camping, you may want to rent the equipment first.

Generic dry bags can also be found, both with and without carrying straps. These are a cheaper alternative ($10 to $75) and may work well if you anticipate little or no portaging. We have also made do with a plastic-bag-lined duffel bag when we were going on a float trip with no portaging.

Safety Gear

Each person in the canoe should wear a lifejacket. Buying a comfortable lifejacket (instead of the cheapest one you can find) will make it easier not to get slack about wearing your PFD (personal flotation device).

A seventy-five-foot rescue line should be readily accessible at all times. An extra paddle should be packed away (in case one is broken or lost), and helmets are required wear for whitewater travel.

What to Pack

Now that you've chosen what you're going to pack your gear in, what do you bring? The items carried on a canoe camping trip are similar to those carried on any camping trip—tent, sleeping bag and pad, cook stove and kit, food and your preference of the other items covered in this book. The only item you may want to consider carrying that you probably wouldn't take on most backpacking and cycling trips is fishing gear. After all, the majority of your time will be spent on or around the water.

Because I am not a fishing expert and because what you will want to carry varies depending on where you are fishing and what for, I will not recommend anything other than: make sure it is in backpack-size proportions and you get the necessary license and permits.

Canoe camping can mean carrying as many as four packs. These are smaller than backpacking packs and are usually organized as the food pack, the housekeeping pack, the shelterpack and the miscellaneous pack. You will want to make sure that you have some food in a pack other than the food pack, however. This will give you an emergency supply if something happens to the food pack. When you know you'll be portaging, it might be tempting to carry fewer packs, but be careful not to stuff too much gear into one or two bags making them hard to carry.

The food pack should carry all your food but should weigh only one-third the weight of the person who is carrying it. For example, were I to portage the food pack, it could weigh no more than thirty to thirty-five pounds. See Chapter 1 on how to pack food. Some people pack their food into a box before inserting it into a pack. Others tote the food in an internal frame pack. Lining your food (and other) packs with heavy-duty plastic will help ensure the food doesn't get wet. It also helps protect against camp critters. Once the food in your pack begins to dwindle, you can add items from other packs to reduce their weight. Stove fuel bottles are prone to leaks. Pack them wrapped so that they cannot damage other gear if they do leak.

The housekeeping pack generally is the heaviest and carries the tent, ground cloth, cooking gear, repair equipment and first aid kit. It, too, can be a large Duluth or internal frame pack. Another pack (the up-dated Duluth called a Voyageur makes a good shelter pack) holds the sleeping bags and pads, extra clothes and toiletries; the miscellaneous pack, usually a day pack, can hold things like rain gear, camera, snacks, etc.

Pack your canoe packs as you would a backpack, with the gear needed the most in the most accessible location. See the section on backpacking on how to pack for easiest trekking.

Loading Your Canoe

A canoe must be loaded properly so that it is not subject to tipping easily. The center of gravity should be near the center of the boat. Settle your packs in the middle of the canoe and closer to the front or back, depending on the weight of the paddlers. For example, if the paddler in the rear weighs more than the paddler in front, the gear should be closer to the front to even the weight up some.

Keep all gear as low as possible to maintain the canoe's natural stability as well giving the canoe less wind resistance. All of the gear should be securely tied into the boat. The more haphazard the loading, the harder it is to unload. You may find it difficult to get in and out of the canoe at portages or beaver dams. If you must crawl over you luggage, keep as low a profile as possible and hold onto both gunwales for support.

If you're carrying a duffer, that is, someone who will not be paddling, make sure they sit on the floor of a canoe or on a pad on the floor of the canoe. If the duffer must sit on a pack, make sure the pack has nothing in it that can be damaged by someone sitting on it. The duffer must also remain lower in profile than the paddlers or otherwise they risk falling out of the canoe and damage the stability of the craft.

Portaging the Canoe

A canoe is always carried on land, never dragged. If possible, portaging the canoe is also a one-person job, freeing the other paddler to carry gear. To portage, the canoe must be turned over and lifted to the portager's shoulders without hurting the portager or the canoe.

There are a number of ways to do this, but the best is to stand alongside the rear of the canoe, facing it. From this point, you stoop down, and using the arm that is closest to the front, reach across and take hold of the far gunwale. The other hand grabs hold of the near gunwale (both hands should be behind the rear seat with thumbs inside, fingers outside the gunwales) and in one smooth motion lift the end of the canoe over your head, turning the canoe bottom-side up at the same time. Simultaneously, turn to face the front of the canoe (still resting on the ground). Lock your arms at the elbow (the canoe is supported at three points) and step forward, sliding your grip along the gunwales until you are in position under the portage pads. Now lower the canoe until the portage pads are resting on your shoulders and lift the front of the canoe slightly until the entire canoe is balanced on your shoulders. Then head 'em up and move 'em out.

Keep in mind that portaging often involves two trips for at least one person. Whoever portages the canoe usually carries just that. The other will either carry all the gear (often in excess of eighty pounds and impossible for many people to carry in one trip) or carry half the gear on the first trip, return and the rest of the gear on the second trip. Life jackets and paddles can be affixed to the canoe to cut down on the amount of gear carried.

If the canoe carrier is fast, the gear porter can carry half the gear halfway and deposit it, returning for the rest of the gear. Meanwhile, the canoe porter has finished the trip with the canoe and returned for the first half of the gear. The gear porter makes the full trip with the second round of gear.

Another option for the gear porter is to carry a load halfway, deposit it and return for the second round of gear. He can then continue on his way with the second round and return (only halfway) for the first round of gear. The length of the portage isn't less, but it is broken into more frequent rests.

Always try to unload (and load) your boat while it is in the water. A gear-filled canoe is practically immovable and can be damaged if dragged across land.

Sanitation

When canoe camping, you must often be more concerned about dealing with your urine and feces than with other forms of camping. The once accepted practice of peeing from a boat (something I never could have managed anyway) is now uniformly frowned upon. When camping on a river bank, you will need to walk far from the river (at least 200 feet) to select a "bathroom." If you are in a canyon or other area where that is not possible, you will have to carry out your waste. Use an empty coffee can or other similar container lined with a resealable plastic bag as a toilet. Instead of "flushing," let the air out of the bag, seal and pack out. Dispose of your wastes at home.

For more information on how to enjoy canoe camping, read Patricia J. Bell's *Roughing It Elegantly* by Cat's-paw Press.

Bicycle Camping

Bicycling America's blue highways is an excellent way to discover your country. Riding the backroads from one campsite to another will leave more time to take in the countryside than when you speed by in a car. The same can be said of touring Canada, Europe, South America, etc.

As with backpacking and canoe camping, what you leave behind is more important than how much you take with you. Also of importance is knowing how to pack what you decide to bring and what to pack it in.

What to take

Assuming that you already are aware of what to carry for your bike and its repair (Rob van der Plas has written a number of helpful books on the subject, including *The Bicycle Touring Manual*), most of the basics are similar to what you would bring on any camping trip.

The clothes you wear when cycling differ only slightly from those you would wear backpacking or canoeing. Rain gear is important for both warm and cold weather. In warm weather, you will need only bike shorts, a jersey or shirt, socks, underwear, shoes, gloves, helmet and visor. In cold weather, you may have to add long pants, a sweater or fleece pullover, thick socks, lined gloves or mittens, helmet liner, long johns, pedal covers, helmet cover, spats or leggings, plastic liners, shoe covers or overshoes. You may also want to carry off-bike clothing such as an additional pair of shoes, socks, shirt, pants or skirt (or dress), swimsuit and sleep wear.

Concerning other equipment, a first aid kit, similar to the one described in Chapter 3, is also important, as are toiletries and most of the other items mentioned in the latter part of that chapter. Cooking on the road will involve gear similar to backpacking gear—a small stove, cook kit, cup, bowl or plate, utensils, etc. You must also carry along some food and in this case, weight and bulk will count greatly. Camping will require a tent, groundsheet, a sleeping bag and pad, all lightweight and easy to pack onto the limited space a bike offers.

Cycle Luggage and Racks
Strong, rigid, weatherproof luggage is important when it comes to cycle touring. You'll have to scour your cycling catalogs to help you to decide what types of bags are necessary for your trip, but all trips will require good gear placement to keep the bike from becoming unbalanced.

Some tips for weight distribution include:

- The weight should be concentrated as close as possible to the bike's center of gravity.
- The luggage load should be stable in relation to the bike's frame.

- If you mount luggage behind the seat, keep it as far forward as possible. On the other hand, it need not necessarily be low.
- Front racks should be attached to the frame if at all possible.
- If you mount luggage in front and on the steering system, the luggage should be as close as possible to the steering axis and as low and as close to the wheel axle as possible.
- Luggage and/or racks should be attached so that they do not shift or sway when the bike is leaned over or when you are turning, accelerating, decelerating, climbing, descending or traveling over bumpy terrain.
- Attach bags and/or racks rigidly to the bike frame, tying not only the top (in at least two points) but at least one point at the bottom.
- A saddle bag is perfect for times when you need carry only a little luggage.
- If you are using a rack, make sure it has a stiffener or brace and is attached very rigidly to avoid lateral deflection.

Racks

Bicycle fatigue failure is an ailment from which your bike will not recover. If luggage and racks are improperly mounted, metal parts will break and the bike will then be subjected to many torturous miles of wear.

Fortunately, there are a number of things to look for when purchasing luggage racks for your bike. Most importantly, know how your bike will perform with the rack. Any rack should be attached at four points, minimum. The rack should be attached with sizable bolts with flat washers under the head. The washers will reduce friction when you are tightening the bolts. Do not use spring washers, which reduce friction and resist turning. Attach the rack to points on the bike that are also solid and stiffen the rack's stays by using braces.

When looking for a rack, those using steel tubing, aluminum rods or steel rods (in that order) are preferable. Aluminum rods should be at least 7 mm thick; steel rods, 6 mm; and tubular steel, 9 mm or more. Tubular steel is light and strong but can be expensive.

Construction of the rack is also important. Racks made of solid steel or aluminum should be welded while tubular steel should be brazed. The former method requires melting the material and then bonding them together. Brazing uses a filler material that melts at a lower temperature and bonds the two solid materials. If welded, the walls of tubular steel would weaken and could break.

If you purchase a folding rack, make sure that the pivot points have a solid metal construction as opposed to plastic joints. The vertical stays on larger racks should be constructed of twin rods or tubes in an inverse V pattern at both ends of the rack. When these stays also have a horizontal stiffener, your rack will function at its greatest strength. If only one pair of stays is used on a smaller rack, make sure the stays are attached just beyond the midpoint of the platform.

Lateral stays should be triangulated laterally. If so braced, the rack will hold up much better under wear. As I mentioned earlier, you should be able to place your load as far forward as possible on your rear rack not as low as possible. As a matter of fact, low-rider racks are of no use at all at the rear of the bike. Rear racks should also provide a vertical plane for the backs of your bags to rest against, which will prevent your bags from swaying as much.

>>Camping Tip<<

To check if your luggage is mounted properly, hold the loaded bicycle by the center of the handlebars and shake it. If everything is mounted well, there will be a minimum of sway.

Front racks should be low and have a centered mounting position that is close to the steering and wheel axes. The racks should possess a maximum of rigidity as well as be supported at the top and the bottom. The combination of being both low-rider and rigid can be difficult to find. Most of these racks feature a strange construction consisting of big loops that extend around and over the top of the front wheel.

Front racks should also be wide and long to carry some luggage atop the rack. Only light items should be carried on top of the rack. To prevent load shifting and thus, interference with the brakes, the rack should have a stop that protrudes from the top.

Bicycle Bags

There are three basic types of bags that can be used to carry luggage while bicycle touring: bags that attach to the rider, bags that attach to the bike, and bags that attach to luggage racks.

Basically, bags that attach to the rider include day packs, rucksacks, backpacks and fanny packs as used in day hiking or backpacking. Although these bags have their uses, they are not really for long-distance touring. Large packs might come in handy when you are traveling overseas and your trip requires a lot of off-bike traveling. In that case, your rackless, bagless bike can be dismantled and packed in a bag while your belongings remain in the backpack. Otherwise, day packs are useful for touring in cases where you leave your bike and wish to take some items with you. They are also good for carrying just-bought groceries before you stop for the night. Fanny packs are great for carrying small items such as sunglasses, sunscreen, lip balm, maps, snacks and a camera on any length trip.

Saddle bags, handlebar bags and frame bags are carried directly on the bike. Saddle bags come in a variety of sizes, the largest of which should be supported by a rack or bracket so that it does not rub against the rear wheel and rear brake. Since these small bags often hold bike tools, they are usually left on the bike even when the bigger bags are removed. Handlebar bags can also be attached under the seat, like saddle bags, by using a clamping bracket sold as the Seat Post Thing.

Handlebar bags are popular and are used to carry light-weight, small items that you want to be easily accessible (such as the items you might carry in a fanny pack). They are not to be used to carry anything heavy and should be purchased in a design that is supported at the top by a bracket that fits on the handlebars. The bottom should be held down to the front fork-ends with bungee cords. If you wish to purchase a handlebar bag, find one with external pockets and a transparent map compartment. For easiest use, the bag should open toward the rider. The bag should in no way interfere with steering, braking or lighting. There are also special handlebar camera bags.

Frame bags are the least common of the bags that attach directly to bikes. They are trapezoidal and usually attach between the frame tubes. They must be carefully packed, or they will interfere with the movement of your legs. These bags are of use primarily to those long-distance travelers who need to use all available space.

Panniers are those that attach to either side of a luggage rack. They come in a variety of shapes and sizes and are the most common cycle touring bag. Because of the variety of shapes and sizes, and the fact that a front bag can also attach to the rear, you will have to experiment with your bike to discover what works best for you. Panniers are generally connected to the luggage rack by means of hooks at two points close to the top of the rack and by a bungee cord at the bottom. For example, the cord can be clipped to the drop-out or fork-end. A relatively large bag can be installed at the rear of the bike while only a flat pouch (or two small ones) is workable on the side of the bag that faces out when installed. Make sure there is still clearance for your heels after you have attached the rear bags, especially once external pockets are stuffed.

You can also purchase combination bags, which are single pieces of luggage made up of three compartments—two side bags and a top compartment. These bags hang over the luggage rack, but are not as practical as one might think. They are often hard to pack and difficult to attach and remove. They are inexpensive, though. Combination bags without the top compartment, having only a layer of fabric in its place, are a bit easier to use but still not as practical as separate panniers.

Bags made to fit atop luggage racks should be used only on the back of the bike. These bags are either of the stuff sack type or a rectangular case, the latter being the most preferable. You can stack the cases and attach them to the rack with long webbing straps that buckle. If possible, it is best to attach bags to your bike by means of webbing straps or leather belts because they do not stretch like bungee cords do. Because bungees stretch, your load can shift, and items can fall off your bike. You also have to be especially careful that the bungee hooks don't get caught in your spokes. This situation could lead to falls and repair work.

What to Look for in a Bike Bag

For touring, you will want your bags to be as waterproof as possible, but you should also plan on lining the insides with platic bags. Canvas is the best material for bags. Unfortunately, canvas bike bags are hard to find. Most bags these days are made of coated synthetics. Look for heavy cloth because it tends to make a sturdier bag. Seal the seams yourself (even if the manufacturer claims they have been sealed) with a seam sealer purchased at an outdoors store. Make sure that the bag has double seams and that there are reinforcements at places that receive a lot of stress—where straps are attached, ends of zippers, points of contact with the bike or rack and all corners.

Inside the bag, "seal" the fabric by melting the edges with a lighter, match or candle. This will form a solid edge that will not fray. Should the fabric fray, you risk the seams eventually coming undone.

For easy access, look also for bags that open as widely as possible by means of a zipper or drawstring. Narrow openings make packing and access that much harder. Zippers should be covered by a flap of material to prevent leaks. Bags should be simple to open and close, and the closure flap should be held down by wide webbing straps with attached buckles, allowing you to compress the bag if it is only half full and further prevent shifting. These straps should be separate from what is used to attach the bag to the bike or luggage rack, mostly because you won't want getting at something in the bag to effect whether or not the bag stays attached to the bike. Rigid backs with stiffener boards help bags retain their shape and keep them from interfering in the operation of the bicycle. If necessary, you can make your own stiffeners by cutting fiber board to fit the back of your bag.

Bags that hang should be held in two points. Plastic-coated metal hooks at the front and rear ends of the bag are best. The hooks should not hang loose on the rack, and the rack should be long enough for both hooks to fit. If they don't, bend them into shape with pliers. The bottom of the bag should be fixed to the bike in at least one point, and the strap that attaches to the bike should be higher on the bag than it is on the bike. This way you place tension on the bag, not the bike, holding the bag more securely.

Test the stability of your luggage on your bike by holding

and shaking it in different positions: upside down, vertically with the front wheel off the ground, vertically with the rear wheel off the ground, horizontally to the left, horizontally to the right and shaking it while holding the handlebars.

Bike Trailer

An unconventional way to carry your luggage is to pull a bike trailer. These mostly two-wheeled trailers are attached to the seatpost by means of a flexible coupling. The trailer should be made for touring, rigid but light, and have large wheels that rotate on ball bearings and pneumatic tires. A built-in suspension will help it ride better. These trailers have little negative effect on the handling of the bike but are difficult to transport and store. Like many things, whether you use a trailer is a matter of personal preference.

How to Pack

Packing for a bicycle tour is similar to packing for backpacking or canoeing. The things you need the most or quickly should be the most accessible. These items should be packed in the outside pockets or outside bags. This would once again include the items you might store in a fanny pack as well as rain gear and other weather-related items.

Pack first the things you'll need last—extra clothing, sleeping bag, etc. Also, pack together things that go together. For example, cooking gear should all be kept in one bag, if possible, because you don't want to have to rummage through a number of bags to gather the things needed to cook your evening meal. However, weight considerations might force you to split some items up.

Did you carry too much on your first trip? When unpacking, divide your gear into four piles. The first pile should contain the things you could not have done without no matter the situation. The second pile will contain items used only in certain situations. The third pile is for things you used during your trip that may or may not be useful on another trip or that can be replaced by smaller and/or lighter items. Finally, make a fourth pile with items that were essentially ballast. Not only did these items serve no purpose on this trip, but there would probably never be an occasion when they would be useful.

When packing, look at every item carefully. Do you really need a clean pair of underwear for each day of the trip? Could you not just bring a couple of pairs and wash them out every night. Think light and spare, ascetic, and your trip will be delightful.

· 15 ·
Special Camping Trips

I went to the woods because I wished to live deliberately, to front only the essential facts of life, and see if I could not learn what it had to teach, and not, when I came to die, discover that I had not lived.

—*Henry David Thoreau*
Walden

Camping with Children

Camping as a child and camping with my child have brought me some of the best experiences of my life. From Canada to Hawaii, I grew up camping in all manner of sites, both private and public. From car camping to backpacking to camping out of an RV and a houseboat, I couldn't wait to share my love of the outdoors with my own child. Now that my daughter, Griffin, has begun to experience all the wonders nature has to offer, from a tent pitched beneath curtains of Spanish-moss on a barrier island, to an RV parked comfortably by a lakeside, she can't wait for our next camping trip.

Children are such an expected part of camping that it almost seems odd to include them in a section on special camping trips. But they do merit some special attention, because in a lot of ways their needs are different from those of adults. For example, while adults can fast for a day with little trouble, children, who are still growing and will continue to grow until they are about twenty-one years of age, should not be expected to get by on an empty stomachs. Similarly, a child's need for sleep differs from an adult's.

Even with these and other differences, children enjoy camping as much if not more than adults. Their open, eager minds will seize the new experience and learn from it.

Most children are extremely adaptable and less prone to feeling the minor discomforts of the outdoors. Anyone who can sleep in a car seat can manage a sleeping bag. Everything in moderation applies as much to children as to life. As long as they are not pushed too hard physically, mentally or emotionally, they will enjoy camping. And, if they are addicted to television, this is a great way to break them of the habit.

Including your children in the planning process will greatly add to their enjoyment of the trip. Allowing them some responsibility is good for all of you. Don't build up a trip to the degree that it can't possibly meet everyone's expectations. Camping allows certain freedoms, but it restricts others, particularly when it comes to living space. Make sure all are aware of the drawbacks as well as the pleasures of being outdoors.

Babies

The youngest of children can enjoy camping as much as toddlers, adolescents, teenagers and adults. Keeping everything small scale is the key. Do not spend too much time in the sun or in the water. Make sure they are neither too hot or too cold. Sun hats and sunscreen will protect them from the sun, a hat and jacket from the wind.

Feel free to let your infant crawl on the ground, but keep an eye out for anything she might put in her mouth—pebbles, bugs, acorns, trash left by prior campers. Keep her away from streams, poison ivy, fire pits, etc. and she will have a rousing good time.

If you do not wish to carry along a small folding bed for your child and feel comfortable doing so, share your sleeping bag. If your child naps outside the tent, you can protect her from insects by covering the bed or blanket with mosquito netting. Bring along a portable car or infant seat so that the child can sit up between naps.

Some strollers fold down so that a baby can lie prone while napping, and can also be used for day hikes if it is sturdy enough for unpaved trails. Infant carriers such as those made by Tough Traveler, Gerry or Kelty are great for carrying children on day hikes or around camp. These packs have a compartment to carry diapers, changing supplies, teething ring and other compact baby needs.

If you are not nursing your baby, plan to bring plenty of formula, juice and/or water with you. Since water varies from place to place, you don't want to risk messing up your infant's digestion with strange water. Bring only practical clothing that will keep the baby warm or cool, depending on the weather. As a matter of fact, try to bring clothing for any possible situation just to be on the safe side.

Think twice about using disposable diapers in the outdoors. Although established campgrounds have means of disposing of trash, disposables are hardly ecologically sound. If you do choose to bring disposable diapers, make sure that if they cannot be disposed of at the site, you carry them back home and dispose of them there. Pack it in, pack it out is always the rule.

Whatever type of diaper you choose, dispose of the feces in a toilet, privy or cathole as you do your own. Several soiled diapers can be packed out in one-gallon size resealable plastic bag or a hard plastic container (such as Tupperware). With cloth diapers, you can cut down on their weight, if you are hiking or biking, by wringing out urine diapers as you dispose of the feces and hanging them out to dry at night. They can't be reused until washed, but they will be lighter to carry.

Finally, if you are worried about camping with your baby, practice. While at home, set up your tent outdoors (or even indoors if that is not possible) and spend a night in it. Some children have no problem falling asleep in a dark tent while others who wake to total darkness will freak out. Keep a flashlight lantern handy (both Coleman and Eveready make good ones). Others may find the confining walls of a tent disconcerting and fuss, but usually they get used to it after a couple of nights.

Toddlers

The only real difference (when it comes to camping) between infants and toddlers is that toddlers can run around. They will enjoy exploring the site, but if you can't keep a constant eye on them, they will need to be confined. A stroller or baby harness is best for the outdoors. If you want to let them roam but are afraid of your child wandering off, try pinning a small bell to their shirt or jacket. That way you can keep track of which direction they are heading. For the extra-cautious—a name tag with pertinent information pinned to the child's clothing will ease your mind. If children can't move around a

---

>>Camping Tip<<

If your child has a security object, such as a blanket, or stuffed animal, make sure you bring it along on the trip. Bedtime story books are also a big plus.

little, why bring them? In fact, actively involve them in the process of camping.

Toddlers are also old enough to begin learning how to set up camp. Holding some stakes or poles and handing them to you as the tent is set up, and other similar tasks, are a way to get toddlers more involved in camping.

As with an infant, keep an eye out for hazardous items and be particularly watchful around the cooking area, since campstoves and boiling water can easily tip over and are often within arm's reach. Any hazardous equipment—knives, insect repellents, gas lanterns, you get the idea—should be put out of reach.

Naps and plenty of sleep are called for in the outdoors as much as at home. Once again, you can share your sleeping bag or carry along a portable crib or a stroller. Do whatever is necessary to make sure your child gets plenty of sleep. Toddlers also will need a stroller or backpack for day hikes.

Parents will find that toddlers get dirty very quickly when camping. Either bring plenty of clothes or keep a spare set for outings. Don't prepare the child for bed until he is about to be tucked in.

On rainy days, toddlers can be entertained in the tent or beneath the dining screen with coloring books and puzzles. Leaf and rock-collecting are fun in good weather. Tailor the toddler's activities to their needs and desires.

Children and Adolescents

This is a wonderful age for camping. Children are much more capable than toddlers and eager to learn as well. They will want to help around camp, can sleep in their own bags, no longer need naps and can be told what to touch and not to touch. The range of games and activities they can participate in is nearly endless.

Adolescents are more independent and will want to leave

the site on their own, occasionally. There is no reason they should not do so, but they should be well versed in the basics, ie. not talking to strangers, etc. If it makes you feel more comfortable, supply each child with a whistle to blow in case of an emergency.

Teenagers

Because thay are even more independent than adolescents, chances are you won't see much of teenagers once you set up camp. On the other hand, some teens enjoy taking part in family projects and will be a huge help as well as a joy to have around.

Don't be surprised if your teen is no longer eager to go camping unless there is something to appeal to their interests. This might mean that your first-choice destination will have to be dumped in preference to a site that will suit your

teen. Or perhaps your teenager can bring a friend along for company. Again, include your child in the planning process.

Keeping Your Child Busy

There are hundreds of ways to entertain your child on a camping trip (some of these will help you out as you travel by car to the campsite or trailhead as well) including:

- Revel in nature. Point out interesting flowers, clouds, trees, mushrooms, etc. Enjoy water by throwing pebbles or floating sticks and leaves. Play in sand or mud or snow. Watch frogs hop, squirrels and chipmunks scuttle from tree to tree, insects going about their business, a deer standing stock still, insects going about their business, a hawk drifting on air currents . . .
- Teach your children geologic and natural history—that Indians once hunted in these woods, that they are walking on what was once hot lava, that a glacier once molded this valley.
- Answer your child's questions—Why is the sky blue? Are there still Indians in these woods? Will the volcano erupt on us?
- Tell stories. Parents can tell stories of past but true events, make up stories or even invite children to tell stories.
- Play games. At-home favorites like hide and seek or freeze tag work well at campgrounds, too. Keep kids away from deep grass and bushes when ticks are in season and check them after play.
- Bring toys. A Barbie doll or frisbee takes up little space in the car trunk compared to the amount of in-camp fun it provides.
- Sing songs. Let the child choose, or take turns choosing.
- Play animals. Pick an animal and tell about it, make its noises, etc.

- Draw the new animals, plants, insects, etc. that you discover. Colored pencils and an art pad will add to the enjoyment.
- Children who can write might enjoy keeping a journal of new things seen, weather, campground routines, emotions, etc.
- Write postcards to friends and family.
- Present your child with a disposable camera with which to document the camping trip.

Camping with Dogs

Although dogs make wonderful camping partners, particularly when you intend to do some day hiking, lots of people say they prefer not to camp around people who are camping with dogs. Unless you have complete control over your animal, you are going to make a lot of people unhappy (and lots of campgrounds, national parks, etc. do not allow pets at campsites).

Unless you keep your dog chained up or unless he minds well, he will be roaming other sites and bothering the poor campers there. Some people love dogs and won't mind at first, but even animal lovers find dogs a nuisance when they beg for food.

Children abound at many campgrounds and many are terrified of dogs and often justifiably so. My daughter has been bit twice by dogs that were house pets and is now extremely wary. Dogs also tend to scare up trouble. They have been bitten by snakes, swatted by porcupines, enraged bears and are keen on rolling in dead animals—not a pleasant odor. If you choose to camp with a dog, you won't see much wildlife.

If you do bring a dog camping, make sure you keep it under control. Many dogs dislike children and are suspicious of strangers (and campgrounds are full of strangers). Bring plenty of food for your animal; keep him supplied with fresh water and he should be happy. And like humans, dogs are susceptible to hot and cold weather. Keep them warm when its cold and wet, cool when its hot, and they should be fine. Taking your pet along on a day hike will give him the exercise he needs. Just hold onto him if you run into other hikers and you will part on friendly terms.

If your dog has a tendency to snap and bite, leave him home. Don't risk the quarantine or death of your pet because you lost control of man's best friend at a campground.

Winter Camping

Experienced campers have discovered that pleasurable camping need not only be found during the spring, summer and fall. Winter camping is possible in many parts of the U.S. and provides much more solitude. It is a way to experience the Earth during its darkest season—to discover a new world both physically and mentally.

Even in the South, where, contrary to popular opinion, it does get cold, and even, occasionally, snow, you'll find the campgrounds (except in Florida) much less crowded. By the same token, you can find snowy places throughout the country where you can camp and hike in peace.

Cold-weather Gear

If you are heading out into the snow, you'll need a four-season tent with a waterproof floor. In the deep South, a three-season tent will probably suffice, since the temperature rarely drops below twenty degrees. For other areas, a free-standing, four-season tent is the best choice.

When pitching your tent in the snow, make sure you level the area and pack the snow down. If this is not done, it is very likely that you will wake up when the tent collapses on your head. If you're backpacking, leaving your pack on while you stamp the ground flat will give you some extra weight that will make the job go more quickly. If you make the base wider than the tent, you will be able to walk around your tent more easily, which will be especially useful should nature call in the middle of the night.

Special tent pegs for snow camping can be purchased from most outdoors stores. Once your tent is pegged, try pouring some water on the pegs. After it freezes, the pegs really won't move. To remove them, pour water warmed in the stove over the pegs, remove and dry before the water cools and freezes. There is more information on pitching a tent in the snow in Chapter 7.

Some four-season tents offer cookholes—a zippered or gathered hole in the bottom of the tent that can be flapped or pulled back so that you may cook directly on the ground. A cookhole is preferable to cooking on the floor of your tent, which can catch fire easily should the stove tip over. Another common option is to cook in your vestibule.

When camping during the winter, you will also need a sleeping bag with a low comfort rating—a zero-degree bag will do for most situations. If you don't want the expense of owning two different sleeping bags, consider using a liner to make your three-season bag warmer. It should go without saying that you will need a mummy-style sleeping bag for winter camping. It will keep you the warmest, and if the temperature really drops, you can tighten the hood until nothing but your nose is showing. Some sleeping bags are available with extra insulation in the foot of the bag to combat cold feet.

Since the bottom of your tent may be on the top of snow, you will want some good insulation between you and the bottom of your tent. While a three-quarter sleeping pad may do for three-season camping, if your feet get cold easily, you may want to consider a full-length pad for winter camping. Bags, liners and pads are discussed in Chapter 6.

But, before you snow seal your boots, keep in mind that winter backpacking requires a little more forethought as well as preparation. Unless you intend to do some extensive snowhiking (with crampons or snowshoes or cross-country skis), a pair of boots will suffice. Hard core snow hiking requires detailed knowledge. Sam Curtis' *Harsh Weather Camping in the 90s* by Menasha Ridge Press offers more information on how to hike in the snow.

As long as the snow is not too deep or if it is hard-packed, boots will more than likely suffice. A pair of gaiters and well-sealed boots will make the trip more comfortable.

Remember that layering your clothing is of utmost importance when camping in the winter. Beginning with a layer of long underwear, you may want to add a warm shirt and pants or a pile or fleece pullover and pants set. You can top these off with a layer that includes a warm parka and waterproof, insulated pants if it is really cold or a rain/wind suit if the temperature is only reasonably cold. Don't forget that you can add greatly to your warmth by donning a hat or balaclava.

If you are sufficiently bundled, the exertion of hiking should keep you warm. If you start feeling hypothermic, stop what you are doing immediately, change into dry clothes if yours are wet, crawl into a sleeping bag and heat yourself a warm drink. Make sure the stove you bring will light (as well as boil water) in frigid weather.

Cold-related hazards are discussed in detail in Chapter 12. Remember that when hiking or moving around on open snow, it is wise to wear sunglasses because the sun reflecting off the bright, white snow can burn your eyes. Snowblindness can occur even on overcast days. If you don't have sunglasses, cut eyeslits in anything (a bandana, for example) that can tie around your head. Should you or someone else become snowblind, cold compresses, a painkiller and a lightproof bandage are needed. Between eighteen and twenty hours later, the blindness should fade.

All the equipment needed for winter camping—warm clothes, four-season tents, sleeping bags, tent pegs, etc.—is available through outdoors stores where you will also find information on how to use the equipment. Although there are certainly hazards when cold-weather camping, don't be deterred. Just leave home well-prepared.

Desert Camping

"In the desert, one is sensible of the passage of time. In that parching heat, a man feels that the day is a voyage towards the goal of evening, towards the promise of a cool breeze that will bathe the limbs and wash away the sweat. Under the heat of the day, beasts and men plod towards the sweet well of night, as confidently as towards death."

—Antoine de St. Exupery

If you enjoy hiking out West, there are lots of opportunities to do some desert camping. Like camping in the winter, the desert offers its own brand of solitude and an awesome beauty described often and most eloquently by the late Edward Abbey. Few people choose to experience the desert, but as long as you take certain precautions, you will find yourself won by what it has to offer.

Because of the intense heat of the desert, there are several problems you face immediately—dehydration, hyperthermia and sunburn. Dehydration and hyperthermia are discussed in detail in Chapter 12.

Sunburn is a potential problem, even in cold weather, because it can do extensive damage to your skin, and constant burning can lead to skin cancer. Burned skin can also retard sweating. Sun block is necessary no matter what part of the day you are moving around. The Arabs know what they are doing when they cover their bodies and heads with long, flowing material. Take a cue from them and wear,‘ at least, loose, long pants and a loose but high-necked and long-sleeved shirt. When it comes to desert camping, clothes made of cotton are your best bet because they get the wettest and the evaporation will cool your body. Keep in mind that the more area you leave uncovered, the more sunscreen you will need to use. Don't wear black out in the sun unless you want to be baked. On the other hand, bring along some warm clothes for night because the desert cools down in the evening except for the hottest part of summer.

Wide-brimmed hats and sunglasses that block the ultra-violet rays are mandatory. The bright light of the desert can burn your eyes as well as your skin.

Obviously, the best time to camp in the desert is during the winter. Avoid the summer months, if possible. If you must desert-camp in the summer, keep in mind that the sun often rises about 5:30 A.M. and does not set until almost sixteen hours later. Three or four hours after sunrise temperatures peak and do not fall until evening.

Most of your activity should take place just before or at dawn, particularly if you are backpacking or day hiking. Move around (if you wish) until the temperatures peak and then rest through the hottest part of the day. You will save yourself a lot of grief this way. Try to find some shade, if possible, under a tree or rock outcroppings. You may also want to try setting up a tarp, but unless your tent is highly ventilated, I wouldn't suggest pitching it because it will heat up like a furnace.

Once the sun begins to set and temperatures fall again, you can start moving around. If you're backpacking, hike in the early evening, when it's cool. Use a flashlight, head lamp or if you're lucky, a full moon. If you're encamped, now is the time to fix a meal, and if you have slept some during the day, you can spend a good part of the night awake, enjoying the vastness and beauty of a desert night.

To keep from getting dehydrated, you must drink at least a gallon of water per day, and unless you have very reliable water sources, don't count on just anyone's word for where you might find it. Although heavy, it is safest to bring all your own water to the campsite even if you are backpacking. And, like they say, don't put all your eggs in one basket. If you carry a one gallon jug and it breaks or leaks, you've lost one entire day's water supply. Spread the water around by carrying it in one- and two-liter bottles.

You can also get water in an emergency by memorizing the following method of distilling water in the desert:

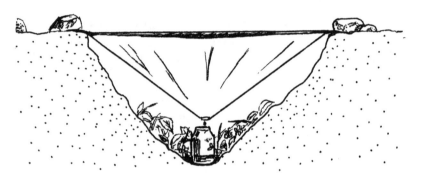

Solar Water Still
- Dig a hole two feet deep by three feet wide.
- Set a wide-mouth bottle or pot in the bottom of the hole.
- Fill the area around the bottle with any plant material you can find.
- Cover the hole with plastic (clear or translucent, if possible).
- Weigh down the edges of a plastic sheet around the hole so that it is "sealed."
- Place a light-weight, insulated rock in the center of the plastic so that a funnel shape is formed over the mouth of the bottle. Water from condensation will then drip from

the "funnel" into the bottle. You can insulate the rock with a bandana or piece of paper.

After three hours, the still will produce about a pint of water.

Also keep in mind that your appetite drops some in the desert, so you don't necessarily have to carry a cook kit. Cold foods will do just fine; besides who wants a hot dinner in the desert heat unless it is eaten in the middle of the night?

Some desert food could include tuna and hard cheese-stuffed pitas, fruit leathers, peanut butter, candy bars, pemmican, beef jerky and so on. Remember, though, that while camping in the desert, it is better for your digestion to eat a bunch of small meals rather than one big meal.

· Appendix 1 ·
Equipment Checklists

This checklist is for tent campers, whether you arrive at your site in a car, on a bicycle, in a canoe or on foot. By combining the Essentials, which are common to any camping trip, with optional equipment, you can create your own equipment checklist. Hobby-specific gear, such as firearms and ammunition for hunting, or binoculars and field guides for birding, is not included.

The Essentials
- ❏ Tent or tarp and groundcloth
- ❏ Sleeping bag or bed roll
- ❏ Sleeping Pad
- ❏ Stove and fuel
- ❏ Lighter and waterproof matches
- ❏ Cooking pot
- ❏ Cooking and eating utensils
- ❏ Knife (pocket)
- ❏ More than adequate food for the length of your trip
- ❏ Containers for water (canteen or water bag)
- ❏ Drinking cup
- ❏ Rain gear (poncho, umbrella, or rain jacket and rain pants)
- ❏ One pair of shorts
- ❏ One pair of long pants
- ❏ One to two short sleeve shirts
- ❏ One long sleeve shirt or sweater
- ❏ Knit Cap+
- ❏ Balaclava+
- ❏ Two pair socks
- ❏ One pair shoes or hiking boots
- ❏ Long Johns+

+ Seasonal

❑ Two pair underwear
❑ Toilet paper and trowel (if no bathroom is available in camp)
❑ Washcloth
❑ Biodegradable soap
❑ Deodorant
❑ Toothbrush and toothpaste
❑ Nylon cord (at least 10 feet)
❑ Trash bag(s)
❑ Repair equipment for stove, tent and other equipment
❑ Flashlight with fresh batteries
❑ First Aid kit
❑ Space blanket+
❑ Sunglasses
❑ Sunscreen+
❑ Insect repellent+

Optional Equipment for Any Camping Trip
❑ Water purification tablets or filter
❑ Watch or clock
❑ Spices for cooking
❑ Swimsuit
❑ Shaving kit

Optional Equipment for Car Camping
❑ Additional clothing
❑ Cot
❑ Cooler
❑ Thermos
❑ Coffee Pot
❑ Griddle and spatula
❑ Lantern
❑ Dining Fly
❑ Chairs

❑ Hibachi or other small grill
❑ Whisk broom
❑ Large sponge

Equipment for a Bicycle Camping Trip
❑ Bike equipped with panniers
❑ Pump
❑ Water Bottles
❑ Bike Lock
❑ Helmet
❑ Bike shorts and jersey
❑ Gloves
❑ Bike shoes
❑ Bike repair equipment and spare parts
❑ Tire patch kit
❑ Map and/or guidebooks

Equipment for Canoe Camping
❑ Canoe
❑ Paddles (including one spare)
❑ PFD for each person
❑ Duffel bags (lined with a trash bag)
❑ Duct tape
❑ Ammo boxes (to waterproof gear, such as cameras)
❑ Helmets (for whitewater)

Equipment for Backpacking
❑ Internal or external frame pack
❑ Pack cover
❑ Gaiters*
❑ Crampons and ice ax+
❑ Maps and/or guidebooks
❑ Compass

* Optional   + Seasonal

· Appendix 2 ·
State Parks and
Parks in Canadian Provinces

By writing or calling the following offices, you can obtain specific information on campgrounds throughout the United States and Canada.

Alabama Department of Conservation
Division of State Parks
Folsom Administration Building
64 North Union Street
Montgomery, AL 36130
(800) 252-7275

Alaska Division of Parks and Outdoor Recreation
Department of Natural Resources
3601 C Street
P.O. Box 107001
Anchorage, AK 99510
(907) 762-2600

Arizona State Parks
800 West Washington Street, Suite 415
Phoenix, AZ 85007
(602) 542-4174

Arkansas State Parks
One Capitol Mall
Little Rock, AR 72201
(501) 371-7743

California Department of Parks and Recreation
P.O. Box 942896
Sacramento, CA 94296-0001
(916) 445-2358

Colorado Department of Natural Resources
Division of State Parks and Outdoor Recreation
1313 Sherman Street, Room 618
Denver, CO 80203
(303) 866-2884

**Connecticut Department
of Environmental Protection**
State Parks Division
165 Capitol Avenue
Hartford, CT 06106
(203) 566-2304

Delaware Department of Natural Resources
Division of Parks and Recreation
P.O. Box 1401
Dover, DE 19903
(302) 739-4702

Florida Department of Natural Resources
Division of Recreation and Parks
3900 Commonwealth Boulevard
Tallahassee, FL 32399
(904) 656-2753

Georgia Department of Natural Resources
205 Butler Street, S.E., Suite 1352
Atlanta, GA 30334
(404) 656-3530

Hawaii Department of Land and Natural Resources
Division of State Parks
P.O. Box 621
Honolulu, HI 96809
(808) 548-7455

Idaho Department of Parks and Recreation
Statehouse Mall
Boise, ID 83720
(208) 334-2154

Illinois Department of Conservation
Division of Land Management
600 North Grand Avenue West
Springfield, IL 62701
(217) 782-1395

Indiana Department of Natural Resources
Division of State Parks
616 State Office Building
Indianapolis, IN 46204
(317) 232-4136

Iowa Department of Natural Resources
Bureau of State Parks
Wallace State Office Building
Des Moines, IA 50319-0034
(515) 281-5886

Kansas Department of Wildlife and Parks
Landon Office Building
900 Jackson Street, Suite 502
Topeka, KS 66612
(913) 296-2281

Kentucky Department of Parks
Capitol Plaza Towers, 10th Floor
Frankfort, KY 40601
(502) 564-2172

**Louisiana Department of Culture,
Recreation and Tourism**
Office of State Parks
P.O. Drawer 44426
Baton Rouge, LA 70804-4426
(504) 342-8111

Maine Department of Conservation
Bureau of Parks and Recreation
Statehouse Station #22
Augusta, ME 04333
(207) 289-3821

Maryland Department of Natural Resources
Forest and Park Operations
Tawes State Office Building
580 Taylor Avenue
Annapolis, MD 21401
(301) 974-3771

**Massachusetts Department of
Environmental Management**
Division of Parks and Forests
Leverett Saltonstall Building
100 Cambridge Street
Boston, MA 02202
(617) 727-3180

Michigan Department of Natural Resources
Parks Division
P.O. Box 30028
Lansing, MI 48909
(517) 373-1270

Minnesota Department of Natural Resources
Division of Parks and Recreation
500 LaFayette Road
St. Paul, MN 55155-4039
(612) 296-2270

Mississippi Department of Natural Resources
Bureau of Recreation and Parks
P.O. Box 10600
Jackson, MS 39209
(601) 961-5240

Missouri Department of Natural Resources
Division of Parks, Recreation and
Historic Preservation
P.O. Box 176
Jefferson City, MO 65102
(314) 751-9392

Montana Department of Fish, Wildlife and Parks
Parks Division
Capitol Station
Helena, MT 59620
(406) 444-3750

Nebraska Game and Parks Commission
P.O. Box 30370
Lincoln, NE 68503
(402) 471-0641

**Nevada Department of Conservation
and Natural Resources**
Division of State Parks
201 South Fall Street, Room 119
Carson City, NV 89710
(702) 885-4370

**New Hampshire Department of
Resources and Economic Development**
Division of Parks and Recreation
P.O. Box 856
Concord, NH 03301
(603) 271-3255

New Jersey Department of Environmental Protection
Division of Parks and Forestry
501 East State Street
Trenton, NJ 08625
(609) 292-2733

**New Mexico Energy, Minerals
and Naural Resources Department**
State Park and Recreation Division
Villagra Building
408 Galisteo Street
Santa Fe, NM 87503-1147
(505) 827-7465

**New York Office of Parks, Recreation
and Historic Preservation**
Agency Building #1
Empire State Plaza
Albany, NY 12238
(518) 474-0463

**North Carolina Department of Natural Resources
and Community Development**
Division of Parks and Recreation
P.O. Box 27687
Raleigh, NC 27611-7687
(919) 733-4181

North Dakota Parks and Recreation Department
1424 West Century Avenue, Suite 202
Bismarck, ND 58501
(701) 224-4887

Ohio Department of Natural Resources
Division of Parks and Recreation
Fountain Square, C-3
Columbus, OH 43224
(614) 265-6511

Oklahoma Tourism and Recreation Department
Division of State Parks
500 Will Rogers Building
Oklahoma City, OK 73105
(405) 521-3411

Oregon Department of Transportation
State Parks and Recreation Division
525 Trade Street, S.E., Room 301
Salem, OR 97310
(503) 378-5019

**Pennsylvania Department of
Environmental Resources**
Bureau of State Parks
2150 Herr Street
Harrisburg, PA 17103-1625
(717) 787-8800

**Rhode Island Department of
Environmental Management**
Division of Parks and Recreation
22 Hayes Street
Providence, RI 02908
(401) 277-2632

**South Carolina Department of Parks,
Recreation and Tourism**
Division of State Parks
Edgar A. Brown Building
1205 Pendleton Street
Columbia, SC 29201
(803) 734-0159

South Dakota Department of Game, Fish and Parks
Division of Parks and Recreation
Sigurd Anderson Building
445 East Capitol Avenue
Pierre, SD 57501
(605) 773-3391

Tennessee Department of Conservation
Customs House
701 Broadway
Nashville, TN 37219-5237
(615) 742-6745

Texas Parks and Wildlife Department
Parks Division
4200 Smith School Road
Austin, TX 78744
(512) 389-4866

Utah Department of Natural Resources
Division of State Parks
1636 West North Temple
Salt Lake City, UT 84116
(801) 538-7362

**Vermont Department of Forests,
Parks and Recreation**
Division of State Parks
103 South Main Street, 10 South
Waterbury, VT 05676
(802) 244-8711

Virginia Department of Conservation and Recreation
Division of State Parks
203 Governor Street, Suite 306
Richmond, VA 23219-2010
(804) 225-3867 (in Richmond)
(800) 933-7275

Washington State Parks and Recreation Commission
7150 Cleanwater Lane, KY-11
Olympia, WA 98504-5711
(206) 753-5757

West Virginia Division of Parks and Recreation
Capitol Complex
Charleston, WV 25305
(304) 348-2764

Wisconsin Department of Natural Resources
Bureau of Parks and Recreation
P.O. Box 7921
Madison, WI 53707
(608) 266-2185

Wyoming Recreation Commission
122 West 25th Street
Cheyenne, WY 82002
(307) 777-6690

Canada

Alberta Department of Tourism
10025 Jasper Avenue
Edmonton, Alberta
Canada T5J 3Z3
(800) 661-8888

Tourism British Columbia
Parliment Buildings
Victoria, BC
Canada V8V 1X4
(604) 382-2127

Travel Manitoba
Department 7271
Winnipeg, Manitoba
Canada R3C 3H8
(800) 665-0040 (ext. 271)

New Brunswick Tourism
P.O. Box 12345
Fredericton, New Brunswick
Canada E3B 5C3
(800) 561-0123

Newfoundland-Labrador Tourism
P.O. Box 8730
St. John's, Newfoundland
Canada A1B 4K2
(800) 563-5353

Northwest Territories Tourism
P.O. Box 2107
Yellowknife, Northwest Territories
Canada X1A 2P6
(800) 661-0788

Nova Scotia Department of Tourism
2695 Dutch Village Road, Suite 501
Halifax, Nova Scotia
Canada B3L 4V2
(800) 341-6096

Ontario Ministry of Tourism and Recreation
Queen's Park
Toronto, Ontario
Canada M7A 2E5

**Prince Edward Island Department
of Tourism and Parks**
P.O. Box 940
Charlottetown, PEI
Canada C1A 7M5
(800) 463-4734

Tourisme Québec
P.O. Box 20,000
Québec City, Québec
Canada G1K 7X2
(800) 443-7000

Tourism Saskatchewan
1900 Albert Street
Regina, Saskatchewan
Canada F4P 4L9
(800) 667-7191

Tourism Yukon
P.O. Box 2703
Whitehorse, Yukon
Canada Y1A 2C6
(403) 667-5340

· Appendix 3 ·
Bibliography

If you would like to read more on subjects covered in *Camping in the 90s*, I suggest the following books and guides.

Backpacking in the 90s: Tips, Techniques and Secrets, by Victoria Logue. Menasha Ridge Press, updated annually.
A comprehensive guide to the sport by the author of *Camping in the 90s*.

Be an Expert with Map and Compass, by Bjorn Kjellstrom. MacMillan, Revised 1994.
The standard text on an important backcountry skill.

The Bicycle Touring Manual, by Rob van der Plas. Bicycle Books, Second Edition, 1993.
Detailed guide to touring and camping on a bicycle by a veteran cyclist and author.

Camping and Backpacking with Children, by Steven Boga. Stackpole Books, 1995.
Practical advice on exploring the outdoors in a 256-page guide.

Emergency Medical Procedures for the Outdoors, by Patient Medical Associates. Menasha Ridge Press, revised 1995.
Unique step-by-step guide to almost all outdoor emergencies.

Harsh Weather Camping in the 90s, by Sam Curtis. Menasha Ridge Press, Second Edition 1993.
From hiking the desert Southwest to cross country skiing

in New England, this book tells you how to keep dry when it's wet, warm when it's cold and cool when it's hot.

Nuts 'n Bolts Guide to Cooking for Campers & Backpackers, by Victoria and Frank Logue. Menasha Ridge Press, 1995.

A 32-page guide to what to eat in the backcountry. Filled with recipes, this book includes information on freeze-dried meals, supermarket food, baking in the backcountry and more.

Nuts 'n Bolts Guide to Knots for Hikers & Backpackers, by Frank Logue. Menasha Ridge Press, 1994.

A 32-page guide to useful knots for camping and backpacking.

Nuts 'n Bolts Guide to Preventing Traveler's Diarrhea, by Donald Sullivan. Menasha Ridge Press, 1995.

A 32-page guide for people who travel at home or overseas, that offers advice on what to eat and drink and what to avoid.

Nuts 'n Bolts Guide to Stretching and Massage for Hikers & Backpackers, by Victoria and Frank Logue. Menasha Ridge Press, 1995.

A 32-page guide for hikers with a pre-hike stretch routine and recommended post-hike massage techniques. Includes self-massage and massages for your hiking partner.

Roughing It Elegantly: A Practical Guide to Canoe Camping, by Patricia Bell. Cat's Paw Press, Second Edition, 1994.

An experienced canoe-camper gives down-to-earth tips and advice.

Woodall's Campground Directory, North American Edition. Simon and Schuster, updated annually.

This campground guide is an official publication of the Family Motor Coach Association, The National Campers and Hikers Association and the Canadian Motor Home and Trailer Association. This guide, which looks like a telephone book for a major metropolitan area, gives specifics on thousands of private campgrounds all over North America. Almost all of the campgrounds are personally inspected by Woodall representatives. Smaller state and regional guides are also sold by Woodall's.

· Index ·

Mittens, 84
Moose, 231
Mosquitos, 237-238
National Forests, 156-157
National Parks, 157-158
No-see-ums, 234-235
Nylon, 76, 81
Outback Oven, 27, 36-37
Pillows, 114-115
PolarGuard, 102, 103
Polarplus, 76-77
Polartec, 76-77
Polypropylene, 75
Porcupines, 231-232
Primaloft, 102, 104, 106
Private campgrounds, 160
Quallofil, 102, 103
Rabies, 204-205
Raccoons, 233
Rain gear, 78-81
    Ponchos, 79
    Rain suits, 79
Rattlesnakes, 228
Razor, 50
Recreational vehicles, 139-154
    Class A motorhome, 143
    Clubs, 153
    Driving, 149-153
    Features, 144-148
    Fifth-wheel trailers, 141-142
    Mini-motorhome, 143
    Packing, 148-149
    Pick-up camper, 143
    Pop-up trailers, 140-141
    Rentals, 153-154
    Travel trailers, 141
Recycled gear, 185
Red bugs, see Chiggers
Repair Equipment, 57-58
Rocky Mountain Spotted
    Fever, 205-206, 238

Rope, 55
Scorpions, 236-237
Shampoo, 49
Shaving Cream, 50
Sheet-bend, 56
Silk, 75
Skunks, 232
Sleeping bags, 99-112
    Care of, 110-111
    Comfort ratings, 101-102
    Fillings, 102-106
    Liners, 111-112
    Mated, 111
    Shape, 106-108
    Shells, 108-109
    Weight, 109-110
Sleeping pads, 113-114
Sleeping under stars, 133, 135
Snacks, 14
Snake-bite kit, 64
Snakes, 227-230
Soap, 48-49, 180-181
Socks, 83, 96-97
Solar still, 278-279
Solitude, 160-161
Spices, 16
Sports sandals, 97
State parks and forests, 159
Stoves, 27-39, 58
    Backpacking stoves, 33-37
    Butane stoves, 37
    Camp stoves, 28-30
    Grills, 30-32
    Operation and maintenance,
        38
    Propane cookers, 33
    Repair kit, 58
    Safety, 38-39
Sunglasses, 66
Sunscreen, 63
Supper, 11-12

· About the author ·

Victoria Logue began her writing career as a newspaper reporter for two small daily newspapers, for whom she garnered several writing awards.

In 1988, with her husband, Frank, Victoria hiked the entire Appalachian Trail. After returning, they wrote *The Appalachian Trail Backpacker's Planning Guide* to help others prepare for a hike of any length on that trail. Since then, they have written and illustrated the *Appalachian Trail Fun Book*, a coloring and activity book for 4-9 year olds. The Logues also collaborated on *The Best of the Appalachian Trail: Dayhikes* and *The Best of the Appalachian Trail: Overnight Hikes*. Their most recent book is *Georgia Outdoors*, published by John F. Blair, Publisher.

The Logues live in north Georgia where they are restoring a 120-year old house and sharing their love of the outdoors with their daughter, Griffin.

· About the illustrator ·

Leigh Ellis is a professional artist, who specializes in illustrating the natural world. She was formally educated as a zoologist and ecologist before pursuing a career in fine arts. In addition to her science training, she has studied art at the University of Hawaii and Montana State University.

Her work has been exhibited in juried and private shows in several states and is sold in galleries. Leigh teaches watercolor and illustration classes for both children and adult audiences focusing on avian and floral illustration. She lives north Georgia with her daughter, Jessie.